THE *Ontario* CRAFT BEER GUIDE

THE *Ontario*
CRAFT
BEER
GUIDE

ROBIN LEBLANC
JORDAN ST. JOHN

DUNDURN
TORONTO

Editors: Cheryl Hawley and Dominic Farrell
Design: Courtney Horner
Cover Design: Courtney Horner
Cover Image: © Atu Studio Atu Studio | Dreamstime.com
Printer: Webcom

Library and Archives Canada Cataloguing in Publication

LeBlanc, Robin, 1984-, author
        The Ontario craft beer guide / Robin LeBlanc, Jordan St. John.

Includes index.
Issued in print and electronic formats.
ISBN 978-1-4597-3566-8 (paperback).--ISBN 978-1-4597-3567-5 (pdf).--
ISBN 978-1-4597-3568-2 (epub)

        1. Microbreweries--Ontario--Guidebooks. 2. Breweries--Ontario--Guidebooks. 3. Beer--Ontario. I. St. John, Jordan, author II. Title.

TP573.C3L43 2016   663'.4209713   C2016-900228-4
                                                C2016-900229-2

2   3   4   5   20   19   18   17   16

We acknowledge the support of the **Canada Council for the Arts** and the **Ontario Arts Council** for our publishing program. We also acknowledge the financial support of the **Government of Canada** through the **Canada Book Fund** and **Livres Canada Books**, and the **Government of Ontario** through the **Ontario Book Publishing Tax Credit** and the **Ontario Media Development Corporation**.

Care has been taken to trace the ownership of copyright material used in this book. The author and the publisher welcome any information enabling them to rectify any references or credits in subsequent editions.

— *J. Kirk Howard, President*

The publisher is not responsible for websites or their content unless they are owned by the publisher.

Printed and bound in Canada.

VISIT US AT
Dundurn.com | @dundurnpress | Facebook.com/dundurnpress | Pinterest.com/dundurnpress

Dundurn
3 Church Street, Suite 500
Toronto, Ontario, Canada
M5E 1M2

CONTENTS

FOREWORD

Twenty-odd years ago, what you are holding in your hands would have been little more than a pamphlet. When I published the first edition of my *Great Canadian Beer Guide* in 1994, Ontario boasted a mere thirteen "microbreweries" and twenty more brewpubs, the latter group being then licensed to sell their beer only on their premises.

That situation scarcely improved over the balance of the decade, with many breweries closing, selling, or otherwise changing course, and the total number of brewpubs actually declining by the time the second edition of the *Guide* hit, in 2001. What's more, while there were some very good beers on the market, the range of styles they represented was limited for the most part to pilsners and pale ales, "dark ales" and "golden lagers." As unlikely as it might seem today, the sighting of an actual IPA was then considered a rare and exciting thing.

Brewery tasting rooms, growler fills, brewpub bottle shops, and the Ontario Craft Brewers association? Double IPAs, barrel-aged imperial stouts, doppelbocks, and saisons? All but dreams, still years away from realization.

However, sometime well after the dawn of the new millennium there occurred a seismic shift in Ontario craft beer and the shock waves were many and far reaching. Suddenly, as if out of nowhere, beer drinkers were spoiled for choice, with local brewers cranking out beers in any number of styles and strengths, from nuanced takes on the German kölsch style to generously hopped IPAs and unapologetically powerful barley wines. And just when we thought we had seen it all, those same brewers discovered yeasts and bacteria that could deliver bold, tart, and fruity flavours, and the excitement started all over again.

Today, of course, we live in the promised land of beer, or at least some sort of government-regulated, made-in-Ontario version of it. While we do remain saddled with the beer-retailing behemoth known as the Beer Store, we have also, thanks to the recent explosion of small breweries and the government's tentative steps into grocery-store beer sales, more brands in more styles than perhaps this province has ever before seen, and more venues from which to buy them.

Simply, it is a good, if occasionally confusing, time for beer drinkers in Ontario.

It is that second part, the confusing side, which makes this book so valuable. With such a plethora of breweries at hand and still more in development all the time, it is a challenge for even a full-time beer specialist to stay on top of things. Add in an endless stream of seasonal brews, special one-off editions, and inter-brewery collaborations, and you have a state of affairs that is as maddening to track as it is rewarding to sample.

What you hold in your hands is a snapshot of the Ontario beer landscape at the start of 2016, written by two of the most knowledgeable and keen observers of that scene. It is not the first word on Ontario beer and neither will it be the last, but it is an excellent jumping-off point for a richly satisfying journey of beer discovery. Your guides are ready, and the beer awaits, so grab your glass and get started!

Cheers!

Stephen Beaumont, Toronto, 2016
Author of *The Beer & Food Companion* and
co-author with Tim Webb of *The World Atlas of Beer*

INTRODUCTION

Until very recently, Ontario's craft beer scene was a fairly manageable affair. The explosion of small breweries that has taken place since 2007 means that it has become very difficult (even for beer writers covering the province) to keep track of what exists, let alone how everything fits together. While it is excellent to have an up-to-date list of breweries from across the province, it became apparent to us in mid-2014 that additional context and information was required if anyone was going to be able to navigate the huge amount of choice that currently exists in the marketplace.

So, in a climate where new breweries are popping up at the rate of one a week, the most frequent question we were asked when writing this book was, "How did you know when to stop?" We chose to make the cut-off point for inclusion two weeks before we had to hand in the manuscript of this book: approximately November 15, 2015.

The second-most-frequent question, and perhaps one of the more loaded ones, was, "How are you defining what makes a craft brewery?"

As you may know, there are a lot of definitions out there, from making small amounts of beer to being independently owned to being community focused. In this book we have included just about any brewery that might be considered "craft," which means breweries, brewpubs, and contract breweries. In all cases, we have denoted the difference in type of business for the sake of clarity. Because contracting is sometimes used as a first step by a brewery before moving into its own facility, some are listed as transitional.

In cases where a brewery has been purchased at some point in the past by a large multinational company, we have included it but made a note of the ownership. Breweries like Creemore and Mill Street have not transitioned yet to become national brands. They are still brewed locally and the historic context they've provided for the craft beer scene in Ontario cannot be ignored.

The purpose of this guide is to assist you in navigating Ontario's craft beer market and finding something that you might like to drink. Each brewery's entry is composed of its contact information and co-ordinates, a brief biography to help give a sense of the brewery's identity, and a series of tasting notes and ratings for the beers that it has on offer.

In producing tasting notes and ratings, we have strived for fairness. That being said, we have offered brewers every opportunity to put their best foot forward by directly consulting with them to see which beers (usually capped at eight examples) they feel best celebrate who they are. In the majority of the entries, we've used samples directly from the brewery itself, avoiding any potential problems that might arise from tasting the beer, from dirty tap lines in a bar or pub or from bottles or cans that have gone stale as a result of languishing too long on the shelves of a retail establishment.

A WORD ABOUT THE RATING SYSTEM

In producing ratings, we have been mostly interested in three things: whether the beer has objective flaws; how well the flavour profile works; and how well the beer accomplishes what it sets out to do, i.e., the extent to which it is what the brewer claims it to be.

Beer preference is subjective. You may like a certain style of beer more than another for just about any reason, and you're not wrong to feel that way. Brewing quality is not subjective. Beer frequently has technical flaws or undesirable qualities that can leave an unpleasant impression. In the case of flavour defects, these might include the presence of diacetyl (which smells like buttered popcorn, leaves a slick, butterscotchy mouthfeel, and causes hangovers), dimethyl sulphide (an aroma of creamed corn, canned vegetables, or tomato sauce), acetaldehyde (overwhelming green apple), butyric character (blue cheese or baby vomit), inappropriate phenolic character (smoke, burnt plastic, or Band-Aid), or just a lack of conditioning resulting in a rough, unpleasant mouthfeel. The beer may be inappropriately carbonated or under attenuated (containing residual sugars that ought to have been fermented).

We have taken into account stylistic convention. The Beer Judge Certification Program style guidelines are a helpful tool in doing exactly that and, combined with context, experience, and the knowledge that it is possible to push the envelope a little, they have helped form the backbone of our rating system.

We have been pleased to reward brewers for balance of flavours. A frequent criticism of websites for beer geeks is that they tend to reward the extreme, favouring beers with higher alcohol and in-your-face flavours. We've tried to eliminate this bias from our thinking, focusing on how balanced a beer is, its progression of flavours, and the overall impression that it leaves. Whether considering a beer in a simple style done well or a complex behemoth that somehow manages to attain balance, we've done our best to treat them similarly.

Finally, writing this book has given us an appreciation for how much the art of brewing has to do with expectation management. When deciding how to market a beer, brewers must decide exactly what that beer is in order to communicate its qualities effectively. If a brewer refers to something as a blonde ale and it has pronounced notes of chocolate and mint, something is seriously wrong. If a brewer has referred to something as "Belgian-style" and it shows no trace of Belgian influence, that's a real problem. If a "kölsch" is more like a blonde ale or a "cream ale" is more like a pale ale, we've taken that into account.

That said, there are always new styles of beer emerging. We have taken seriously the description of the beer provided. To give an example, the term *breakfast stout* may not be widely known enough to connote an actual style of beer, but it conveys the impression that it will taste like oats, coffee, and chocolate. It lets you know what you're getting, which is of ultimate importance to the consumer.

The rating system is a simple five-point system that includes half stars for emphasis and versatility. The ratings describe the following properties:

1 – POOR

A deeply flawed beer. Likely contains off flavours or does not seem to be well-made from a technical perspective. May be off-style or poorly conceived. Not recommended.

2 – FAIR

Beer may contain noticeable flaws in terms of flavour or technical elements. Beer approaches stylistic guidelines. Beer may not quite work from a conceptual standpoint.

3 – GOOD

Stylistically accurate. Beer does not contain off flavours. Beer may have issues with balance in its flavour profile. Technical proficiency is not an issue.

4 – VERY GOOD

A memorable example of the style. Very much in balance. Flavours are appropriate and the beer has managed a distinct character that sets it apart from other examples.

5 – EXCELLENT

A beer of quality such that it would hold its own against the best examples of its style in the world.

In some cases we've been unable to taste a particular beer. In these cases, we have not provided ratings, but rather a simple description of the beer followed by **"NR"** for "no rating."

LEGEND

In each brewery entry the contact information uses these symbols:

 ADDRESS   WEBSITE

 PHONE NUMBER   VISITING HOURS

 TWITTER   RETAIL STORE HOURS

TOP BREWERIES
IN ONTARIO

Here are the breweries that got the highest average ratings.

1. Side Launch Brewing Company
2. Folly Brewpub and Burdock Brewing (two-way tie)
3. Tooth and Nail Brewing Company
4. Bellwoods Brewery
5. Stone City Ales

TIED FOR SIXTH PLACE: Collective Arts Brewing, Creemore Springs Brewery, Great Lakes Brewery, Muddy York Brewing Company, Sawdust City Brewing Company

(We have excluded contract brewers from consideration.)

You'll find the beers that received the highest ratings on pages 20–27.

ONTARIO'S CRAFT BEER HISTORY

The renaissance of brewing in Ontario has taken place in approximately the same time frame during which the rest of North America's brewing industry has blossomed again. All across the continent, there has been an immense growth in the number of breweries operating and the number and types of beers available.

For the most part, however, the history of the brewing industry in North America has been about the consolidation and shuttering of various plants under larger banners. In Canada, throughout the middle of the twentieth century, one of our most successful businessmen, E.P. Taylor, built Canadian Breweries, an empire that thrived on this model, reducing the number of players in the market and the selection of products available to beer drinkers. His empire was not limited solely to North America. In the United Kingdom,

Taylor's consolidation of breweries and their tied houses led to a situation where Carling Lager was served in over eleven thousand pubs by 1967.

By the end of the 1970s, the number of players in the Ontario beer market was the smallest since the advent of industrialized brewing in the province. Molson, Labatt, Carling O'Keefe, Northern Breweries, and Henninger were all that was left of an industry that a hundred years earlier had boasted nearly two hundred companies. The lack of selection in the marketplace briefly created a boom in sales. The late 1970s represent the historical high point of beer sales across North America.

TOP FIVE IPAS		
1.	THRUST! AN IPA	p.175
2.	BRONAN IPA	p.180
3.	KARMA CITRA IPA	p.175
4.	BLACK SWAN IPA	p.86
5.	HEADSTOCK IPA	p.257

An indirect effect of E.P. Taylor's empire building was the founding in 1971 of England's Campaign for Real Ale (CAMRA). Concerned by the shrinking amount of diversity in brewing, CAMRA strived to preserve traditional brewing methods and more flavourful ale styles. CAMRA in turn inspired many of the microbrewery start-ups in Ontario. Germany had similarly been a bastion for quality and full-flavoured beer due to the protections of the *Reinheitsgebot*, or beer purity law (which limited the ingredients permitted to be used in the making of beer to water, hops, barley, and yeast), and its influence can be seen in our early brewers.

New craft beers from both of these traditions have found receptive markets in Ontario. In the early days of the craft beer revival in the province, there was a claim by some that the beer market in Ontario was separated by Yonge Street. To the east, it was said, customers preferred ales, due to their British traditions and heritage. To the west, drinkers supposedly preferred lagers, due to their Germanic roots. Whatever truth there might have been to this claim has, as the market diversified over the last thirty years, become diminishingly accurate to the point of irrelevance. However, the central premise that lies at the heart of this insight does help to illustrate why Ontario has provided such a robust market for

TOP FIVE PALE ALES	
1. GOLDEN BEACH	p.300
2. RHYME & REASON	p.136
3. 504 PALE ALE	p.212
4. JUTSU	p.73
5. CANUCK PALE ALE	p.175

beer in the twentieth century and why so many beer lovers in the province were so quick to take up brewing in the 1980s: the majority of the population had come from beer-drinking nations.

There has been a tremendous growth in the business of brewing beer in Ontario since the 1980s. It is helpful to think of this modern brewing history in Ontario as three distinct periods: the founding of the first wave of small brewers (approximately 1984 to 1995); a second period following failure and shakeout when conservatism reigned (approximately 1996 to 2007); and the current period (2007 to the present day), signified largely by enthusiasm, expansion, and change to the market.

THE FIRST WAVE (1984–1995)

Ontario's first craft brewery, Brick, was founded in Waterloo in 1984, literally in the shadow of Labatt's converted Kuntz facility. Upper Canada opened in Toronto the same year, brewing a mixed selection of ales and lagers. Overall, the selection of styles on offer in the province was very basic, with the varieties being direct lifts of English and German tradition.

TOP FIVE PILSNERS	
1. VIM AND VIGOR	p.346
2. PILS-SINNER	p.192
3. WEST COAST PILSNER	p.111
4. STARKE PILSNER	p.50
5. STEAM WHISTLE (UNFILTERED)	p.320

Frequently, brewers would cite their travels in Europe as inspiration for a particular recipe. Latching on to any tradition, be it the "real ale" movement or the *Reinheitsgebot* regulations, provided ready-made talking points and a defined marketing context for small-brewery products. These specialty products helped to differentiate small brewers from their much larger, and more established, counterparts. The 1980s may well prove to have been the only period in Ontario history when people anticipated the annual release of a bock beer.

Small brewers were helped in their battle to capture the imagination of the market by a labour dispute at the Beer Store, which closed down for the month of February in 1985. At the time, the LCBO (Liquor Control Board of Ontario) had not fully diversified into beer sales, offering only inexpensive

American imports like Pabst Blue Ribbon and Lonestar. With the province's only real outlet for beer sales closed and the LCBO struggling to keep up with orders, small local breweries became important in the short term. Customers were lining up in order to purchase their beer, and sales were so strong that the small breweries were pleading in newspaper interviews for the return of empties so that they could bottle more beer.

One of the hallmarks of this period was the ambitious attitude toward the market. For decades, the beer industry model in Ontario involved an attempt to sell beer to the whole province through the Beer Store. It was a model dictated by the largest players in the market and many start-up breweries attempted to

TOP FIVE STOUTS		
1.	COBBLESTONE STOUT	p.237
2.	SHIPS IN THE NIGHT OATMEAL STOUT	p.322
3.	OR DUBH STOUT	p.270
4.	LUCK & CHARM OATMEAL STOUT	p.224
5.	BLAK KATT STOUT	p.140

emulate it. The small breweries founded in this period were huge by today's standards. By the end of its first decade of operation, Brick was producing 40,000 HL of beer annually and was publicly traded. Sleeman, partially funded by Stroh's in Michigan, began producing beer in 1988 at 200,000 HL annually. In point of fact, of the thirteen microbreweries listed in 1993's *Ontario Beer Guide*, the very smallest produced just under 10,000 HL of beer and the majority were vastly larger.

Toward the end of this period, the industry was plagued by two issues. The first was quality. The drive to create large volumes of beer for sale led to issues with consistency on the part of brewers who were, after all, relatively inexperienced, having started only a decade previously. Adding to the problem of inconsistent quality was the proliferation of extract brewing systems in brewpubs across the province. By 1993, Ontario had thirty-one brewpubs, many of which operated with these systems. Extract brewing was touted as something anyone could do, as replacing all-grain brewing with malt extract removed much of the effort from the process. A small number of these brewpubs simplified things even further by simply using imported wort, removing even the necessity of adding extract to hot water and making them responsible only for fermenting it on premises. Without sufficient training, information, and respect for cleanliness, however, the quality of the beer being served suffered enormously. It is not a surprise that the majority of those that survived employed all-grain brewing methods.

The second issue was the emergence of the discount beer segment at approximately the same time. In late 1992, President's Choice launched its own brand, which managed to

TOP FIVE SAISONS	
1. FLEMISH CAP	p.162
2. BRETT FARMHOUSE SAISON	p.111
3. FARMAGEDDON	p.73
4. PRAXIS	p.161
5. PENGO PALLY	p.113

capture fully 2 percent of the market by spring of the following year. Loblaws, which had commissioned the beer, struggled to keep up with demand. Imitators were spawned and the large brewers entered the discount-beer market. Ontarians, perhaps sensibly in the wake of a recession, decided that, rather than paying a premium for inconsistent beer produced by small brewers, they would prefer to pay much less for a dependable product that was somewhat inferior in flavour. Even those who enjoyed a more flavourful beer increasingly avoided the not-always-dependable small breweries and brewpubs. Instead, they began taking advantage of the numerous brew-on-premises outlets that opened at the time.

TOP FIVE PORTERS		
1.	ROBUST PORTER	p.128
2.	MUDDY YORK PORTER	p.241
3.	BRICKS & MORTAR COFFEE PORTER	p.211
4.	NUTCRACKER	p.84
5.	CLIFFORD PORTER	p.131

These allowed anyone to walk in off the street and make small batches of beer of a relatively high quality at a massive discount.

As a result of these issues, sales in the craft beer market declined significantly. Brewpubs folded left and right. Small breweries closed or were consolidated into the holdings of larger companies. The effects of the shakeout of the mid-1990s can be seen to this day. Some of Ontario's early craft brands are owned by odd companies. Brick has ended up with Conners and Northern Algonquin. Sleeman still produces Upper Canada Lager and Dark Ale (which are shells of their former selves).

THE SECOND WAVE (1996–2007)

If the second period in our recent history has a theme, it is that of caution.

As one might expect following such a period of tribulation, the late 1990s saw craft breweries reining in experimentation. Instead, the surviving breweries focused on quality and consistency. It had become apparent that the key to long-term success in the beer market in Ontario was not the size of the brewery, but rather the ability to grow predictably while maintaining the quality of the product.

The good news was that the first generation of small brewers in Ontario had produced a significant number of personnel capable of running breweries that conformed to this model. Of the relatively small number of start-ups that emerged following the shakeout, the majority had employees that had formerly worked in successful breweries. Steam Whistle is the most famous example, with founding partners who had worked at Upper Canada. The "3FG" code on its bottles stands for Three Fired Guys. Mill Street was founded by personnel from Amsterdam. Magnotta entered the beer industry having already developed expertise in wine production. Other new ventures were frequently staffed by veterans of existing breweries who had outgrown their positions or found themselves without an employer. The pattern repeated throughout the industry, creating a sense of continuity in the slow but steady recovery.

During this period, the quality of the beer on offer increased dramatically. However, the variety of beer styles being brewed remained approximately the same and, at various points, may even be said to have decreased. Ontario developed a reputation internationally for beers that were of high quality even if they were not particularly interesting. By way of contrast, in the United States, which had always been a more adventurous market and somewhat less bound up in tradition than Ontario, brewers created mould-breaking, highly experimental beers.

ROBIN'S PICKS

In the defence of Ontario's craft brewers, it can be said that, chastened more than a little by the troubles of the mid-1990s, they were justifiably timid. The decision to offer a new brand was not taken lightly. However, experimentation was minimal. After all, the beer was selling, and many brewers saw little benefit in developing new recipes. A residual effect of this, which persists to this day, is the sentiment among beer geeks that Ontario lags behind the United States in terms of interesting beer.

ONTARIO'S CRAFT BEER HISTORY

THE THIRD WAVE (2007–PRESENT)

The term *craft beer* entered into popular usage midway through the first decade of the twenty-first century. The change in language helped to differentiate a category in which small brewers could participate. The Ontario Small Brewers Association, originally founded in 2003, changed its name in 2005 to Ontario Craft Brewers in order to take advantage of this development.

Gradually, over the course of the decade, the number of kinds of beer being offered began to expand. The hop-forward ales that had been popular in the United States began to have additional influence on recipe design north of the border. The earliest commercially available examples were still malt-heavy. The now retired Devil's Pale Ale from Great Lakes was considered extreme at its launch in 2006, containing a whopping 66.6 International Bittering Units' (IBU) worth of hopping.

Slowly, confidence returned to the market and new breweries began to crop up. The build-up was slow, however. In the first half of the decade there were entire years that went by without a brewery launch. From 2006 to 2010, the average was approximately four a year. An increase in the status of craft beer was helped by the addition of bars and pubs focused specifically on the category. Events like Bar Volo's Cask Days and an increasing number of other festivals provided showcases for experimentation and challenged brewers to come up with something new to delight the public.

The focus of the business began to change. Rather than intending to sell beer to the entire province, brewers focused on specific localities, due in part to the expense of dealing with the foreign-owned Beer Store chain. Distribution through the LCBO has increased and the focus in packaging has shifted from the traditional six-pack of bottles to a system that prefers single cans of beer. For the most part, very small craft breweries prefer to do business out their front doors. Compared to the early brewers of the 1980s, the ambition of Ontario's new craft brewers is somewhat smaller. The size of these companies may not be as large, but the imagination on display is infinitely greater.

The caution that followed the shakeout of the 1990s has served us well. Many of the young brewers opening their own facilities gained experience under long-time industry veterans and have had the idea that quality matters drilled into them as a mantra. The cumulative wisdom is having a real effect.

The addition of the Niagara College Brewmaster and Brewery Operations Management program helps to ensure that brewery start-ups will survive, and has engendered a greater sense of community in an already collegial industry.

Between 2012 and 2016, Ontario will have added 150 breweries to the roster of brewing operations in the province, including individual brewpub locations, contract brewers, and bricks-and-mortar breweries. That surpasses the high point of the nineteenth century. During the five-month period in which this book was written, Ontario launched more breweries than it did during the 1990s in total.

At the moment, there are very few styles of beer in the world that are not brewed in Ontario. In addition to the brewing industry, there is currently a burgeoning hop industry, a handful of maltsters, and suppliers of yeast starting up. The brewing renaissance is in full swing and the province has taken notice. Recent changes to the retail system will ensure that this development continues.

BUYING BEER IN ONTARIO

As a result of a combination of factors, the Ontario beer market has changed relatively drastically in a very short time. The addition of 150 breweries over the last four years created a situation in which reform to the existing beer-retailing system was necessary in order to provide the provinces' breweries a road to the market. The political will to make these changes was helped somewhat by the geographic allocation of breweries. There is now a small brewer in just about every riding in the province, which makes their survival an important issue for local government representatives.

In this section we will attempt to outline the players in the market. This comes with a caveat. Change to the retail portion of the Ontario beer market is going to come relatively slowly over the next decade. This is likely by design. Critics of the recent changes that have taken place assume that the laggard nature of change is designed to help the large brewers. More probably, the changes to the market are designed to be gradual and predictable in order to create dependable tax revenues for the Ontario government. In life, sometimes we get boring policy instead of exciting conspiracies.

THE BEER STORE

In principle, the Beer Store is a good idea. Founded in 1927, it was a post-Prohibition answer to beer retailing. The twelve-year experiment with prohibiting alcohol left a market in which there was no system for retailing beer. The Province of Ontario created the Liquor Control Board of Ontario (LCBO) in order to retail wine and liquor, but was stymied somewhat by one of the ever-present realities of brewers throughout history: beer takes up a lot of space. Beer is heavy and the roads are poor. In order to sell beer, it is necessary to warehouse it and deliver it. Consider the cost of starting the LCBO from scratch and then tack on additional warehousing.

Brewer's Warehousing, as the Beer Store was called when it was first created, was an attempt to outsource the warehousing and delivery of beer. Originally, it delivered to mom-and-pop stores, which actually handled the retailing. The warehousing system was partially owned by each of the brewers in the province — a format that made it a co-operative.

Some brewers were larger than others, but that is a persistent market reality. Eventually, Brewers Warehousing became Brewers Retail and the warehouses developed their own network of stores. The cost savings for brewers as a result of the vertical integration of the business was part of the appeal.

With the benefit of hindsight, it is easy to see that the consolidation of Ontario's breweries was an inevitability following Prohibition. Many of them had been turned into vinegar factories or soft-drink bottling plants and were not really solvent. Prohibition had driven nearly all of Ontario's brewers out of business, but the creation of Brewers Warehousing in 1927 was not the ideal answer for many of the new breweries that were opened following the relaxation of the province's liquor laws; in fact, it compounded the pressure on some brewers. While the beer retailing co-op provided savings to the brewers who jointly owned it, the size of the operation and the fact that participating brewers were expected to be able to provide enough beer to stock stores across the province meant that many brewers could not afford to be part of it. As a result, larger, better-financed companies, such as E.P. Taylor's Canadian Breweries, were able to lessen competition by buying up the smaller, failing brewing operations.

While companies like Canadian Breweries certainly got the ball rolling, consolidation was happening in markets all over the world. This practice continued over the next few decades until, by the 1980s, there were only a handful of giant brewers left in Canada. In Ontario, this extreme consolidation of the brewery business resulted in the Beer Store having just two majority owners by 1989: Molson and Labatt.

By 2014, additional mergers and acquisitions in the international market meant that Molson had become Molson Coors and was therefore partially American owned. Labatt had been purchased by InBev in 1995 and subsequently became part of the Belgian-based Anheuser-Busch InBev. A small percentage is owned by Japan's Sapporo, which was able to make inroads into the market by purchasing Sleeman. As a consequence of corporate consolidations, the means of distribution and retailing of beer in the province of Ontario, originally intended to be a co-operative for the province's brewers, was completely owned by three entities based outside the province. It was estimated by various analysts that the owners realized between $400 and $700 million worth of cost reductions annually as a result of this arrangement.

The 150 breweries that existed in Ontario at the end of 2014 had no ownership stake or decision-making ability in the system with which they were meant to do business. Criticisms included exorbitant listing fees and unequal representation on shelves and in displays, both of which were entirely justified. Additionally, the Beer Store represents a mid-twentieth-century model of retail designed for a small number of year-round brands to be sold in large packaging formats. The craft beer model, which includes numerous seasonal releases throughout the course of the year, was completely ignored.

The Beer Store's failure to acknowledge the realities of the market have led to some mandated changes. Small brewers will be entitled to purchase nominal ownership. The board structure has been revamped to include independent members and representatives for non-majority owners. The creation of the position of beer ombudsman will hopefully shed light on any abuses customers witness. A reduction in the fee structure and a mandate dedicating 20 percent of products be from small brewers may make the stores more accessible, but the question remains as to whether small brewers will want to do business with an entity that did not consider their needs until forced to by the government.

In light of other developments, the Beer Store's overall business will likely continue to wane. The LCBO diversified into beer two generations ago, and polling commissioned by the authors suggests that 50 percent of customers under the age of forty-five are unlikely to shop for beer at the Beer Store. Its unwillingness to cater to an emerging market rendered the Beer Store irrelevant to Ontario's brewers as a retailer for years and did serious damage to it with beer drinkers. It remains to be seen whether brewers will do business with it and whether customers can be persuaded to shop there again.

THE LCBO

As mentioned, the LCBO was not designed to handle beer. Its mandate was to sell the province wine and liquor. There was a time when it did so begrudgingly, forcing people to carry liquor-permit books with them until 1962. In the modern era, it supplies a glossy magazine that highlights the qualities of various types of alcohol and provides food-pairing possibilities. This suggests that change is possible as long as the government gets a cut of the profits.

The LCBO has done quite a good job with the beer segment, especially when you consider that it was not designed for that purpose. Its position as the largest purchaser of beverage alcohol in the world means that it has frequently achieved economies of scale in dealing with foreign producers. That means Ontarians have access to world-class Belgian and German beers at incredibly reasonable prices. In fact, the LCBO is the only retail organization in Ontario that actively imports beer from other countries. While the choices it makes in terms of which beers to import is certainly a bone of contention, it hits on winners about 50 percent of the time.

The real difficulty with the LCBO is the fact that it is limited in terms of retail space. Traditional beer-packaging formats are large and cumbersome. An agreement from the year 2000 arranged that the LCBO would limit itself to six packs as the maximum volume in the majority of its stores (agency stores excluded), allowing the Beer Store exclusivity on twelve- and twenty-four-bottle formats. While this caused public outcry upon revelation, it's not an insensible policy. The Beer Store was designed to handle those volumes. The LCBO was not.

The LCBO has done quite well for Ontario's small brewers, which have been one of the fastest-growing segments in the store for a number of years. In fact, the explosion of Ontario's craft scene could not have happened without the LCBO as a partner. There are, however, a few intrinsic problems. For one thing, brewers are not guaranteed shelf space at the LCBO and frequently profess a desire for a more transparent product-selection process. For another, limitations in shelf space mean that the preferred formats for craft beer are cans and single bottles. A side effect of this limitation is that people experiment with different products more willingly — a real positive if you're a small brewer.

The LCBO has recently launched the Craft Beer Zone, a specialty area in a small number of stores that will focus on showcasing Ontario's brewers and giv them the attention that the exploding industry deserves. That being said, the LCBO is ill-equipped to deal with the approximately 200 breweries that currently exist, let alone the hundred that are in the planning.

GROCERY STORES

The announcement in April of 2015 that grocery stores would be permitted to sell beer in Ontario was met with skepticism.

It has been so long since there was any change to the structure of beer retailing in the province that a certain amount of wariness was understandable. According to the new framework, over the course of the next decade 450 grocery stores will be allowed licences to sell beer, creating approximately the same number of retailers as currently exist in the Beer Store chain. While the initial bidding process has allowed for sixty grocery stores to obtain licenses at time of writing, 150 stores will have the ability to sell beer by May 1, 2017. A reasonable effort has been made to ensure the distribution of licences is equitable and that they do not fall solely to larger chains of stores.

There are justifiable concerns about the manner in which beer is going to be sold. An upper limit of 7.1% alcohol on products to be sold at grocery stores seems somewhat arbitrary but should not represent a barrier to the vast majority of brands. Stores will apparently not be allowed to sell their own brand of products. A soft cap on volumes of beer being sold through each location means grocery stores will pay a 1-percent penalty beyond a certain amount of beer sold, with that penalty going to the brewer owners of the Beer Store. The authors suspect that this amount will in no way be large enough to compensate the Beer Store for its loss of business. The convenience of being able to purchase beer and food in a single trip should prove to be extremely attractive to beer drinkers.

A mandated 20-percent quota for small-brewer inventory and the massive increase in shelf space that grocery stores represent means that this development is likely to disproportionately benefit craft brewers in Ontario. If one views grocery store sales in the United States or other provinces as an example, it's likely that while large international breweries will be represented, they will not be able to dominate. Grocery stores are prohibited from accepting money or inducements for shelf space. In point of fact, most grocers have indicated that they plan to exceed the quota significantly. This development represents a huge amount of potential growth for Ontario's brewing industry and should be exciting to watch over the next few years.

BARS AND RESTAURANTS

One of the best places to enjoy craft beer is at a bar that specializes in serving it. To that end, we have created an appendix with a list of some of the better destinations in Ontario for your delectation. Because craft breweries tend to sell and deliver directly to bars and pubs, that's where you're likely to find their most interesting products. Seasonals and one-off beers are in high demand across the province for rotating taps, and offerings can change daily. Many better pubs post daily changes on Twitter or Instagram.

Some of the better bars will have dozens of choices. A word of caution: beyond a certain point you may notice diminishing returns on taplist size. A bar with over a hundred craft beers on tap is almost certainly not turning over kegs at the speed of a bar with a dozen. Although this is not a certainty, you may want to keep in mind that variety has drawbacks as well as advantages.

Bars that do not carry some manner of craft beer are becoming increasingly rare in urban parts of Ontario. That said, brewery incentivization remains a real problem in the province. Doubtless you will have walked into a bar in which all of the taps are from a single large brewing company. Perhaps you have witnessed the annual blossoming of the promotional patio umbrellas.

Theoretically, the practice of incentivizing bars to carry your product is illegal. In practice it remains very difficult to enforce. The Alcohol and Gaming Commission of Ontario does not currently have a realistic path to the enforcement of this policy. As a consumer, you do. We urge you to vote with your dollar. Choose to drink in a bar with more flavourful beer that's made in Ontario by a small producer. Not only will you be helping the province's economy, the food will probably be better and the people will almost certainly be more interesting.

BREWERIES

If you enjoy beer and you'd like to support Ontario's craft breweries, the place that makes the most sense to buy beer is at the brewery. Whether it's a brewpub that sells growlers out of its retail store or a full-size brewery with bottles, cans, and a selection of novelty glassware and bottle openers, the reality is this: The beer is going to be better coming out of the brewery. It will be fresher and tastier.

While buying through a retail channel may be more convenient, depending on where you live there may be issues with freshness when you're buying a product from a store that stocks several hundred different items. In the case of craft beer, which is almost always unpasteurized and frequently unfiltered, the product is probably shelf stable for up to four months. That said, the difference between a fresh can and a four-month-old can is probably noticeable in a side-by-side tasting, even to the uninitiated.

Many small breweries have tasting bars that will allow you to try a small amount of a beer before you purchase it, just in case you want to be sure that you'll like it. In some parts of Ontario you could put together a pretty good afternoon wandering from brewery to brewery and doing just that. The majority of these breweries will have knowledgeable employees behind the bar, willing to talk you through the finer points of their products. In some cases it may be the owner of the brewery manning the bar. It's always good to know the person whose product you're buying.

Also, because the beer at the brewery is not subject to retail markups, brewers will make a better margin on beer that they sell out their front door. This, in turn, will allow them to invest in their businesses and improve the beer that you're buying from them. When you buy beer from the brewery retail store, you're part of a delicious economic cycle.

Ontario
CRAFT
BREWERIES

ABE ERB BREWERY & RESTAURANT

📍 15 King Street S, Waterloo

📞 (519) 886-4518

🐦 @abe_erb

🌐 abeerb.com

🕐 Mon–Thu 11a.m.–1a.m., Fri 11a.m.–2a.m.,
Sat–Sun 9a.m.–12a.m. No tours necessary,
as equipment is prominently displayed.

🛒 Open daily 11a.m.–11p.m.

Named after Waterloo's first settler, Mennonite Abraham Erb, this brewpub opened in 2014. The owners have gone for a visual effect that they refer to as "boutique industrial," and the design is a thoughtful use of the space. The airy, high-ceilinged room has a windowed garage door as a front wall and chandeliers made out of repurposed barrels from the now-defunct Seagram's distillery. The brewery cellar is unique in that its fermenters are housed on a catwalk above the dining area, supported by steel beams driven eight feet into the concrete floor. Within this rough space are elegant touches such as repurposed window sashes fitted with stained glass, custom leather couches, and even specially commissioned wallpaper.

The menu is restrained and focuses on the use of local produce in traditional pub fare, making good use of the in-house smoker for barbecue dishes. The staff is welcoming and enthusiastic.

―――

1857 KÖLSCH is a refreshing version of the hybrid style served from a bright tank positioned directly above the bar. It has a crisp, grainy body with white grape, green apple, and lavender accents (4). **ALTERIOR MOTIVE** is also a German hybrid beer but eschews the traditional earthiness, instead deriving light chocolate and biscuit from the specialty malts, with a hint of tart raspberry jammy-ness in the middle, not unlike a Viva Puff (3.5). **WALKABOUT** is a session IPA made entirely with Australian hops and packed full of tropical-fruit character (3.5). **BUGGYWHIP** IPA, although only 45 IBU, is a journey through low-country pine scrub and juniper (3), while its big brother **WHIPLASH** double IPA balances that character with additional sweetness and body (3.5).

ALL OR NOTHING BREWHOUSE

📍 1100 Skae Drive, Oshawa

📞 (416) 238-6760

🐦 @allornothingbh

🌐 allornothing.beer

Since the summer of 2014, All or Nothing has been a staple of the Toronto beer scene, appearing on tap at a number of the better bars around the city. Brothers Jeff and Eric Dornan manage the distribution of their contract-brewed hopfenweisse from their headquarters in Oshawa. The name of the brewery ties nicely into the sentiment shared by many small brewers in Ontario about their place in a market dominated by large international conglomerates. In November of 2015, the brewery was forced to change their name from Underdogs as part of a trademark dispute; the beer remains identical.

———

ALL OR NOTHING HOPFENWEISSE is a hop-forward take on German wheat beer. The smooth, wheaty body produces a doughy aroma highlighted by banana, tropical fruits, and freshly juiced oranges (3.5).

AMBER BREWERY

📍 130 Riviera Drive, Markham

📞 (905) 305-8383

🌐 www.amberbrewery.com

🛒 Sales by phone and email for kegs,
including free delivery within the GTA.

Located in Markham, Amber is a brand that you're unlikely to run into at retail. The brewery itself does not currently have a retail store, preferring to deal with small mom-and-pop businesses in the restaurant and bar trade. The brewery has a 20-HL brewhouse and is therefore significantly larger than many new craft brewers in Ontario, and has been producing beer for over two decades.

———

The focus at Amber is on value, with its two brands, **TORONTO HOUSE LAGER** (NR) and **CHICAGO DARK** (NR) being positioned as competitively priced compared to similar choices in the Toronto market.

THE ONTARIO CRAFT BEER GUIDE

AMSTERDAM BREWING COMPANY

AMSTERDAM BREWERY

- 📍 45 Esandar Drive, Toronto
- 📞 (416) 504-6882
- 🐦 @amsterdambeer
- 🌐 www.amsterdambeer.com
- 🕐 Tours Sat 1p.m.–5p.m.
- 🛒 Mon–Sat 11a.m.–10p.m., Sun 11a.m.–6p.m.

AMSTERDAM BREWHOUSE

- 📍 245 Queens Quay W, Toronto
- 📞 (416) 504-1020
- 🐦 @AmsterdamBH
- 🌐 amsterdambrewhouse.com
- 🕐 Tours Mon–Tues 4p.m., Wed–Sun 11a.m.–6p.m.
- 🛒 Mon–Wed 3p.m.–10p.m., Thu–Sun 11a.m.–10p.m.

Toronto's oldest craft brewery has had its share of change over the years. Beginning as a brewpub under Roel Bramer at 133 John Street in 1986, a second location, The Rotterdam, was added on King Street West in 1988. In 2003, they acquired Kawartha Lakes Brewery and their current brew-master, Iain McOustra. From 2005 to 2012 the brewery occupied a space at the bottom of Bathurst. The current incarnation includes a large-scale production facility in Leaside and a massive brewpub on Queen's Quay West.

Amsterdam's core product lineup has changed significantly since the beginning of the decade; only three of their nine year-round offerings existed before 2010. Under McOustra, the brewing team has proved to be as versatile as any in the province in creating beers for their Seasonal and Adventure Brew ranges, with farmhouse ales and barrel-aging programs being specialities. Amsterdam now walks the line between providing extremely affordable beer for the masses and specialty products for enthusiasts, while slowly converting the former to the latter.

————

ALL NATURAL BLONDE is a brewery staple representing the older mentality at Amsterdam. A competently made pale lager, it's a step up from macro beers (2.5). **FRAMBOISE** is a long-time seasonal wheat beer using a huge number of raspberries in fermentation to good effect (3.5). **CRUISER** is a contemporary pale ale with bright lemon and grape-fruit from Citra and Sorachi Ace hops (4). **BONESHAKER** is more an oversized red ale than an IPA and fits a huge amount of pine and zest into its wide body (3.5). **STARKE**

PILS is a recent addition to the mix that merges a massive Hallertau lime bite with a crisp finish (4). **HOWL** is a mixed-fermentation farmhouse ale with a sharp peppery aroma and dry tail (4), while **TESTIFY** combines tropical hop character with an all-Brettanomyces fermentation (4.5). **TEMPEST** is a rye-heavy imperial stout with notes of smoke, coffee, and deep, dark roasted grain (4), while **BARREL AGED DOUBLE TEMPEST** will hold its own against any of North America's super-heavyweight imperial stouts and ought to be shared (5).

ARCH BREWING COMPANY

📞 (1-888) 391-7670

🐦 @ArchBrewingCo

🌐 www.archbrewing.ca

For Suzie and Billy King, the road to Arch has been a long one. It took eight years for them to realize their dream of opening a brewery, testing the waters with a contract-brewed product before jumping into the market with both feet. Retaining Paul Dickey as their brewer, Arch produces a single beer out of Wellington Brewery in Guelph. However, plans are currently in place for a brewery of their own in Newmarket, which should open in early 2016. They intend it to be a boutique brewery with a 10-BBL brew-house producing experimental brands, and they have hired Andrew Anker, a graduate of Niagara College, as their brewer.

———

Their initial product, **DINNER JACKET O'RED IPA**, is a complicated number. A combination of an IPA and an Irish red ale, the nose is strongly pine while the body is nutty caramel and toasted oat with a whiff of wet leather on the finish (2.5).

ASHTON BREWING COMPANY

📍 113 Old Mill Road, Ashton

📞 (613) 257-4423

🐦 @AshtonBrew

🌐 ashtonbrewpub.ca

🕐 Mon–Sun 11:30a.m.–11:00p.m.

Originally built as a grist mill on the bank of the Jock River, the Old Mill at Ashton is a brewpub with a historic feel. Some of the original wooden foundation still shows signs of a fire. The brewery is owned by the Hodgins family, who began pouring their beers to the public in 2011. The Hodgins patriarch, Art, has had a long career as a publican, having owned many establishments in the area since 1975. This, his first brewpub, required additional expertise. To set up the brewing side of the Old Mill, the family enlisted the help of Lorne Hart, founder and owner of the famous Hart Brewery, which opened in 1991 and closed its doors in 2005, to the upset of many.

Under the hand of brewmaster Eric Dubec, the Ashton Brewing Company (using the ABC brand throughout their lineup) makes accessible, flavourful beers. While ABC beers

ONTARIO CRAFT BREWERIES

are poured across the Ottawa region, they can also be found in the Bank Street tied houses of Patty's Pub and Quinn's Ale House, as well as the Old Mill itself.

If you find yourself at the Old Mill, keep a look out for George, the resident ghost.

———

SESSION ALE is a mild and easy beer that has many of the malt characteristics of a blonde ale (4). **CREAM ALE** has a pilsner-like aroma, thanks to the Saaz hops (3). **AMBER** has robust roasted-coffee notes complementing citrus tones (3.5). **HARVEST BROWN** features unmistakable creamy chocolate notes (2.5). **HOPSTRAVAGANZA** is an English-influenced IPA with a medium body, citrus undertones, and a lingering bitter aftertaste (4). **VANILLA STOUT** is served on nitro and features intense coffee notes with a smooth mouthfeel (2).

BANCROFT BREWING COMPANY

📍 2 Hastings Street N, Bancroft

📞 (613) 334-8154

🌐 www.bancroftbrewing.ca

🕐 Re-opening summer 2016.

In 2014 the Bancroft Brewing Company, under the ownership of the Krupa family, took over the Southern Algonquin Pub and Eatery and installed a brewpub. One of the first breweries to take advantage of the Hastings County Economic Development Office's handbook on starting up a brewery, Bancroft Brewing supplies beer to their eatery. After starting with a small system, the brewery was expanded in the summer of 2015 and now supports a retail store, which launched in August. Their brewpub is still the best place to enjoy Bancroft's beers.

———

To date, Bancroft's lineup includes four beers. **BLONDE LADY** is a light blonde ale that fills the role of being the brewery's accessible beer for those who may be new to craft (NR). **IRON**

MAN IPA fits squarely into the Ontario pale ale category with a selection of West Coast hops meeting sweet malt and roasted character (NR). **BLACK QUARTZ ALE** is a dark ale named after a gem specific to the region. Containing six malts, it has notes of coffee and caramel (NR). **LOGGERS ALE** is a straight-ahead English brown ale (NR).

BANDED GOOSE BREWING COMPANY

📍 31 Division Street S, Kingsville

📞 (519) 733-6900

🐦 @jacksgastropub

🌐 www.facebook.com/bandedgoosebrewing

🕐 Sun–Mon 11:30a.m.–8p.m., Tue–Sat 11:30a.m.–9p.m.

Started in early 2014, Banded Goose is a nanobrewery-sized expansion to Jack's Gastropub and Inn 31 in Kingsville, themed to take advantage of the migratory patterns of birds over Lake Erie. The brewing set-up at Banded Goose is diminutive even by nanobrewing standards, coming in initially at just under fifty litres per batch. The goal for Banded Goose is not to brew enough to sell off-site, but rather to brew beers that complement the pub's menu, using seasonal ingredients where possible. They are often able to take advantage of local hop yards in Leamington. At present they are usually able to manage two draught taps of their own beer at once to go alongside eight other taps of Ontario offerings. The menu features produce from local farms and artisans, and provides pairing suggestions of both wine and beer.

NOTTY BLONDE is a citrus-forward blonde ale that uses zest and Saaz hops to add punch (NR). **POT O' GOLD AMBER ALE** is a slightly sweet amber that uses Cascade hops and locally grown Centennial for dry hopping (NR). **FALSE ALARM IPA** is a single-hop Centennial beer that develops grapefruit bitterness (NR). Seasonal offerings in 2015 included a pumpkin brown and an apple cinnamon saison.

BARLEY DAYS BREWERY

📍 13730 Loyalist Parkway, Picton

📞 (613) 476-7468

🐦 @BarleyDaysBrews

🌐 barleydaysbrewery.com

🕐 Summer: Open daily 10:30a.m.–6p.m.
Winter: Fri–Sun 10:30a.m.–5p.m., Mon–Thurs by chance.

First opening as Glenora Springs Brewery in 2000, Barley Days changed their name in 2007 to commemorate the period in Prince Edward County's history as a producer of malted barley. Barley Days has long been regarded as the brewing ambassador of their home region, and is featured prominently on promotional material to promote Prince Edward County tourism. In light of new ownership in 2015, Barley Days has moved operations to a new facility and, with brewmaster Brett French, are doing their bit to spread awareness of the rich history and brewing talent that the county has.

———

Most of Barley Days' beer names feature a common theme, referencing the rich history of Prince Edward County.

ONTARIO CRAFT BREWERIES

Their selection includes **LOYALIST LAGER**, with a light biscuit finish and a delicate toffee note (2.5); **WIND & SAIL DARK ALE**, with its very prominent roasted-caramel notes and light to medium mouthfeel (3); **SACRED MULE SPARKING ALE**, a Czech pilsner perplexingly brewed with sparkling-wine yeast that showcases how yeast can change the profile of a beer, contributing a bitter flavour not unlike mustard seed in the finish (1); and **HARVEST GOLD PALE ALE**, a nicely bitter beer with dry floral notes and a mild, bitter finish (2.5).

BARNSTORMER BREWING COMPANY

- 📍 384 Yonge Street #3, Barrie
- 📞 (705) 481-1701
- 🐦 @BarnstormerBeer
- 🌐 barnstormerbrewing.com
- 🕐 Sun–Thu 11a.m.–11p.m., Fri–Sat 11a.m.–1a.m.
- 🛒 Daily 11a.m.–11p.m

Opened late in 2013 in a shopping plaza on the south side of Kempenfelt Bay, Barnstormer Brewing is Barrie's first brewpub. The restaurant has an aeronautical motif that extends across the entire enterprise, from the nose-cone pin-up mascot through to the names of the spelt-crust pizzas on the menu. Featuring walls covered with diagrams of aircraft, despite cozy wooden fixtures, the bar-area has the feel of a small aircraft hangar. At present the brewhouse is a relatively small 3-BBL system built into the space by original brewer Dustin Norland, but there are plans to expand to a bigger 10-BBL model with new brewer Jeff Woodworth. Barnstormer is planning for that increase by attending beer festivals across Ontario in order to build a following.

FLIGHT 400 is a lightly fruity blonde ale with a touch of strawberry and garden herbs over a straight-ahead cereal body (2.5). **WINDSHEAR WATERMELON SUMMER ALE** is a light-bodied American wheat made with watermelon juice that comes across more as rind than pulp due to the wheaty tang (2). **CIRRUS SESSION PALE ALE** is a light pale ale with bright lemon, orange, and tropical fruit character from the hopping schedule (4). **LATE ALL DAY PALE ALE** is an English take with an earthy, spicy hop character although mild in bitterness (2.5). **BILLY BISHOP BROWN** fits somewhere between a brown ale and a mild due to its relatively low alcohol, but features toasted grain, chocolate, toffee, and a gentle finish (3.5). **FLIGHT DELAY IPA** is a West Coast IPA that neatly balances northwest pine and orange with mango and guava in the aroma (3.5). **COCKY CAPTAIN** is a nineties-throwback American strong ale with a deep dried-fruit and caramel malt body, and a woody, earthy bite (3). **BLACK BOX** is a restrained oatmeal stout with light roasted mocha notes and a hint of toffee sweetness (3.5).

BAYSIDE BREWING COMPANY

BAYSIDE BREWING Cᵒ

ERIEAU 🍁 CANADA

📍 970 Ross Lane, Erieau

📞 (519) 676-1888

🐦 @BaysideBrewery

🌐 baysidebrewing.com

🕐 Daily 12p.m.–9p.m.

🛒 Daily 11a.m.–9p.m.

Located on the Erieau peninsula at the south end of Rondeau Bay, the Bayside Brewing Company has been a very popular addition to the Erie coast. Opened in 2013, with equipment repurposed from noted Windsor brewpub Charly's and with the same brewer, Bayside is something of a summer destination due to its large patio and proximity to the beach. The menu largely consists of standard pub fare, although the selection of pizzas from their wood-fired oven is a clear highlight.

———

The beers on offer are in fairly basic, accessible styles, possibly due to the extract brewhouse currently in use. **LIGHTHOUSE**

ONTARIO CRAFT BREWERIES

LAGER is a light lager with a banana-chip ester and a dry finish (1), while its big brother **LONG POND LAGER** produces juicy fruit and melon character with its more substantial body (1.5). The most successful offering is their **HONEY CREAM ALE**. Made with honey from a local Chatham-Kent apiary, it has a floral nose and a balanced sweetness (2.5).

BEAU'S ALL NATURAL BREWING COMPANY

📍 10 Terry Fox Drive, Vankleek Hill

📞 (866) 585-2337

🐦 @beausallnatural

🌐 beaus.ca

🕐 Daily 10a.m.–6p.m.

You would be hard-pressed to find anyone in Ontario who hasn't heard, in some way or another, of Vankleek Hill's Beau's. They have earned awards and critical acclaim for everything from their eye-catching packaging, environmental sustainability efforts, and 100 percent organic status to their continual releases of new beers, unique and well-publicized collaborations, and almost cult-like fan base.

Beau's was started by father and son Tim and Steve Beauchesne, who left their respective jobs (Tim was the owner of a long-running textile company and Steve ran Go! Go! Go! Records and kept a government job) in order to pursue their dream of running a brewery. Since opening in 2007, they have already seen tremendous success in sales and have managed to do what few breweries have been able to

ONTARIO CRAFT BREWERIES

do: stretch their distribution borders outside of Ontario and into New York and Quebec. Additionally, Beau's has managed to become the face of Ontario craft beer and environmental sustainability, pushing strongly on the importance of supporting local businesses, remaining active in their community through charity work, and doing their best to encourage green practices in other businesses.

———

Beau's flagship beer, **LUG-TREAD LAGERED ALE**, is a very approachable beer for newcomers to the brewery, with mild grain notes in a slightly sweet finish (3). **THE TOM GREEN BEER!**, a milk stout brewed in collaboration with famed Canadian comedian and cow "milker" Tom Green, is smooth and chocolatey, with strong flavours of roasted coffee and sweet lactose (3). **SCREAMIN' BEAVER** is an oak-aged imperial IPA with a very dry, malt-forward flavour profile, including notes of pine and lemon (3). **WAG THE WOLF** is a wheat beer with New Zealand hops added, creating a cocktail of banana, clove, papaya, and mango (3.5). **MATT'S SLEEPY TIME** is a Belgian imperial stout from the brewery's Wild Oats series. Expect espresso, rich cocoa, and dark fruits with a warming note toward the end (2.5). Part of Beau's Farm Table series is the **NIGHT MÄRZEN**, containing nice toasted caramel with raisin and brown sugar (3.5). **BOG WATER** is a beer in the gruit style that has been brewed with hand-picked bog myrtle. The resulting flavours are that of a very earthy and sweet herbal tea soda, with notes of plum and a touch of lemon (2). **KISSMEYER: NORDIC PALE ALE** is a beer made in collaboration with Danish brewer Anders Kissmeyer, and part of the Beau's B-Side Brewing Label. The beer has a distinct herbal and citrus character, with a crisp finish and grassy aftertaste (4).

BEER LAB LONDON

📍 420 Talbot Street, London

🌐 www.facebook.com/Beer-Lab-London-212759812268247

A collaboration between London's extremely popular venue for craft beer, Milos' Craft Beer Emporium, and talented brewers the Denim Brothers (Adil Ahmed and Nick Baird) has resulted in a small bespoke line of beers. Currently, Beer Lab is brewing under contract at London's Forked River Brewing on the outskirts of town. To date, the focus has been on extremely experimental small-batch beers, frequently brewed on a diminutive pilot system. As the brewery is only required to supply beer to one bar, this might not seem like a problem, but demand is still extremely high due to the quality of the product and excitement of the patrons.

With such a small operation that concentrates on variety, it is difficult to suggest what will change between the writing and publication of this guide. The following ratings are included as examples of where the brewery is likely to go in the future.

———

BRETT LAM BERLINER is a Brettanomyces-finished Berliner weisse, light in alcohol with a refreshing, bone-dry finish. The aroma is peach, apricot, and light barnyard funk (4.5). **GALAXY SAISON** has a nose of papaya, mango, and passion fruit and delicate peppery Belgian yeast over a light wheat cracker (4). **MIMOSA GOSE** is bright orange peel and fresh-squeezed juice with an understated salinity throughout the core of the palate and a scrubbing carbonation (4). **BREAKFAST STOUT** is full of chocolate syrup depth, but may be a little overwhelmed by roast on the finish (3.5).

BELL CITY BREWING COMPANY

📍 51 Woodyatt Drive, Unit 9, Brantford

📞 (519) 900-6204

🐦 @bellcitybeer

🌐 bellcitybrewing.com

🕐 Wed–Sat 11a.m.–8p.m., Sun 11a.m.–6p.m.
Tours Sat–Sun 1p.m., 2p.m.

🛒 Wed–Sat 11a.m.–8p.m., Sun 11a.m.–6p.m.

Located in Brantford and inspired by the works of that city's most famous resident, Alexander Graham Bell, Bell City has taken on the theme of famous inventors for their lineup of beers. Beginning as a contract player with a single brand in May of 2013, Bell City opened their bricks-and-mortar location in February of 2015. The result has been a sharp increase in the number of brands supported and the addition of a retail store and taproom that has made the brewery a part of the Brantford community. They continue, for the time being, to contract brew their flagship products out of Railway City Brewing in St. Thomas.

———

While Bell City is still in the first year of producing seasonal products, they have expanded their core range to four beers. **EUREKA CREAM ALE** is, stylistically speaking, more like a pale ale, but is accented by lemon, meadow grasses, and a robust toasted malt character (3). **LENOIR BELGIAN ALE** (named for the inventor of the combustion engine) is a take on Belgian golden ale that combines a deep malt and unsubtle candied sugar sweetness with a tart yeast character (2). **GALAXY HOPPER IPA** uses the Galaxy hop to bring tropical fruit character to a lightly hopped session IPA (NR), while **A CAUTIONARY ALE** is a relatively low-alcohol IPA featuring rye and a significant hop presence (NR).

BELLWOODS BREWERY

📍 124 Ossington Avenue, Toronto

📞 (416) 535-4586

🐦 @bellwoodsbeer

🌐 bellwoodsbrewery.com

🕐 Mon–Wed 5p.m.–12a.m., Thu 5p.m.–1a.m.,
   Fri 4p.m.–1a.m., Sat 2p.m.–1a.m., Sun 2p.m.–12a.m.

🛒 Daily 11a.m.–11p.m.

Opened in April 2012 in a converted garage near Dundas and Ossington, Bellwoods has rapidly developed an international reputation as one of Canada's best breweries. The small space that the brewery began in proved insufficient to keep up with local demand, and by their second year Bellwoods had expanded next door, adding additional fermentation capacity and a permanent bottle shop. Demand for their beer rightly remains high, periodically causing the bottle shop to sell out completely, while special releases now result in polite queues.

The lasting popularity is explained by the combination of high-concept and high-quality products, a clean yet playful branding aesthetic, and aggressively flavourful beers that, despite their punch, never quite overbalance. Barrel aging and blending and wild fermentations have become real strengths for the brewery, with a number of variations showing the range of ideas at play. Fans will be rewarded with additional product availability when Bellwoods expands to a second facility on Dupont, a project slated to be completed in 2017.

———

STAY CLASSY LIGHT SESSION ALE is a low-alcohol summer favourite with pineapple and passion fruit aromas (3.5). **WIZARD WOLF SESSION ALE** combines a pleasant cereal body with a snappy grapefruit bitterness (3.5). **JUTSU PALE ALE** manages to combine nearly every manner of fruit under the sun in its hazy orange body (4). **WITCHSHARK IMPERIAL IPA** progresses from tropical to northwestern, beginning with red mango, citrus, and lychee and ending in spruce (4.5). **WARP AND WEFT SOUR BRETT ALE**, aged in tequila barrels, cleverly combines the best elements of tequila with sour lime and a bone-dry mouthfeel (4). **FARMHOUSE CLASSIC** pours a hazy golden yellow and features a distinctly grassy character blended well with flowery spices and a subtle honey note (4). **FARMAGEDDON** is a special version of the farmhouse classic, aged in barrels with Brettanomyces and bottle conditioned with champagne yeast. Although there is some batch variation, most versions include a dry, wooden, and fairly tart mouthfeel, with fruit notes and a delicately sweet finish (4.5).

The Barn Owl series is a fine example of the brewery's continuing innovation. **BARN OWL NO.1**, a sour brett ale barrel aged on ginger, apricot, and cranberry highlights tart stone fruit and spiky acidity with its explosive carbonation into a drying brett finish with almost ethereal barrel char (5).

BENTLEY BREWERS

 @BentleyBrewers

bentleybrewers.com

Technically, Bentley has been in existence since 1991, operating as a brew-on-premises service called Brewer's Delight. However, in early 2015 news of the Beer Store opening up ownership to Ontario brewers enticed them to make the switch to being a commercial brewery.

CEO and brewmaster Daniel Herweyer has a background in farming, which really drives his focus on natural ingredients in his beers.

———

Their sole offering, the **COPPER LAGER**, is a Vienna lager that features a large amount of toffee flavours finishing with a subtle note of pine (2).

ONTARIO CRAFT BREWERIES

BEYOND THE PALE BREWING COMPANY

📍 5 Hamilton Avenue N, Ottawa

📞 (613) 695-2991

🐦 @BTPBrewing

🌐 beyondthepale.ca

🕐 Tues–Sat 12p.m.–8p.m., Sun 12p.m.–5p.m.

🛒 Tues–Sat 12p.m.–8p.m., Sun 12p.m.–5p.m.

One of the early success stories from Ottawa's recent explosion of breweries is Beyond the Pale. Their initial goal was simple: brew more adventurous beer than what existed in Ottawa at the time — beer the brewers wanted to drink. Beginning in 2012, in a Hintonburg location barely 1,000 square feet in size, the brewery expanded rapidly with the loan of some fermenters from Beau's All Natural in Vankleek Hill.

On opening day, owners Shane and Al Clark and Rob McIsaac sold through the entire volume of beer they had produced, initially having estimated it would last three weeks. The fanaticism for locally brewed beer in Ottawa means that they have been able to open a much larger facility at City

Centre, with a 15-BBL brewhouse five times the size of their original equipment. With recent changes to Ontario law, it is likely that the second location will have a retail store of its own. Additionally, 2015 saw the expansion of Beyond the Pale into LCBOs across Ottawa.

———

BREAKING BITTER is a fairly carbonated take on an English bitter, with a malty whole-grain mouthfeel and a floral, grassy nose with a small hint of coffee (3). **PINK FUZZ** is an American wheat ale that is deceivingly light in body, given its 6% alcohol. Each batch includes the zest of twelve boxes of grapefruit, creating a bright, vibrant citrus character (4). **RYE GUY** is a West Coast IPA that uses rye as an accent grain, lending a spicy character and also a mellow mouthfeel that balances the orange and pine from Cascade hops (4). **IMPERIAL SUPER GUY** is Rye Guy's big brother, taking the same flavour profile toward the extreme at 9% (3.5). **THE DARKNESS** is an American-style stout with a heavy coffee and chocolate character, and with a whiff of asphalt and a hint of salted caramel in the body (3.5).

BICYCLE CRAFT BREWERY

OTTAWA | ONTARIO

📍 850 Industrial Avenue, Unit 12, Ottawa

📞 (613) 408-3326

🐦 @BicycleBrewery

🌐 bicyclecraftbrewery.ca

🕐 Thu–Fri 12p.m.–7p.m., Sat 11a.m.–7p.m., Sun 12p.m.–4p.m.

Located on Industrial Avenue in Ottawa, Bicycle Craft Brewery is operated by husband-and-wife team Laura and Fariborz Behzadi. Started in 2014, their love for the outdoors inspired the name and general theme of their brewery, and great care has been taken to decrease their carbon footprint and be cost-efficient.

———

Bicycle's flagship beer is the **VELOCIPEDE** IPA, dry-hopped with Centennial and featuring a lot of tropical fruit, notes of pine, and brown sugar (2). Other beers include the **CRIMSON CASCADE** American amber, with a thin mouthfeel and distinct flavours of toasted caramel, chocolate, and orange zest (2), the creamy and chocolatey **BASE CAMP OATMEAL PORTER** (2), and the unfiltered **BELLE RIVER BLONDE**, with a grassy bitterness balanced with a nice biscuity malt backbone (2).

BIG RIG BREWERY

BIG RIG BREWERY & TAPROOM

- 📍 103 Schneider Road, Kanata
- 📞 (613) 591-6262
- 🐦 @BigRigBrewery
- 🌐 www.bigrigbeer.com
- 🕐 Tues–Thurs 11:30a.m.–6p.m., Fri 11:30a.m.–8p.m., Sat 12p.m.–4p.m.

BIG RIG KITCHEN & BREWERY

- 📍 2750A Iris Street, Kanata
- 📞 (613) 688-3336
- 🐦 @BigRigBrewery
- 🌐 www.bigrigbrew.com
- 🕐 Mon–Wed 11a.m.–11p.m., Thu–Fri 11a.m.–1a.m.,
  Sat 8p.m.–1a.m., Sun 8p.m.–11a.m.

BIG RIG KITCHEN & BREWERY

- 📍 1980 Ogilvie Road, Gloucester
- 📞 (613) 552-3336
- 🐦 @bigrigbrew
- 🌐 www.bigrigbrew.com
- 🕐 Mon 11a.m.–10p.m., Tue–Wed 11a.m. –11p.m.,
  Thu–Fri 11a.m. –12p.m., Sat 8a.m. –12p.m., Sun 8a.m. –11p.m.

ONTARIO CRAFT BREWERIES

Award-winning Big Rig is perhaps one of the fastest-growing breweries in the city of Ottawa. Opened in 2013 by brewmaster Lon Ladell, Clocktower Brewpub co-founder Pierre Cleroux, restaurateurs Jimmy Zourntos and Angelis Koutsos, and famed Ottawa Senators defenceman Chris "Big Rig" Phillips, Big Rig has seen tremendous growth. The brewery now boasts two brewpub locations and a full-on brewery and taproom in Kanata, which has become one the top contract-brewing facilities in the province, along with Cool Beer Brewing.

———

Big Rig's signature flagship beer is the **GOLD**, which has sweet bready and cereal notes with a delicate hop presence (3). The **RIDEAU RED** pours a hazy amber and features distinct grain notes with a clean finish (2.5). The **INDIA PALE ALE** is of the American variety of IPAs, with lots of grapefruit backed by pine with a malt backbone (3). **BYWARD BROWN** predominantly contains roasted notes, with hazelnut, coffee, and light chocolate notes (3.5). **MIDNIGHT KISSED MY COW** is a double-chocolate milk stout with creamy notes of chocolate with warming roasted and alcohol notes (4). **RELEASE THE HOUNDS BLACK IPA** contains traces of chocolate, roasted coffee, and leather with pine bitterness (4). The **HEFEWEIZEN** is a remarkable example of the style, featuring the usual banana and clove with a hint of vanilla (4). **BOCK ME GENTLY** is a traditionally dry beer that contains lightly toasted grain and caramel notes with dried fruit and cinnamon (4).

BLACK CREEK HISTORIC BREWERY

📍 1000 Murray Ross Parkway, Toronto

📞 (416) 736-1733

🐦 @blackcreekbeer

🌐 blackcreekbrewery.ca

🕐 Times vary seasonally. Daily tours at 2p.m. and tasting at 3p.m., with additional tasting at 12:30p.m. Sat–Sun.

Located within the much-loved open-air heritage museum that is Black Creek Pioneer Village, the Historic Brewery is located in the town's Half Way House Inn and Restaurant. Making use of brewing methods commonly used in the 1800s, award-winning brewer Ed Koren has been creating historically themed beers for Black Creek since the brewery's inception in 2009. While the public can purchase their beers at liquor stores, thanks to large-scale contract brewing at Trafalgar Brewing, the real treat is to visit Pioneer Village, learn about the brewing landscape and methods of the 1800s, and sample the beers made with the brewery's historical equipment.

———

ONTARIO CRAFT BREWERIES

For the benefit of readers, ratings for Black Creek's beers will be of their offerings made at Trafalgar Brewing, as the more modern technology yields a more consistent end product. The **PORTER** is the brewery's first commercial offering and yields notes of espresso, roasted nuts, and cocoa in a light to medium body (3). **RIFLEMAN'S RATION** is a brown ale with flavours of toffee and brown sugar blending nicely with a roasted malt character (3.5). The **PALE ALE** pours a clear copper with flavours of caramel and a subtle hint of citrus (2). **LEMON BALM** is a herbal offering, with biscuity and earthy characters and a subtle lemon-balm tea undertone (1). The **STOUT** contains light coffee and roasted wood notes with a drawn-out finish (2).

BLACK OAK BREWING COMPANY

📍 75 Horner Avenue, Unit 1, Toronto

📞 (416) 252-2739

🐦 @BlackOakBrewing

🌐 www.blackoakbeer.com

🕐 Tours available on Saturdays.

🛒 Mon–Fri 9a.m.–5p.m., Sat 10a.m.–3p.m.

Founded in Oakville in the last days of 1999, Black Oak was one of a handful of breweries to open in Ontario during the period following the brewing industry shakeout of the mid-1990s. Although the brewery's two core brands have always been available, an early experiment with a premium lager proved something of a setback and it was discontinued in 2004. Ken Woods, owner and president, has frequently acted as a spokesman for small breweries in Ontario.

Black Oak has been based out of Etobicoke since 2008, a move that did the brewery good. While the core range of seasonals has always been stable, the new facility has allowed for expansion and experimentation. Changes in staff over the last half decade have resulted in additional one-offs and seasonal products, the vast majority of which have hit their mark and driven new customers to the brewery. The switch to cans for core products in 2015 was met with universal approval and is a positive sign for the brewery's prospects.

———

PALE ALE has a light, bready body and has leaned more toward North American citrus and pine hop character over the last few years (3). **NUT BROWN ALE** is, as the name suggests, nutty and toasted in body with chocolate and toffee accents and a balanced bitterness (4). **10 BITTER YEARS** holds the distinction of having been the first regularly available double IPA in Ontario, dank with piney resin and brightened by clementine and tangerine citrus (4.5). **NUTCRACKER** porter is a perennial holiday favorite (4.5), while **OAKTOBERFEST** has a bread-crust body and a mild herbal, grassy character (4). **SUMMER SAISON** is something of a masquerading witbier, but a pleasantly lemony summer quaffer nonetheless (3). **TRIPLE CHOCOLATE CHERRY STOUT** performs as advertised, with deep kirsch and black cherry notes (4), while **NOX AETERNA** is a full-bodied and lightly smoky take on the oatmeal stout made with locally roasted coffee (4).

BLACK SWAN BREWING COMPANY

📍 144 Downie Street, Stratford

📞 (519) 814-7926

🐦 @blackswanbeer

🌐 www.blackswanbrewing.ca

🕐 Tue–Sat 11a.m.–7p.m.

🛒 Tue–Sat 11a.m.–7p.m.

Both owners of Black Swan were teachers in Stratford before they decided to venture into brewing professionally. As younger men, Bruce Pepper and Ryan Stokes had become aware of good beer in Montreal and Detroit respectively, and the duo have been home-brewing for a significant period of time. The brewery location was, until recently, a lingerie store, which may not have been its highest and best use in a town of 30,000. The shop now fits a 10-HL brewhouse into an ultra-low-budget, DIY set-up that still manages to produce beers that have captured the imagination of Stratford's beer scene. Black Swan has come a long way in a very short time.

BERLINER WEISSE develops its sourness in the kettle, but in practice it mostly lives in the aroma. On the palate, it's bright lemon and citric acidity that ends abruptly in a dry finish (3.5). **ENGLISH PALE ALE** is properly British, with earthy allotment-garden flowers and hedgerow hops over biscuity, bready malts, but still fairly light in body (4). **PORTER** is lightly sooty in the aroma with a touch of freshly roasted espresso. Brown malt lends a touch of sweetness and a friable snap to the body (4). **IPA** is dominated by pineapple and juicy fruit, quince and clementine, and relatively light in body in the southern California manner (4.5). **TRENT SEVERN RYE PALE ALE** is practically marmalade on light rye toast (3.5).

BLOCK THREE BREWING COMPANY

📍 1430 King Street N, Unit 2, St. Jacobs

📞 (519) 664-1001

🐦 @BlockThree

🌐 www.blockthreebrewing.com

🕐 Tours available during retail store hours.
   Call ahead for groups larger than ten.

🛒 Sun–Thu 11a.m.–6p.m., Fri–Sat 11a.m.–8p.m.

Block Three's story begins in earnest in 2012, when four friends (a brewer and three accountants) decided to expand their monthly beer club in a drastic way. By April of 2013 renovations on their chosen site had begun, and by September beer was flowing out the front door. Block Three has continued to upgrade and expand as they go along, adding fermenters and a barrel-aging program. Their tasteful tile-accented taproom frequently hosts open-mic nights and features board games for the entertainment of their fans, whom they refer to as "Blockheads."

Listed are some of the most frequently offered Block Three beers. This does not come close to representing the

ONTARIO CRAFT BREWERIES

entirety of the huge number of options available over the course of the year. The brewers conveniently provide a form on their website that will allow you to be updated about the identity of the next batch.

———

KING STREET SAISON is a bright, citrusy saison with spicy yeast and herbal characteristics thanks to the addition of coriander and peppercorn (3.5). **KAMIKAZE MONK** is claimed as a variant Japanese-Belgian saison due to the use of Sorachi Ace hops, which impart a touch of lemon, dill, and cedar to the light, dry body (2.5). **NOON ON A WEEKDAY** is a light American pale ale with a character of lemon, grapefruit, and mango (3). **PUSHBROOM PORTER** is a thick chocolate-and-molasses-accented porter with a small amount of mildly bitter roast (3.5).

BLOOD BROTHERS BREWING

📍 344 Westmoreland Avenue,
Unit 104C, Toronto

🐦 @bloodbrothersto

🌐 www.bloodbrothersbrewing.com

🕐 Wed–Fri 4p.m.–8p.m., Sat 12p.m.–6p.m., Sun 12p.m.–4p.m.

Located in the basement of an industrial warehouse off Dupont and Dufferin in Toronto, Blood Brothers Brewing gives an almost literal meaning to the term "hidden gem," with only two signs indicating the location of their taproom. The brewery was started in the fall of 2015 by brothers Dustin and Brayden Jones. Making use of retrofitted dairy equipment, Blood Brothers' intention is to provide small-batch innovative beers along with distinctive year-round offerings.

––––

The two year-round beers on offer are the **SHUMEI IPA**, with hints of orange and grapefruit zest and a growing bitterness that continues in the finish (3), and the **INNER IPA**, a brett IPA with a tart peachy quality, a predominantly dry mouthfeel, and a gradual finish (3.5).

THE BLUE ELEPHANT CRAFT BREW HOUSE

📍 96 Norfolk Street S, Simcoe

📞 (519) 428-2886

🐦 @BlueElephantInc

🌐 blueelephant.ca

🕐 Mon–Sat 11:30a.m.–12a.m.

Heather Pond-Manorome has been the proprietor of the Blue Elephant since 1992. Since the restaurant's shift to brewpub in 2012, it has become a destination for beer drinkers. The Blue Elephant's elegant menu features local Norfolk County produce wherever possible. This ethos may be what accounts for their success in using fresh hops; their relationship with Carolinian Hop Yard resulted in a victory in the 2014 Great Ontario-Hopped Craft Beer Competition.

The brewpub's enthusiasm for creating better beer (not just their own, but in general) is impressive. They offer customers the opportunity to participate in a monthly brew camp with interesting ingredients, and designed their own Ale Trail to help promote other breweries in Ontario's southwest.

———

GENTLEMEN'S PILSNER was originally brewed for the Simcoe stopover of Gentlemen of the Road. It is a light, grainy North American pilsner with a slightly sour finish (2.5). **RED DEVIL** is an earthy amber ale with a caramel and toast-grain body (3). **SWEET LEAF** is a brown ale with an earthy, vegetal hop presence and a deep malt body leaning toward Tootsie Roll and molasses (3).

BOBCAYGEON BREWING COMPANY

 (705) 243-7077

@bobcaygeonbeer

bobcaygeonbrewing.ca

Founded in 2015 in Bobcaygeon and contract brewed in Ottawa, the Bobcaygeon Brewing Company is enjoying some early success on draught around Toronto.

———

Their single offering, **COMMON LOON APA**, has a citrus and tropical-fruit aroma and a light bitterness that is slightly over-balanced by the nutty malt in the body (3).

BOSHKUNG BREWING COMPANY

📍 9201 Highway 118, Minden Hills

📞 (705) 489-4554

🐦 @BoshkungBrewing

🌐 boshkungbrewing.com

🕐 Tue–Thu 12p.m.–8p.m., Fri 12p.m.–10p.m., Sat–Sun 11a.m.–8p.m.

🛒 Tue–Thu 12p.m.–8p.m., Fri 12p.m.–10p.m., Sat–Sun 11a.m.–8p.m.

Catering both to locals and the cottage crowd, Boshkung has seen so much success since opening in 2014 that they have already added fermenters to increase their volume. The brewery is an ideal destination for visitors to the Haliburton region. In addition to a tasting room and retail store, Boshkung has licensed seating at picnic tables on Mirror Lake and takeout pizza for customers looking for a bite to eat. Couple that with neighbouring restaurant Rhubarb, which is under the same ownership, and this Carnarvon brewery is a must-visit.

Founding brewmaster Johnny Briggs is an early graduate of the Niagara College brewing program and has nicely judged the balance between flavour and accessibility in the core lineup of beers.

NORTH COUNTRY KELLERBIER is deeply bready for a kellerbier, verging into the sweetness of a Vienna lager. The leafy, lightly spicy noble-hop character imparts a light herbal bitterness with lime in the aroma (3). **35 & 118 CREAM ALE** is gently fruity to the nose with pear, apple, and peach fading into a light cereal body with no real bitterness to speak of (3.5). **BLACK ROCK DARK ALE** has a sweet malt character, smooth and creamy but full of dried berries and milk chocolate on the palate (3). **KUNGAROO IPA** is a fair representation of the classic American pale ale, balancing earthy spruce and orange above a crackery malt body with caramel accents (3.5).

BREW WINDSOR

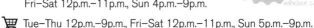

📍 635 University Avenue E, Windsor

📞 (226) 246-0720

🌐 brewwindsor.com

🕐 Tue–Thu 12p.m.–9p.m.,
Fri–Sat 12p.m.–11p.m., Sun 4p.m.–9p.m.

🛒 Tue–Thu 12p.m.–9p.m., Fri–Sat 12p.m.–11p.m., Sun 5p.m.–9p.m.

Started in 2014 by hospitality-industry veterans Joseph and Jordan Goure, Brew is one of a handful of recently opened breweries in Windsor. The brewhouse itself is a rarity: one of a very few recently commissioned extract systems in Ontario. It is partitioned off from the taproom by a glass wall, which fits seamlessly into the retro-industrial look of the building. Many of the food items on the taproom's tightly focused menu integrate beer into the recipe, including spent-grain pizza crust and lager-braised brisket. In summer a rooftop beer garden provides a comfortable patio for customers. In colder weather, beer to go is available in the brewery's custom blue-glass swing-top bottles.

———

Brew is thoroughly focused on the crowd just arriving at craft beer. As such, their main offerings are what you might

ONTARIO CRAFT BREWERIES

consider gateway beers. **PROPER LAGER** is a light-bodied take on a pale lager, with a hit of rising bread dough (2). **BERLINER WEISSE** leans into witbier territory, the sourness not quite up to the moniker (1). **THE WALKING RED**, a spiced red ale, approximates a gingerbread cookie nicely, a good fit for autumn (3.5). **BLACK 'N' BREW** chocolate stout is slightly thin, but redeemed by dry cocoa on the finish (2.5).

BRICK BREWING COMPANY

📍 400 Bingemans Centre Drive, Kitchener

📞 (519) 742-2732

🐦 @Brickbrewery

🌐 www.brickbeer.com

🕐 Mon–Sat 10a.m.–7p.m., Sun 10a.m.–6 p.m.

Brick Brewing was Ontario's first craft brewery, founded by Jim Brickman in 1984 in the shadow of a much-larger Labatt plant. While the focus of Brick's portfolio has shifted over the years (not very long ago they led the discount segment with their buck-a-beer brand Laker Lager and its variants), the company has invariably enjoyed a great deal of success. Their sadly discontinued Anniversary Bock has attained legendary status within Ontario's short craft-brewing history. With changes to the structure of beer pricing in the province and the emergence of the craft sector since 2007, Brick's focus has become their Waterloo brands. Don't assume the shift has diminished their size; they still brew nearly 350,000 HL a year. The new facility in Kitchener-Waterloo contains state-of-the-art equipment, beginning operations just as the brewery entered their fourth decade.

___

The shift in attention to craft brands has created some significant improvement in recent years. **CLASSIC PILSNER** has a gentle bready body and a grassy hop aroma with lime accents from the Hallertau hops (4). **WATERLOO DARK** has gained roast and is currently fuller bodied than it has been in a decade (3.5). **IPA** is a muted British expression of the style (2.5), while the **AMBER** is a practically unclassifiable oaked rye bock weighing in at 6.8% and suitable for autumn sipping (3). The biggest success the brewery has enjoyed in the craft segment has come from its line of radlers, which have sold incredibly well over the last two summers. The **GRAPEFRUIT** (4) is preferable to the **LEMONADE** (2.5) in terms of balancing sweetness with refreshment.

BRIMSTONE BREWING COMPANY

📍 209 Ridge Road N, Ridgeway

📞 (289) 821-2738

🐦 @BrimstoneBrew

🌐 www.brimstonebrewing.ca

🕐 Wed 4p.m.–9p.m., Thu–Fri 4p.m.–11p.m., Sat 12p.m.–11p.m., Sun 11a.m.–5p.m. Contact in advance for tours.

🛒 Mon–Tues 12p.m.–6p.m., Wed 12p.m.–9p.m., Thu–Sat 12p.m.–11p.m., Sun 12p.m.–5p.m.

The goal of any small brewery is to fit into the community that it serves. Brimstone has been aided in achieving that end by operating out of the basement of Ridgeway's Sanctuary Centre for the Arts, which routinely hosts everything from yoga classes and gallery shows to live music. In its first two years the brewery has expanded from a modest nanobrew set-up to a much larger system, and maintains a taproom catered by Crave Local Fresh Catering, which occupies the same building. In summer, a patio extends the taproom to the outside of the converted church.

ONTARIO CRAFT BREWERIES

Given the name of the brewery and the fact that it occupies a converted church basement, it is no surprise that the beer names have taken on a darkly liturgical theme. **ENLIGHTENMENT** blonde ale is sweet and lightly grainy with a mild hop bitterness, an approachable offering for initiates to the order (2). **MIDNIGHT MASS** oatmeal stout takes the step of using chicory in the fermenter in place of the more traditional coffee in order to deepen roast character and add bitterness, becoming somewhat overwhelming (2.5). **SINISTER MINISTER** is an extremely assertive India pale ale, pine and vine with a hint of lime, but nonetheless somewhat overmatched by caramel malt sweetness (3).

BROADHEAD BREWING COMPANY

📍 81 Auriga Drive, Unit 13, Nepean

📞 (613) 695-9444

🐦 @broadheadbeer

🌐 broadheadbeer.com

🕐 Tue–Thu 10a.m.–6p.m., Fri 10a.m.–8p.m., Sat 10a.m.–5p.m.

Located in Nepean, just outside the borders of Ottawa, Broadhead's brewing facility and taproom will make any DIY enthusiast go green with envy. The walls, flooring, bar, grain-mill chute, and much of the equipment was hand built by home-brewing friends Shane Matte, Jason Smale, Jamie White, and head brewer Josh Larocque. Even the computer system that controls the brewery was developed from scratch (and includes a *Star Trek: The Next Generation* interface that makes the nerd inside of us smile approvingly). Brewing out of their own facility, as well as at Big Rig, Broadhead's distribution goes as far north as Temiskaming and can be found in most bars in the Ottawa region.

——

Broadhead has six year-round beers. **BACKBONE STANDARD** is a golden ale with a crisp, medium body and a slight bitterness rounded out with a sweet finish (3). **LONG SHOT WHITE** is a fairly sweet and spicy wheat beer with a lot of coriander and orange character (2). **GRINDSTONE AMBER** has a fairly light body, with a bit of graham cracker sweetness and a touch of grassy bitterness in a rather clean finish (2). **UNDERDOG PALE** has a lot of sweet caramel notes with a grounded, earthy undertone and a balanced mouthfeel (3). **WILDCARD ALE** is a pale ale with a frequently changed hop addition in each batch. The one that had Centennial hops has a very light body with bitter tangerine character (1.5). **DARK HORSE STOUT** features a lot of rich espresso and brown sugar, with a creaminess brought on by the addition of oatmeal (3).

BROCK STREET BREWING COMPANY

📍 1501 Hopkins Street, Unit 3, Whitby

📞 (905) 668-5347

🐦 @Brockstbeer

🌐 www.brockstreetbrewing.com

🕐 Mon–Wed 11a.m.–8p.m., Thu–Sat 9a.m.–8p.m., Sun 11a.m.–5p.m.

Named for the historical downtown street that was the stopping point for travelling dignitaries, politicians, and even royalty, Brock Street Brewing was opened in the spring of 2015 by partners Mark Woitzik, Chris Vanclief, Victor Leone, and Scott Pepin and proved to be just what Whitby needed. In the first six months an outpouring of support saw sales rise 20 to 30 percent each month. Brock Street has already announced plans to open a second location to further expand capacity beyond their 60 BBL and become a central hot spot in the downtown area.

———

BLONDE is a simple North American take on the style, with an aroma of sweet citrus and apricot with a lightly bitter crest

ONTARIO CRAFT BREWERIES

in the mid-palate (2). **AMBER** has a toffeeish body with a hint of dried fruit and a lightly earthy hop presence in the tail (3). **PORTER** has a whiff of mocha in the aroma and a vinous build through the body to a dry, roasty finish (3.5). **BROKTOBERFEST LAGER** plays white grape off deeper dark fruits and herbal noble hops into a lightly smoky finish (3.5). **ESB** is roundly fruity with prune and mincemeat playing off earthy floral tones and drying hay (3). **IRISH RED ALE** has a very light hop spiciness in advance of a full, round sweetly toasted body with a leathery hop waft (3). **PILSNER** is a faithful replica of the northern German style, with a full cereal body accented by crisp noble-hop aromas and a medium bitter finish (4).

BROKEN STICK BREWING COMPANY

📍 78–5450 Canotek Road, Ottawa

🐦 @BrokenStickBrew

🌐 www.brokenstickbrewing.com

🕐 Thu 12p.m.–6p.m., Fri 12p.m.–8p.m.,
Sat 11a.m.–6p.m., Sun 11a.m.–4p.m.

🛒 Thu 12p.m.–6p.m., Fri 12p.m.–8p.m.,
Sat 11a.m.–6p.m., Sun 11a.m.–4p.m.

While Broken Stick did not open until 2014, the plans for the brewery had been in development since 2007, when much of the necessary equipment was sourced from Quebec. Located in an industrial park in the Orleans section of Ottawa, Broken Stick has already seen production triple. Special attention has been given to the retail section of the small brewery, which has a custom refrigeration unit nearly as wide as the store, featuring a wide selection of growlers for take-home consumption. Custom equipment is part of Broken Stick's modus operandi, since one of the owners, Eric, operates an industrial controls business, ensuring that the brewery will see incremental improvement in processes for the foreseeable future.

ONTARIO CRAFT BREWERIES

WANDERLUST AMERICAN WHEAT is a fairly light-bodied wheat ale, hopped with Citra and Amarillo, which gives it a tangerine and grapefruit citrus presence (2.5). **TIPSY PALE ALE** has notes of brown bread and raisin and leans English in style with minimal hop character (2). **SPRING FLING** red ale has some malt sweetness and enough roast character that it comes through as Tootsie Roll sweet on the finish (3). **SOCKS AND SANDALS IPA** has an orange and sage aromatic bitterness before settling into a long copse of pine bitterness (3). **DOWNTOWN LEROY BROWN PORTER** is full of chocolate and hazelnut, smooth on the way to a dry finish (3).

BROTHERS BREWING COMPANY

 @BrothersBrewery

 www.brothersbrewingcompany.ca

While many brewers come to the trade later in life, by their senior year of high school Asa and Colton Proveau had a plan in place to open a brewery. Goal-directed learning led them to brewing and business school respectively, and allowed them to convert a music studio on the family farm in Pelham into a nanobrewing facility. Just a few years later they are poised to open Brothers Ale House in downtown Guelph in the spring of 2016, with the help of Niagara College graduate Michael Bevan. In the meantime, their beer is available at a handful of accounts around Toronto and Guelph.

———

TROPIC THUNDER, a glimpse into the potential of the Ale House location, is an American pale ale with Mosaic, Amarillo, and Citra developing a relatively mellow fruit-salad character: pineapple, mango, peach, and tangerine (3.5).

BRUX HOUSE

📍 137 Locke Street S, Hamilton

📞 (905) 527-2789

🐦 @BruxHouse

🌐 bruxhouse.com

🕐 Tue–Sat 12p.m.–12a.m.

Located on a resurgent part of Hamilton's Locke Street, Brux is the sister location of noted fine-dining restaurant Quatrefoil in Dundas. Brux focuses predominantly on the cuisine of Europe's beer belt, with executive chef Fraser Macfarlane at the helm. The menu tends toward beer-friendly bistro and pub fare and is ably assisted by the draught and bottle selection curated by Mark Horsley.

———

Horsley contributes to the draught list with his own recipes that are brewed in small batches at Nickel Brook in nearby Burlington. With selections from other breweries doing the lifting on what one might consider flagship styles, Brux's house beers are freed up to play in more complex territory. **VANESSA**, a lemon hibiscus saison, practically comes across as a Berliner weisse due to the kettle souring in the brewing process. It is tart, citric, and scrubbing, with the delicate hibiscus appearing at the head of each sip (3.5). **GRAPEFRUIT BREAKFAST IPA** does exactly what it proclaims it is going to, with Citra and Amarillo hops bolstering grapefruit zest used in fermentation for a tart, puckering pink-grapefruit bitterness (4).

BURDOCK BREWERY

📍 1184 Bloor Street W, Toronto
📞 (416) 546-4033
🐦 @BurdockTO
🌐 burdockto.com
🕐 Mon–Sat 5p.m.–2a.m., Sun 5a.m.–12a.m.
🛒 Daily 11a.m.–11p.m.

Burdock
BREWERY & MUSIC HALL

Despite only having opened in the summer of 2015, Burdock, located near Dufferin and Bloor, has already earned itself a strong reputation in Toronto's beer scene from hardened critics and picky drinkers alike — a very strong debut after two years of planning. While many factors have gone into making Burdock so popular so fast (convenient location, excellent atmosphere, and seasonal, locally focused food), it can't be understated how much is due to the artistic efforts of brewer Siobhan McPherson, who previously worked at Mill Street and Amsterdam Brewery and has an extensive background in microbiology that gives her an understanding of how yeast affects beer. To further focus on utilizing yeast to pull off her vision, McPherson's top priority, beyond acquiring a fully capable brewing facility, was to set up her own yeast lab, located upstairs.

———

While there are several beers that Burdock will keep year-round, the recipes will be tweaked seasonally. As of writing, the **WEST COAST PILSNER** is a hoppy take on the pilsner style, with notes of pineapple and lemon amongst a dry mouthfeel (4.5). **BLOOR LITE** is a blonde lager with a somewhat citric aroma, a hint of lemon zest flavour, and a smooth, biscuity taste that rises the further down the palate it goes (4.5). The **DARK SAISON** features notes of chocolate, caramel, and dark fruits, with tart cherry character in a moderately dry finish (3.5). **BRETT FARMHOUSE SAISON** is beautifully dry, with a presence of grapes, lemon zest, and spiced fruit dancing with the peppery tartness brought on by the brett (5).

BUSH PILOT BREWING COMPANY

📞 (905) 399-5885

🐦 @BushPilotBeers

🌐 bushpilotbrewing.com

Among contract breweries in Ontario, Bush Pilot has a significant advantage in context and in collaborating brewers. Founded by Vlado and Liliana Pavicic from Roland + Russell, importers of beer, wine, and spirits, Bush Pilot has relationships with some of the best brewers in Scandinavia and takes advantage of them with their high-quality, high-concept brews. Each beer pays tribute to a plane or pilot that has braved the Canadian wild.

———

STORMY MONDAY, brewed in collaboration with Danish brewer Anders Kissmeyer, Niagara College, and Nickel Brook, is a barley wine aged in Calvados barrels. With a plethora of fruits and spices involved in the brewing process, it's a complex fireside sipper reminiscent of mulled cider and meant to be lingered over (4). **NORSEMAN**, a collaboration involving

THE ONTARIO CRAFT BEER GUIDE

Nøgne Ø and Nickel Brook, is an eisbock aged in Armagnac barrels. The massive 14.5% eisbock has a sticky sweetness from aroma to finish and is ideal as a sipper on a cold winter evening (4). **PENGO PALLY** is a vibrant saison including herbs one might find in the tundra. The complex aroma of grass, lemon, and peppery botanicals and wheaty body make for a refreshing, food-friendly beer (4.5).

CALABOGIE BREWING COMPANY

📍 12612 Lanark Road, Calabogie

📞 (613) 752-2739

🐦 @calabogiebrewco

🌐 calabogiebrewingco.ca

🕐 Mon–Thu 1p.m.–5p.m., Fri 11a.m.–6p.m., Sat–Sun 11a.m.–5p.m.

🛒 Mon–Thu 1p.m.–5p.m., Fri 11a.m.–6p.m., Sat–Sun 11a.m.–5p.m.

Started in 2015, Calabogie is a new project from three friends (Mike Wagner, Ken McCafferty, and Greg Gilson) who were serious enough about their brewing venture to bring in a ringer. Head brewer Jamie Maxwell has had stints at Harpoon in Vermont and Union Station in Rhode Island. Brewing commenced during the late spring of 2015. The facility itself is carefully laid out and features a tasting station situated in the middle of the brewery's cellar, juxtaposing industrial steel and concrete with an elegant bar and tiled backsplash. Across the road is the Redneck Bistro, owned by the same partnership that runs Calabogie, which features their beer and the beer of other local breweries. The brewery's approach to funding includes a founders club, which gives members first dibs on special releases throughout the year and a number of other benefits.

———

While the brewery has produced a number of beers thus far, the most popular have been: **FRONT PORCH**, a light and accessible German kölsch–style ale (NR); **DOUBLE BOGIE**, a 90-IBU West Coast Double IPA that leans into heavy citrus and pine bitterness (NR); and **HIGHLANDER** nut brown ale, which attempts to play up the fruit and nut character of the style (NR). Most recently, they have launched their Downstream series, whose inaugural member is an **APRICOT SOUR** (NR), a sign that more wild and funky beers are in the future of this exciting brewery.

CAMERON'S BREWING COMPANY

📍 1165 Invicta Drive, Oakville

📞 (905) 849-8282

🐦 @CameronsBrewing

🌐 www.cameronsbrewing.com

🕐 Mon–Fri 9a.m.–5p.m., Sat 12p.m.–5p.m.

Founded by former chemical engineer Cameron Howe, this brewery truly is an example of a hobby flourishing in to a sustainable business. In the early days, Cameron's was most well known for selling their initial beer — an award-winning cream ale — in packs of nine. Called the "Cameron's Cube" and personally signed by Howe himself, the packaging format was enough to plant the name of the brewery into the minds of the public. In 2003 the brewery moved out of their small location in Etobicoke and relocated to a larger facility in Oakville.

In 2010 Bill Coleman, an experienced marketing pro who, notably, was involved in the Molson's "I Am Canadian" ad campaign, purchased a stake in Cameron's and became president and co-owner. Under his leadership, the brewery began hosting cask nights and brought forth more adventurous beers to accompany their original core lineup.

––––––

The brewery's first offering, the **COSMIC CREAM ALE**, pours a lovely golden colour and contains notes of sweet malts, biscuity grain, and a touch of honey (3). The **AMBEAR ALE** contains lightly toasted caramel and a fruity sweetness that lingers after the finish (3). The **RPA** is a rye pale ale that is overall floral and includes grapefruit and orange zest with jab of sharp and spicy rye in the finish (3.5). **RESURRECTION ROGGENBIER** is almost reminiscent of a fruitcake, with notes of plum, bread, brown sugar, and nutmeg, with a hint of banana (2.5). **OBSIDIAN IMPERIAL PORTER — RUM BARREL AGED** is as dark as its namesake and contains prominent flavours of cocoa, dark cherries, and vanilla in a dry mouthfeel (3.5).

CARTWRIGHT SPRINGS BREWERY

📍 239 Deer Run Road, Pakenham

📞 (613) 295-3377

🐦 @CSBbeer

🌐 csbeer.ca

🕐 Tours are not offered, but the taproom is open at the same times as the retail store.

🛒 Mon 11a.m.–5p.m., Fri–Sun 11a.m.–5p.m.

Opened in the late spring of 2015, Cartwright Springs is a partnership between brewer Andre Rieux, and co-owners Eduardo Guerra and Hien Hoang. Named for the freshwater spring from which the brewery sources its water, Cartwright Springs has also been able to harness another resource: the Internet. One of a very few breweries in the province with a Kickstarter success story, they were able to fund the addition of a taproom to their Quonset-housed brewery in July of 2015.

The brewery has opted to sell their beer in custom blue-glass, returnable, swing-top bottles that give their product a distinctive look and tie into the ecologically responsible theme that runs through their facility, from spring water to advanced effluent treatment.

So far, Cartwright Springs' most popular beers have been their **KÖLSCH**, which they profess is light and grassy in terms of hop character (NR); their **SMASH**, a single-malt, single-hop session ale with a pleasant citrusy aroma (NR); and their **MAPLE PORTER**, an 8.5% strong beer brewed entirely with maple sap in place of water, creating a walnutty sledgehammer of a beer (NR).

CASSEL BREWERY COMPANY LTD.

📍 715 Principale Street, Casselman
📞 (613) 369-4394
🐦 @CasselBrewery
🌐 casselbrewery.ca
🕐 Tours offered for groups of four or more, $5.00 per person.
🛒 Wed–Fri 1p.m.–6p.m., Sat–Sun 10a.m.–5p.m.

Opened just in time for the first edition of the National Capital Craft Beer Festival in July of 2012, Cassel is the result of Mario Bourgeois's long-term interest in home-brewing. Beginning in 2000 with extract kits, he graduated to all-grain brewing and eventually to opening a shop of his own. While Cassel was initially something of a DIY affair, piecing together odd bits of equipment, the 3-BBL brewhouse is slated to be replaced with a brand new 15-BBL system and a number of additional fermenters. The brewery has expanded to take on a second building, and the number of offerings has steadily increased since opening. A new website and an improving presence in LCBO locations across the province suggest that Cassel will continue to be an important player, not only in Ottawa's beer scene but in Ontario's, in the foreseeable future.

WHITE FOG is the brewery's take on Belgian witbier, complete with orange peel and coriander. In addition to that light citrus and spice, there's a hint of field berry on the aroma ahead of the full wheaty texture of the body (3). **GOLDEN RAIL** is a honey brown ale that takes on a deeply nutty malt presence in the aroma, fruity with a touch of clove on the palate (2.5). **LIL' RED STEAMER** is full of robust toffee malt, almost nutty brittle, with fruit and light milk chocolate (3). **STATION HOPPY PALE LAGER** would be a pilsner if not for the use of Mosaic and New Zealand hops that give it a bright, vibrant minerality with sharp herbal leaf and bright lemongrass notes (3.5). **CABOOSE IPA** is slightly berryish, leading into tangerine and bitter scrub pine over a nutty caramel body (3). **SLEEPER CAR** is a double-chocolate porter with bittersweet chocolate, Swedish Berries, and hazelnut, and is a good choice as a seasonal fireside sipper (3.5).

CECIL'S BREWHOUSE & KITCHEN

📍 300 Wyld Street, North Bay

📞 (705) 472-7510

🐦 @cecilsebs

🌐 www.cecils.ca

🕐 Mon–Thu 11a.m.–1a.m., Fri–Sat 11a.m.–2a.m., Sun 10a.m.–2a.m.

Cecil's Brewhouse & Kitchen is one of the few places in North America that makes use of New Zealand brewer Brian Watson's "SmartBrew" automated brewing technology. Essentially custom, pre-fermented beer (known as wort) is brewed and delivered to a location, leaving the employees with little to do except load the wort into on-site fermentation tanks, add yeast and hops, press Start, and wait until the beer is ready. The food on offer at Cecil's is traditional pub fare. The highlight is their famous double-dusted chicken wings.

———

The mainstays of Cecil's are **NIPISSING LIGHT**, with hints of lime and a dry, somewhat sweet finish (3); **ALGONQUIN WHITE CAP**, a filtered wheat ale with hints of coriander along with slight notes of banana and vanilla (2.5); **NIPISSING LAGER**, with a distinct grapefruit note and a swirl of malt at the end (2); **TEMAGAMI AMBER**, a fairly respectable representation of the style with nice low-roasted caramel and brown-bread flavours to it (3); and **SHAMUS IPA**, an English-style IPA with a fairly light body and distinct tones of lemon and orange zest and a warming, caramel-like body (3).

CEEPS

📍 671 Richmond Street, London

📞 (519) 432-1425

🐦 @Theceeps

🌐 www.ceeps.com

🕐 Daily 11a.m.–2p.m.

Housed in an 1890 building, the Ceeps (previously the Canadian Pacific Railway tavern) is a very popular destination for students of the University of Western Ontario. The brewing system was installed during the brewpub craze of the early 1990s, making the Ceeps one of the oldest brewpubs in Ontario. The ambience is campus pub and the clientele are mostly young people out for a good time on the weekend. In that sense, it does not cater to the typical craft beer audience. It has been, in the past, a Coors Light Mystery Mansion location. However, the beer on offer, a house-made lager, seems to have improved in quality over the last decade.

———

The most frequently available choice is the **CEEPS LAGER** (NR), which is reportedly better than you might expect from a university watering hole.

C'EST WHAT?

📍 67 Front Street E, Toronto

📞 (416) 867-9499

🐦 @cestwhattoronto

🌐 www.cestwhat.com

🕐 Sun–Mon 11:30a.m.–1a.m.,
Tue–Sat 11:30a.m.–2a.m.

Since opening in 1988, C'est What has been a force in the Toronto scene, not only as a purveyor of the province's small brewers but also, at different points, as a live-music venue and an early adopter of Ontario wines. The basement pub features a large number of Ontario taps and one of the most consistently impressive lineups of cask-conditioned beers in the province. The exposed limestone walls, cozy fireplace area, and eclectic menu of beer-friendly fare make C'est What a perennial favourite in Toronto. Owner George Milbrandt has been important in providing the public with exposure to better beer as the host of the annual Festival of Craft Breweries, now in its twenty-seventh consecutive year.

———

The beers served under the C'est What brand are no longer brewed on the premises. They are manufactured on a contract

125

ONTARIO CRAFT BREWERIES

basis, in most cases by Bruce Halstead from County Durham Brewing in Pickering, Ontario. This is a good fit, especially given the focus on cask-conditioned ales. **JOAN'S DARK SECRET** is the notable exception; this dark mild with a touch of peat smoke is brewed by Toronto's Granite Brewery (3). **AL'S CASK** is a straightforward English-style bitter with spicy, herbal bitterness poking through over lightly toasted grains (4). **CARAWAY RYE** achieves what it sets out to, bringing rye spiciness to the fore over hints of leather, tobacco, and saddle soap (2.5). **MOTHER PUCKER'S** is a refreshing North American wheat brewed with ginger that leans toward the candied end of the ginger spectrum, with a touch of lemon-drop brightness (3). **HOMEGROWN HEMP** ale really shows off its character in the mouthfeel, with smooth vegetal bitterness on the finish (2.5). **STEVE'S DREADED CHOCOLATE ORANGE ALE** nicely manages to retain the milk-chocolate character of the whack and unwrap variety (3.5), while the **COFFEE PORTER** has a massive espresso aroma with a lightly sour finish that nicely sates the caffeine jones (3.5).

CHEETAH INTERNATIONAL BREWERS INC.

📍 #12-75 Milliken Boulevard, Toronto

📞 (416) 292-3434

Based in the Toronto suburb of Scarborough, Cheetah International Brewers began operations in 2004 with a focus on creating beers that would complement a broad range of food, with a specific focus on spicy Indian cuisine. Their beer is contract brewed at Great Lakes Brewery, with distribution stretching throughout North America and Europe.

———

Their two primary beers include the **CHEETAH LAGER**, which has a light mouthfeel and slight hint of honey, with a subtle hop character (NR), and **CHEETAH DARK LAGER**, which is distinctly sweet, with notes of honey and caramel (NR).

ONTARIO CRAFT BREWERIES

CHESHIRE VALLEY BREWING

 @CheshireValley

 www.cheshirevalleybrewing.com

Cheshire Valley
BREWING CO.

Housed at Black Oak Brewing in Etobicoke, Cheshire Valley is the project of long-time brewer and respected beer judge Paul Dickey. Over the years, he has brewed for Black Oak and Pepperwood Bistro in Burlington, and has developed recipes and provided guidance for several start-up breweries in Ontario. While Cheshire Valley's footprint is more modest than that of some of the breweries Dickey has influenced, the beers have generated substantial respect. It's not surprising that he has kept some of his best ideas for his own brand.

———

While the summer and fall offerings change from year to year, they typically involve variations on cream ale and single-hop pale ale respectively. More frequently available are **MILDLY AMUSING**, a highly sessionable, dark English mild ale with nutty toasted grain, chocolate, and coffee that is even better on cask (4), and the American-style **ROBUST PORTER**, featuring coffee, chocolate, and roasted malt with a vinous fruitiness and a full, smooth body (4.5).

CHURCH-KEY BREWING COMPANY

📍 1678 County Road, #38, Campbellford

📞 (877) 314-2337

🐦 @churchkeybeer

🌐 www.churchkeybrewing.com

🕐 Mon–Sun 10a.m.–dusk

Church-Key Brewing can be found in the small hamlet of Pethericks Corners in Campbellford, with the brewery itself occupying a beautifully renovated 1878 Methodist church, which makes it a popular destination for tours. Owner John Graham originally started brewing in 1989 and eventually became a shift brewer at Amsterdam Brewery in Toronto, where he honed his skills and developed his talents. In 1999 Church-Key became a registered brewery, and the first beers were ready in July of 2000. Since then John has kept busy running the Church-Key Pub & Grindhouse (formally known as the Stinking Rose), maintaining his status as a founding member of the Ontario Craft Brewers association, and continuing to push his message of "Think globally, drink locally."

ONTARIO CRAFT BREWERIES

Church-Key has three main flagships that are brewed year-round. The **WEST COAST PALE ALE** has a light texture that is complemented well by the decent grain balance found within (2.5). The **NORTHUMBERLAND ALE** pours a golden straw colour. This standard cream ale's strength is its lack of complexity, with decent malt presence making way for a smooth mouthfeel and a gentle finish (3.5). Finally, the **HOLY SMOKE SCOTCH ALE** features intense smoked malts, making for a very leathery note combined with a dark-fruit sweetness to give it further definition (2.5).

CLIFFORD BREWING COMPANY

 (416) 575-6512

 @CliffordBrewing

 www.cliffordbrewing.com

Clifford Brewing Company is the solo project of Brad Clifford, an award-winning home brewer, co-founder of the Ontario Beer Company, and brewmaster of the now defunct brewing side of Toronto's arcade/bar Get Well. Officially launched in 2015, Clifford brews his beers out of Grand River Brewing and Cool Beer Brewing, though plans are set to brew all beers at Cool.

———

Clifford has three mainstays. **BASTARD LANDLORD** is an ESB that has a significant roasted character with a distinctive note of pine (3). **PINBALL WIZARD** is an American pale ale brought over from Clifford's Get Well days, featuring a lot of earthy notes blended with pine and grapefruit (3.5). The award-winning **CLIFFORD PORTER** is a very creamy beer with notes of leather, tobacco, chocolate, and espresso (4.5).

CLOCKTOWER BREWPUBS

 @The_Clocktower

 clocktower.ca

CLOCKTOWER GLEBE (BREW HOUSE)

📍 575 Bank Street, Ottawa

📞 (613) 233-7849

🕐 Mon–Fri 11:30a.m.–12a.m., Sat 10:30a.m.–12a.m., Sun 10:30a.m.–11:45p.m.

CLOCKTOWER ELGIN STREET

📍 200 Elgin Street, Ottawa

📞 (613) 724-4561

🕐 Mon–Fri 11a.m.–12a.m., Sat–Sun 10a.m.-12a.m.

CLOCKTOWER NEW EDINBURGH

📍 422 MacKay Street, Ottawa

📞 (613) 742-3169

🕐 Mon–Fri 11:30a.m.–12a.m., Sat 10:30a.m.–12a.m., Sun 10:30a.m.–11:45p.m.

CLOCKTOWER BYWARD MARKET

📍 89 Clarence Street, Ottawa

📞 (613) 241-8783

🕐 Mon–Fri 11:30a.m.–12a.m., Sat 10:30a.m.–12a.m.,
Sun 10:30a.m.–11:45p.m.

CLOCKTOWER WESTBORO

📍 418 Richmond Road, Ottawa

📞 (613) 680-5983

🕐 Mon–Fri 11:30a.m.–12a.m., Sat 10:30a.m.–12a.m.,
Sun 10:30a.m.–11:45p.m.

Clocktower is a chain of brewpubs located in Ottawa. Their first location, on Bank Street, opened in 1996 and is considered the city's oldest brewpub. Award-winning brewmaster Patrick Fiori joined Clocktower in 2007 with a master's in brewing and distilling from Scotland's Heriot-Watt University, and over the course of his first two years began tweaking the recipes for the house beers until they were up to his standard.

Today Clocktower has five locations throughout Ottawa and Fiori continues to develop his focus on special one-off beers and collaborations, a notable example being HefeWheaton, a hefeweizen brewed with famed *Star Trek: The Next Generation* star and uber-geek Wil Wheaton for Ottawa Comiccon.

The **KÖLSCH** has a very light body with flavours of graham cracker and honey, with a slight hint of fruit (1.5). The **RASPBERRY WHEAT** has a light to medium body with dominant raspberry notes blending nicely with the dry characteristics of the wheat (3). **WISHART'S ESB** has a very strong and somewhat chalky malt character with a very dry finish (2). The **RED** is a North American amber ale and tastes distinctly of spiced caramel with notes of citrus and pine (2.5). Finally, the **BYTOWN BROWN** is reminiscent of roasted coffee and nutty caramel in an altogether smooth mouthfeel (3).

COLLECTIVE ARTS BREWING

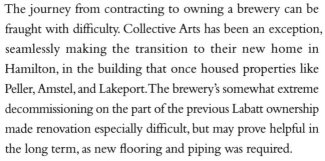

📍 207 Burlington Street E, Hamilton

📞 (289) 426-2374

🐦 @CollectiveBrew

🌐 collectiveartsbrewing.com

🕐 Tours are not currently available, although samples are available at the retail store.

🛒 Sun–Wed 11a.m.–7p.m., Thu–Sat 11a.m.–9p.m.

The journey from contracting to owning a brewery can be fraught with difficulty. Collective Arts has been an exception, seamlessly making the transition to their new home in Hamilton, in the building that once housed properties like Peller, Amstel, and Lakeport. The brewery's somewhat extreme decommissioning on the part of the previous Labatt ownership made renovation especially difficult, but may prove helpful in the long term, as new flooring and piping was required.

Much of the brewery's image is tied up in association with artists in various media, which has resulted in several series of vibrant labels that give the bottles a distinct look and the brewery indie-rock cred. Partnering with Toronto's Indie 88.1 for their Black Box Sessions has certainly delivered Collective

Arts an audience. It would have been easy for skeptics to dismiss the colourful wrapper had the contents of the bottle not measured up. Fortunately, in the hands of brewer Ryan Morrow, the product has been uniformly impressive. With an annual capacity of 35,000 HL at their newly completed facility and the potential for expansion, Collective Arts has become ubiquitous on shelves in just under two years; an impressive accomplishment when one considers the number of breweries founded during that time.

———

The hallmark of Collective Arts' lineup has been the aroma generated by late hopping additions. **STATE OF MIND** is a light session IPA with orange, grapefruit, and pineapple, with very little bitterness (3.5). **SAINT OF CIRCUMSTANCE** incorporates citrus zest along with hops, becoming lemony with a floral presence (4). **RHYME & REASON** is billed as an extra-pale ale and is surprisingly complex: the bitterness is mostly herb and pine but the aroma is full of grapefruit and pineapple (4.5). **RANSACK THE UNIVERSE** features Galaxy and Mosaic hops, becoming a tropical fruit salad in a bottle (4). **STRANGER THAN FICTION** is the first departure from the lineup of hoppy pale ales; a full-bodied porter with a smooth, round mouthfeel and deep roasted grain notes, it displays range as yet unexplored (4).

COOL BEER BREWING COMPANY INC.

9 164 Evans Avenue, Toronto

📞 (416) 255-7100

🐦 @CoolBeerBrewery

🌐 coolbeer.com

🕐 Mon–Fri 10a.m.–7p.m., Sat 10a.m.–5p.m.

Founded in 1997 by Bobby Crecouzos, Cool Beer Brewing Company originally set up operations in Brampton, but outgrew the facility in under a decade. Since 2005 they have been based in Etobicoke, with a 28,000-square-foot facility, having found much success in their three award-winning core brands. Brewmaster Adrian Popowycz, a graduate of VLB in Berlin, and a former employee of fellow Etobicoke breweries Black Oak Brewing and Great Lakes Brewery, oversees operations with skill and puts his many years of experience in biotechnology and brewing to good use. While the beers and the brewery itself have fallen under the radar for many, Cool is better known for utilizing their sizeable facility to become one of the most prominent contract breweries in the province.

ONTARIO CRAFT BREWERIES

Cool's three award-winning core brands are **COOL BEER**, a lager with a very light mouthfeel and subtle cereal character, ending off with a slightly carbonated dry note (2); **MILLENNIUM BUZZ**, a North American amber lager brewed with B.C. hemp, which brings forth a unique and subtle earthy character along with the bready malt notes (2.5); and **STONEWALL LIGHT**, a fairly well-put-together light beer, with delicate floral hop notes hidden in a cereal and corn sweetness (3).

COUNTY DURHAM BREWING COMPANY

📍 1885 Clements Road, Pickering

📞 (905) 686-3022

🕐 Please call ahead for tours.

Founded in 1996 by three partners with experience in home-brewing, County Durham became a one-man show over the course of the last two decades. Brewer Bruce Halstead produces ales that draw influence from both North America and England. While the year-round brands tend toward the American end of the spectrum, Durham's greatest strength are cask ales in traditional English styles and cellared properly. Much of the interest in the cask ales in Toronto can be explained by the consistency and quality of Durham's wares, which have been a constant presence on the city's beer engines for years. Perhaps the only difficulty in enjoying Durham's beer is getting to the pub before its devoted fans drain the firkin.

COUNTY DURHAM SIGNATURE ALE is an English pale ale with nutty amber malts and a fragrant floral, earthy bouquet

(3.5). **BLACK KATT STOUT** is best enjoyed on a nitro tap. It's a deeply roasty Irish dry stout with a slightly smoky whiff around autumn leaves and brandy beans (4). **HOP ADDICT** has had more low-end malt character in recent years, with spruce and citrus hopping underpinned by a touch of roast (3.5). **RED DRAGON** is included here as a single example of a range of cask-only ales. This amber ale is toasty and bready with a certain amount of toffee-apple sweetness and hops that run to bark and orange, with a slightly lingering finish after a full mouthfeel (4.5).

COVERED BRIDGE BREWING COMPANY

📍 6-119 Iber Road, Ottawa

📞 (613) 915-2337

🐦 @CBBeer

🌐 www.coveredbridgebrewing.com

🕐 Thu 3p.m.–7p.m., Fri 12p.m.–7p.m.,
　　Sat 11a.m.–6p.m., Sun 12p.m.–4p.m.

Since late 2013 biochemist and brewer John VanDyk has been selling his beers at the brewery's storefront in the small Ottawa suburb of Stittsville. Starting out as an avid home brewer, VanDyk's love for the limitless variation of flavours using limited ingredients led to him to take the leap into commercial brewing. Since then, Covered Bridge (named after an area on his home street) has made regular appearances at local beer festivals and has become an active member of the local community by taking part in various charity functions.

———

The **DIRTY BLONDE ALE** features a bready, toasted malt flavour with a floral and citrus hop character (NR). **THE MSB** is regarded as an imperial brown ale, chocolate and nut profiles standing up with significant notes of pine in a 9.1% ABV behemoth (NR). **ETERNALLY HOPTIMISTIC** is a dry-hopped American pale ale with significant notes of citrus and a floral character (NR). **AMBER ROSE** is an American amber with a heavy-caramel malt backbone that backs a significant bitterness brought in by American hops (NR). The very Canadian-themed **DOUBLE-DOUBLE** is a very sweet stout that is made with chocolate and coffee added before and after fermentation (NR).

CRAFT HEADS BREWING COMPANY

📍 89 University Avenue W, Windsor

📞 (226) 246-3925

🐦 @CraftHeadsBrew

🌐 www.craftheads.ca

🕐 Mon–Thu 8a.m.–1a.m., Fri 8a.m.–2a.m.,
Sat 11a.m.–2a.m., Sun 12p.m.–10p.m.

Located in Windsor's downtown core, Craft Heads is a small-batch brewery that focuses on experimentation and offers a variety of beer styles, as befits the owners' half decade of home-brewing experience. They will frequently have as many as thirty different variants on tap in their brewery-adjacent barroom. That's an astounding feat considering the diminutive size of the brewhouse — it's situated in a corner basement. You can watch the brewer at work from the street prior to sampling his wares.

The feel of the somewhat sparsely decorated taproom leans heavily toward coffeehouse, due in part to the inclusion of a full barista set-up, including pour-over coffee. Wood-oven pizza is catered from the nearby Terra Cotta Gourmet Pizzeria, although there have been collaborative pairing events with Sushi Guru. The brewery frequently hosts live comedy nights.

While time will allow for focus and refinement of the beer, the enthusiasm here is nearly palpable. The brewery is frequently in operation past midnight to keep up with demand.

———

While it's difficult to properly represent the sheer scope of the lineup toward the end of the brewery's first year, some staples have emerged. **SQUIRREL NUT BROWN** is a thickly flavoured American brown ale that incorporates house-made cold-brew coffee and is dry hazelnutted for extra character (4). **MOTOWN HONEY BROWN** leads from a berryish nose into a thin, floral body (2). **AARDVARK BLONDE** is sweet malt accented by raspberry cane and garden herbs (2.5). **HEFEWEIZEN WHEAT** is tartly wheaty with a spicy clove yeast character (2.5). **NEXT ON STAGE AMBER** is toasted grain, light chocolate, and caramel with a pine and tea accent (3). **FEATHER HAT GUY.P.A.** is a straight-ahead pale ale named after a local figure. It has a pronounced clementine citrus character (3).

CREEMORE SPRINGS BREWERY

📍 139 Mill Street, Creemore

📞 (844) 887-3022

🐦 @creemoresprings

🌐 www.creemoresprings.com

🕐 Daily, on the hour 12p.m–4p.m.

🛒 Mon–Sat 10a.m.–6p.m., Sun 11a.m.–5p.m.

Founded in 1987, Creemore Springs had become one of the most important small breweries in Ontario by the turn of the century. Depending largely on the production of a single flagship lager, the brewery not only survived the industry crash of the mid-1990s but continued to grow incrementally, right up until their purchase in 2005 by Molson Coors.

Partially due to the new ownership, Creemore has become a ubiquitous brand in Ontario, with Molson Coors having wisely added resources while leaving an already successful product alone. The quality of Creemore's beer has remained stable or (arguably) improved since the purchase over a decade ago, which has seen an expansion of brewing capacity to just under 150,000 HL annually. The way the expansion was completed in partnership with the municipality and residents of Creemore may prove a useful

ONTARIO CRAFT BREWERIES

example for Ontario's small breweries as they continue to thrive.

Creemore's focus has always been on beers made according to traditional German brewing practices, and for that reason the Creemore lineup is dominated by lagers, many of which were introduced after the Molson Coors acquisition. The brewery's water is acquired from an artesian well three kilometres away and constantly trucked in.

———

PREMIUM LAGER has a small prickle of dry, herbal bitterness on the tongue surrounded by fairly complex bread-crust malt character and a full body (3.5). **LOT 9 PILSNER** replaced their Traditional Pilsner in early 2015 and is slightly lighter in alcohol and brighter in profile, with wildflowers and peppery herbs settling in above crackery, bready malts (4). **URBOCK** is a dunkel bock with a creamy mouthfeel and a dark brown bread character highlighted by molasses sweetness and baker's chocolate (4). **KELLERBIER** has a hefty dose of dry leaves, spicy pepper, and bready caramel finishing in a bitter snap (4.5). **ALTBIER**, a collaboration with Dusseldorf's Zum Schlüssel, features an aroma of rain on dry earth and coniferous shrubs amid a lightly sweet, mildly roasty body (4). **OKTOBERFEST LAGER** is a simple take on the Munich festival beer with a Grape-Nut and cereal malt character and mild bitterness (3.5). **HOPS & BOLTS** is a sort of India pale lager sold under the Mad & Noisy label, a tangle of fruit and floral hop character above a light caramel body (3.5).

DESCENDANTS BEER & BEVERAGE COMPANY LTD.

DESCENDANTS
BEER & BEVERAGE CO.
—— LTD ——

📍 319 Victoria Street N, Kitchener

📞 (519) 581-7871

🐦 @Descendantsbeer

🌐 www.descendantsbeer.com

One of a handful of breweries that began as contractors while attempting to locate a site for a bricks–and–mortar facility, Descendants has experienced more difficulty than most on the road to that goal. Plans for an initial site in a historic building may have fallen through, but a more suitable location was found in downtown Kitchener in October of 2015. While the 15-HL brewhouse will be installed at some point in the near future, partners Robin Molloy and Carin Lee Brooks continue to contract brew two brands out of Railway City in St. Thomas and participate in festivals around the province, frequently producing one-off beers specifically for that purpose. With their own brewery in place, they will hopefully be able to produce these brands on a more frequent basis.

ONTARIO CRAFT BREWERIES

At the moment Descendants has two brands available in the LCBO. **HARBINGER** is an American pale ale showing bready, caramel grain roughly around the edges of the body, with an aroma of light grapefruit and orange (3). **REYNARD THE FOX** is a golden ale using rye as part of the grist, which peppers and bolsters a light, spicy hop character resulting in a crisp finish (3.5).

DOMINION CITY BREWING COMPANY

DOMINION CITY
BREWING CO.

📍 15-5510 Canotek Road, Ottawa

📞 (613) 688-6207

🐦 @dominioncitybc

🌐 www.dominioncity.ca

🛒 Thu–Fri 12p.m.–7p.m., Sat 11a.m.–6p.m.,
Sun 12p.m.–5p.m. Samples available.

Housed in a business park in the Orleans neighbourhood of Ottawa, in just over a year Dominion City has become one of the best representatives of Ottawa's brewing scene. While the owners Josh McJannett, Adam Monk, and Andrew Kent are home brewers from way back, the most impressive part of Dominion City's business is the commitment to community and representation of the area. Dominion is partnered with local farms and hop growers, coffee roasters, and food banks. The taproom at the brewery is panelled with boards from a recently dismantled local barn, and the bar itself is made of logs recovered from the bottom of the Ottawa River. The theme is completed by an annual celebration of Canadiana on July 1.

EARL GREY MARMALADE SAISON contains the zest of twenty-five cases of oranges in every batch along with Earl Grey tea from Ottawa's Bridgehead Coffee. The pronounced orange sweetness melds with the bergamot in order to create a wildflower character that elongates the finish on the Belgian yeast (4). A **CHARDONNAY BARREL-AGED** variant adds oaky vanilla to the body and a lightly barnyard funk to the aroma, an ideal pairing for blue cheese (3.5). **EARNSCLIFFE ESB** has an aroma of toffee, raisin, and prune, with hazelnut and cocoa notes in the body (3.5). **TOWN & COUNTRY BLONDE ALE** is freshly grainy due to the use of red fife wheat and has a grassy hop presence (3). **TWO FLAGS IPA** is about the balance between sweet and bitter with burnt demerara sugar underpinning grapefruit and pineapple and outlasting it on the finish (3.5). **BEACON ALE** uses 100-percent Ontario-grown Galena hops and develops vinous and floral character from them, full of lemon balm, chrysanthemum, goldenrod, and blackcurrant (4). **DEVIL'S BRIGADE** is a take on a traditional Belgian golden ale, deceptively strong with a vigorous carbonation and an assertive citrus-and-pepper bitterness (3.5).

DOUBLE TROUBLE BREWING COMPANY

 (855) 467-5683

 @HopsandRobbers

 doubletroublebrewing.com

Launched in 2012, Double Trouble is the brainchild of long-time friends Claude Lefebvre and Nathan Dunsmoor, who between them have worked for other breweries such as Sleeman and Mill Street. Lefebvre is also the owner of North American Craft, a beer importer that works closely with the LCBO and the Beer Store. Together, Lefebvre and Dunsmoor have contracted famed brewer Paul Dickey (Cheshire Valley) to formulate and brew Double Trouble's brands at Wellington Brewery's facility in Guelph.

———

Their first offering was **HOPS & ROBBERS** sessionable IPA, which clearly has a strong English influence, with bready malts and brown sugar and a nice jab of pine (3). Further beers include **PRISON BREAK PILSNER**, a dry-hopped pilsner with herbal honey and lemon zest paving the way to a bitter finish

(3); **REVENGE OF THE GINGER: KICKIN' GINGER RED IPA**, offers the fiery note of pure ginger in its aroma and taste, along with apricot and caramel (2.5); and **FIRE IN THE RYE ROASTED RYE PALE ALE**, which features a very spiced and toasted-bread character along with grapefruit and pine, finishing with a distinct bitterness at the back of the throat (4).

DUGGAN'S BREWERY

📍 1346 Queen Street W, Toronto

📞 (416) 588-1086

🐦 @duggansbrewery

🌐 www.duggansbreweryparkdale.com

🕐 Tue–Wed 5p.m.–12a.m., Thurs 12p.m.–12a.m.,
Fri–Sat 12p.m.–1a.m., Sun 2p.m.–11p.m.

🛒 Tue–Sat 12p.m.–11p.m.

Michael Duggan has had a long brewing career in Ontario, serving time at Mill Street before launching a brewpub at 75 Victoria Street in the last days of 2009 after winning Bar Volo's inaugural Cask Days IPA Challenge. The closure of that initial location, after just under two years, left a small number of brands on the market, contracted out of Etobicoke's Cool Beer Brewing.

In late 2014, Duggan opened a new facility in Parkdale at the corner of Queen and Brock. The new brewpub is smaller than the old one, seating maybe one hundred, and works with a far more tightly focused menu featuring local Ontario produce. The good news is that the lineup of products has not changed substantially. There is a lot of depth for

ONTARIO CRAFT BREWERIES

the brewpub to draw on, and a game local audience on which to try out experimental batches.

———

NUMBER 9 is an IPA with nine different varieties of malt, reminiscent of toasted brown bread and raisin, with punchy Cascade pine and citrus (3.5). **NUMBER 5 SORACHI** lager is a pale lager that takes advantage of the Sorachi Ace hop to impart a bright dill and lemon character to the aroma (3.5). **NUMBER 13 HEFEWEIZEN** leans toward kristalweizen territory, with only light wheat haze and significant banana esters in the aroma (3). **NUMBER 46 PARKDALE BOMBER** is a throwback malt liquor, named as a tip of the hat to the neighbourhood's bad old days (3). **NUMBER 7 IRISH STOUT** is full bodied with a heavy roast and bittersweet cocoa, yet dry with a finish that doesn't become acrid (4).

ELORA BREWING COMPANY

📍 107 Geddes Street, Elora

📞 (519) 805-2829

🐦 @EloraBrewingCo

🌐 www.elorabrewingcompany.ca

🕐 Sun–Thu 12p.m.–9p.m., Fri–Sat 12p.m.–11p.m.

🛒 Sun–Thu 12p.m.–9p.m., Fri–Sat 12p.m.–11p.m.

A combination brewery, gastropub, and bottle shop set in the scenic city north of Guelph, Elora Brewing Company was founded by a diverse group of local friends, Matt Lawson, Jonathan Laurencic, Don Smith, Jim Murphy, and former head brewer of Barley Days Brewery Alex Nichols. Having set up shop in the summer of 2015 on historic Geddes Street in the downtown area, Elora Brewing Company's large space includes beer-inspired comfort food and in-house butchery by chef Ben Sachse, with a focus on local and seasonal dining.

———

THREE FIELDS unfiltered triple-grain lager, which utilizes barley, wheat, and rye, has many of the characteristics of a

ONTARIO CRAFT BREWERIES

155

light beer in terms of mouthfeel, resulting in very thin flavours along with a distinctive earthiness toward the end (2.5).
LADY FRIEND IPA has a surprisingly light mouthfeel with large caramel and pine notes rounded out with a roasted cereal character (3).

5 PADDLES BREWING COMPANY

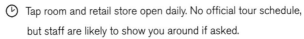

📍 1390 Hopkins Street, Unit 3, Whitby

📞 (905) 665-3042

🐦 @5PaddlesBrewing

🌐 5paddlesbrewing.com

🕐 Tap room and retail store open daily. No official tour schedule, but staff are likely to show you around if asked.

🛒 Mon–Fri 11a.m.–7p.m., Sat 9a.m.–5p.m., Sun 12p.m.–5p.m.

Started in 2013 by a group of friends who come from home-brewing backgrounds, 5 Paddles has retained much of the experimentation that comes with taking that route into the industry. Batches are fairly small, and the versatility of a 300-HL brew system results in more variety than would be offered by a traditional brewery. To date, 5 Paddles has produced a hundred different recipes, with each of the owners focusing on a specialty area, be it English, Belgian, or dark beer. They have gained a reputation for outlandish beers with interesting ingredients.

The small taproom offers very reasonably priced flights of three or five beers in specially made canoe-shaped service trays. The discussion in the taproom frequently turns to the technical aspects of brewing, suggesting that the customers are as invested in brewing as the staff. 5 Paddles is one of the only breweries in the province to have hosted their own home-brewing competition.

The ratings and tasting notes included here are by no means extensive. The beers available from the brewery may change from week to week, and it is worth calling ahead to confirm stock.

———

HOME SWEET HOME is a honey vanilla wheat beer, as close as they have to a flagship. The flavour is citrus and wildflower on the palate, with an extremely light vanilla character on the finish that lingers beyond bitterness (3). **DUGGER** is a lightly peachy cream ale with a juicy, sticky finish; a late-summer lawn-mowing affair (2.5). **PADDLER'S PRIDE** has a light molasses Tootsie Roll character backing plum and quince on the palate and fading to a medium-length finish (3.5). **CAMP-X**, named for the Second World War code-breaking camp down the road in Ajax, is an English IPA with a nose of apple and pear ahead of grassy ground-level hops and honeyed toasted malt (3). **BROTHER IAN'S BELGIAN 8** is a dark Belgian strong, relatively light in body, clovey with a hint of cherrywood, raisin, quince, deep caramelized sugar, and a warming, boozy glow in its aftermath (3.5). **THE DOMINATRIX** is dank Cascade with orange and grass, roasted malt character submissively taking a backseat (4.5). **MIDNIGHT PADDLER** is a sweet stout that has the aroma of poppyseed Bundt cake and very ripe banana backed with chocolate and a round, fruity mouthfeel (3.5).

FLYING MONKEYS CRAFT BREWERY

📍 107 Dunlop Street E, Barrie

📞 (705) 721-8989

🐦 @FlyingMonkeys

🌐 flyingmonkeys.ca

🕐 Mon–Thu 11a.m.–7p.m., Fri–Sat 11a.m.–9p.m., Sun 11a.m.–6p.m.

Founded in 2005 and originally named after Barrie's first mayor, a complete rebranding from the traditional look and feel of the Robert Simpson Brewing Company to the outlandish and bizarre Flying Monkeys was implemented in 2009 to more properly represent the brewery's ethos of "normal is weird." While in the early years the brewery gained popularity through their core brands and unmistakable branding, they have perhaps become best known for coming out with collaborations and esoterically flavoured one-offs concocted by founder and brewer Peter Chiodo.

Core brands include **ANTIGRAVITY LAGER**, with a light straw colour and subtle grassy notes in a crisp finish (2.5); **AMBER ALE**, with a soothing caramel warmth and a touch of lemon and a slightly dry finish (3); **SMASHBOMB ATOMIC IPA**, containing distinct pine aroma and notes of mango, pineapple, grapefruit, and orange (3.5); **HOPTICAL ILLUSION ALMOST PALE ALE**, with a smooth mouthfeel and flavours of grapefruit and pine wrapped up with creamy caramel (3); and **NETHERWORLD CASCADIAN DARK ALE**, which features notes of pineapple, tangerine, and grapefruit combined with dark-roasted coffee and light chocolate (3.5).

Bolder, more recent offerings include **GENIUS OF SUBURBIA INDIA-STYLE SESSION ALE**, with lots of tangerine sherbet and pine with a bone-dry finish (2.5); the **MATADOR VERSION 2.0 EL TORO BRAVO IMPERIAL DARK RYE ALE**, which has intense flavours of cedar, peppercorn, and pine in the taste that go against the very sweet, bready, vanilla aroma (3); and the **CHOCOLATE MANIFESTO TRIPLE CHOCOLATE MILK STOUT**, which is by all accounts like a delicious organic chocolate cake in a glass (4.5).

FOLLY BREWPUB

📍 928 College Street, Toronto

📞 (416) 533-7272

🐦 @FollyBrewing

🌐 www.follybrewing.com

🕐 Mon–Tue 4p.m.–1a.m., Wed–Fri 4p.m.–2a.m.,
Sat 1p.m.–2a.m., Sun 1p.m.–12a.m.

Folly Brewpub is the evolution of the former Habits Gastropub into a more beer-focused space, where there was originally only a small pilot system. Brewers Christina Coady and Chris Conway, former home brewers who were encouraged by Habits owners Michelle Genttner and Luis Martins to brew on their system, have interestingly taken a special focus on farmhouse ales, showcasing the wonderful changes farmhouse yeasts can produce in beer by consistently creating beers within the open-book definition of the style.

———

While Folly has a number of rotating beers available, they have four flagships that are year-round. **PRAXIS** "new world" saison is dry, with a balanced sweetness and a quick finish (4.5). **INKHORN FARMHOUSE BRUIN** is a delicately tart bruin with the distinct taste of raspberry (4). **IMPOSTER SYNDROME**

FARMHOUSE IPA is a hazy orange beer with incredible tropical fruit notes (4). **FLEMISH CAP OLD WORLD SAISON** is a wonderful example of the effect a good yeast (in this case from Guelph's Escarpment Labs) can have on simple ingredents. The beer is crisp, with subtle citrus hints and a drifting finish that fades into dryness (5).

FORKED RIVER BREWING COMPANY

📍 45 Pacific Court, Unit 4, London

📞 (519) 913-2337

🐦 @forkedriverbrew

🌐 forkedriverbrewing.com

🕐 Tours at noon and 2p.m. every Saturday

🛒 Tue–Fri 11:30a.m.–6p.m., Sat 11a.m.–6p.m.

Although still a relatively young brewery, having poured its first beers in the summer of 2013, Forked River has quickly established a reputation in western Ontario and on tap in the GTA. Part of the reason is the backgrounds of owners Andrew Peters, David Reed, and Steven Nazarian, which include engineering and biotech, and the shared enthusiasm for home-brewing that prompted them to start the company. Each of them has won regional awards for their brews.

They also have a sophisticated understanding of their market. London has both a fanatical set of craft beer enthusiasts and a large number of beer drinkers who have not yet made the transition to more interesting offerings. Forked River's lineup includes two accessible standards, but also far more complex seasonal offerings and a highly impressive barrel-aging program

ONTARIO CRAFT BREWERIES

with surprisingly positive results, given the short time frame during which it has existed. Forked River has recently undergone a 150-percent expansion (including a new retail store) after a social media campaign helped change provincial regulations.

———

CAPITAL BLONDE ALE is a lightly sweet, crackery ale with notes of wildflower, hay, and a touch of lemon (3). **RIPTIDE RYE PALE ALE** features a light-rye-toast spiciness in addition to toffee and a light earthy bitterness (3). **MOJO CITRA RHUBARB WHEAT** approximates the summery flavours of lemonade and strawberry pie, slightly malic in sourness but quenching (3.5). **FULL CITY PORTER** features vibrant light-roast coffee above a complex body of woody, nutty roast, chocolate, vanilla and subtle berry (4). **WEENDIGO IMPERIAL STOUT** takes on barrel and bourbon character courtesy of Jack Daniels, but features dark fruit in addition to the inevitable deep roast character (3.5).

Worth mentioning are barrel projects like **HANSEL AND BRETT'EL**, a lightly sour Brettanomyces fermented farmhouse ale (3.5), and **CATHARSIS**, a Belgian-style abbey beer made with the same yeast, deeply fruity and roundly sweet on the palate with a drying, vinous, nearly tannic finish (4).

GANANOQUE BREWING COMPANY

📍 9 King Street E, Gananoque

📞 (613) 463-9131

🐦 @GanBeerCo

🌐 ganbeer.com

🕐 Tours are available by appointment during the winter, and daily at 1p.m., 3p.m., 5p.m., and 7p.m. in summer.

🛒 Summer: daily 12p.m.–9p.m.
Winter: Thu–Sun 1p.m.–8p.m.

Housed in a historic bell tower next to the Gananoque River, Gananoque Brewing strives to express the local terroir through the use of organic, locally sourced grains. The company, founded in 2011, went through an early period as a contract brewery before beginning to produce their own beers on-site in 2013. While their products are popular locally, a significant part of their success hinges on supplying a custom pale ale for the Toronto-based Grand Electric group of restaurants.

Their flagship, **NAUGHTY OTTER LAGER**, leans toward the sweet end of the pale ale spectrum with sweet grain being the main attraction (2). **EAGER BEAVER** is lightly sweet and gently malty in the style of a Mexican amber cerveza (2.5), while **THURSTY PIKE PILSNER** is very light in body with a grassy bitterness and fresh grain aroma (3). **COOPERSHAWK AMERICAN PALE ALE** is lightly crackery with some small caramel and a grass and grapefruit aroma (3), while **BELL RINGER IPA** hits the C-hop trifecta in its malt-forward toffeeish body (3). The pleasant surprise here is the full-bodied **BLACK BEAR BOCK**, an eisbock full of coffee, raisin, and light roasted grain (3.5).

GARDEN BREWERS

 @GardenBrewers
🌐 gardenbrewers.ca

Owned and operated by Victor and Sonja North, Garden's beers are currently brewed at Black Oak in Etobicoke, although the plan is to eventually build a facility in Hamilton. The couple has a credible brewing pedigree, with Sonja having worked in an administrative capacity at Black Oak and Victor having brewed for the 3 Brewers chain of brewpubs. Thematically, the focus is on beer that exploits ingredients usually found in a pantry rather than a pint glass. The creative process for each offering is explained on the brewery's website in admirably transparent detail, sometimes going so far as to include recipes for home-brew versions.

———

PIPERALES is a smoked amber ale with cracked black peppercorns that exaggerate the spicy hop character in combination with a plume of beechwood smoke, leading to a dry conflagration of a finish (3). **GREEN-THUMB** is a dry-gingered IPA using the blackcurranty Bullion hop in order to deflate the heat and spice of the ginger-root character (3.5).

GONGSHOW BEAUTY BEER

📞 (613) 415-7966

🐦 @BeautyBeers

🌐 www.beautybeer.ca

Gongshow is an Ottawa-based hockey apparel company that got into brewing in 2014. Their only brew is meant to be consumed after a hockey game with friends. They have been contracting out the production of their beer to a select few locations and plan on expanding to stores in the near future.

———

Their sole offering, **BEAUTY BEER**, is a fairly light offering, with distinct malt and fruit sweetness mingling with subtle grassy bitterness (2).

GRAND RIVER BREWING

📍 295 Ainslie Street, Cambridge

📞 (519) 620-3233

🐦 @GrandRiverBeer

🌐 grandriverbrewing.com

🕐 Tours are available for groups of ten or more
   when booked in advance. Please call ahead.

🛒 Mon–Sat 10a.m.–6p.m., Sun 11a.m.–4p.m.

Housed in the shell of the Galt Knife Factory in Cambridge, Grand River Brewing was founded just before the current explosion of Ontario breweries in 2007. Grand River's initial focus was on brewing low-alcohol beers for those worried about overindulgence. While many of those initial beers were successful, such a project is limiting in scope and the focus has since broadened. The brewery's beers are frequently cited as an example of the qualities hard-water minerality can impart in brewing, and are noteworthy for their enhanced grain characters. In 2015 Grand River saw its first canned beers and changed its graphic design to a more contemporary logo, which now features prominently on its new labels.

ONTARIO CRAFT BREWERIES

The core products at the moment include **PLOWMAN'S ALE**, a toffeeish yet floral amber ale (3.5), and **PUGNACIOUS PALE ALE**, which comes across as a turbocharged, citrusy English pale ale reminiscent of Fuller's London Pride (3.5). **TAILGATE MUNICH HELLES** is a light and accessible lager with lemon and pepper accents (2.5). **MILL RACE MILD** is an example of the infrequently seen English dark mild, with slightly roasty, husky grain, notes of cocoa, raisin, and roasted nuts (3.5).

In season, you may find **CURMUDGEON IPA**, which changes hop character from year to year at the brewer's whim (3-3.5). **HIGHBALLER PUMPKIN ALE** features the character of the pumpkins grown by brewery owner Bob Hannenberg over pumpkin-pie spice (3). **DOGSTALKER BOCK** has an aroma full of field berries supported by significant caramel grain character (3). **RUSSIAN GUN IMPERIAL STOUT**, named for a local Crimean-era cannon, is deep dark roast with dried fruit, licorice, coffee, and chocolate (4).

GRANITE BREWERY

📍 245 Eglinton Avenue E, Toronto

📞 (416) 322-0723

🐦 @GraniteBrewTO

🌐 www.granitebrewery.ca

🕐 Mon–Thu 11:30a.m.–12a.m.,
Fri–Sat 11:30a.m.–1a.m., Sun 11a.m.–12a.m.

🛒 Mon–Sat 11:30a.m.–11p.m., Sun 11a.m.–11p.m.

Started in 1991, the Granite is actually the second location of this brewpub, originally opened in Halifax. Ron Keefe, with help from his brother Kevin and legendary consulting brewer Alan Pugsley, has created one of Toronto's most enduring destinations for good beer. The Granite's open-fermented ales are made with their house Ringwood yeast, which is especially good for producing cask-conditioned beers (a house specialty). It's an infrequently seen technique in Ontario and worth a look into the glass-walled brewing area. The brewpub has a cozy front room styled as a library, a large back room frequently used to host gatherings, and a patio, which has become a popular venue for weddings in the summer months.

Change has occurred at the Granite over the last half decade, with Mary Beth Keefe, the landlord's daughter, taking over the majority of the brewing duties and adding newer styles of beer to a fairly traditional English lineup. For the first time, Peculiar is available at the LCBO, due to an expansion of the brewery's cellar. The purchase of a small canning line has allowed for a limited number of canned products in the on-site beer store in addition to 64-ounce returnable growlers, a packaging format in which the brewery led the Ontario market for years.

———

RINGWOOD is an English blonde ale with a pear and proofing-dough yeast character with earthy hops that come across as grass and apple-cured tobacco (3.5). **RINGBERRY** is a light, raspberry-dominated blonde ale suitable for the patio in summer (3). **BEST BITTER** on tap is an English bitter, with twiggy, tea-like hops, biscuit, and a touch of marmalade (3.5), while the cask version, **BEST BITTER SPECIAL**, has a fuller mouthfeel and a brighter dry-hopped character, and should ideally be paired with the brewpub's lamb curry (4). **HOPPING MAD** replaces some of the English hop character with Cascade, adding orange peel and peppery bitterness to a full, grainy toffee body (3.5). **PECULIAR** is somewhere between a northern English ESB and an old ale: deep fruity malts with red berries, mincemeat, and quince are balanced by chocolatey roast and a whiff of creosote (4).

More recent additions to the lineup are **DARKSIDE BLACK IPA**, which leans heavily into the dark malt, playing almost as though it were a bitter porter (3), and **GALACTIC PALE ALE**, which uses Galaxy hops, developing pineapple, grapefruit, guava, and a mild touch of spearmint leaf (3.5).

GREAT LAKES BREWERY

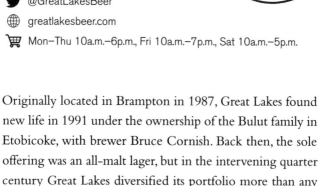

📍 30 Queen Elizabeth Boulevard, Toronto

📞 (416) 255-4510

🐦 @GreatLakesBeer

🌐 greatlakesbeer.com

🛒 Mon–Thu 10a.m.–6p.m., Fri 10a.m.–7p.m., Sat 10a.m.–5p.m.

Originally located in Brampton in 1987, Great Lakes found new life in 1991 under the ownership of the Bulut family in Etobicoke, with brewer Bruce Cornish. Back then, the sole offering was an all-malt lager, but in the intervening quarter century Great Lakes diversified its portfolio more than any other brewery in Ontario. In some ways the introduction of their Devil's Pale Ale, in 2006, signalled the beginning of a long-term change in the Ontario beer market.

Currently, Great Lakes is best known for their IPAs and innovative one-offs released under the Tank Ten label. Much of that success stems from the work of brewer Mike Lackey and the advent in 2009 of their Project X experimental beer series. Many of the Tank Ten recipes have been upsized from the hundred-litre pilot brewery and have earned the brewery serious credibility in the form of consecutive Canadian

Brewery of the Year awards and a sweep of the Canadian Brewing Awards IPA category in 2014.

——

CANUCK PALE ALE is a fine example of a light-bodied West Coast American pale ale with significant pine and grapefruit character (4). **POMPOUS ASS ENGLISH PALE ALE** has a nutty, light crystal malt base supporting dank, earthy tea-like hops (4). **RED LEAF LAGER**, a holdover from the brewery's past, is a clean, lightly bready Vienna lager (3). New to the core lineup in 2016 is **KARMA CITRA IPA**, redolent with exotic tropical fruits and exquisitely balanced (4.5).

Standard seasonals like the heavily spiced **WINTER ALE** (3) and **PUMPKIN ALE** (3.5) remain popular, although the highlights are within the Tank Ten series. **THRUST! AN IPA** heavily features Nelson Sauvin hops, with a profile of white grape, mango, and stone fruit (5); while the imperial IPA **ROBOHOP** is full of grapefruit, pine, and resin while retaining balance throughout the body despite its size (5).

HALIBURTON HIGHLANDS BREWING COMPANY

📍 1067 Garden Gate Drive, Haliburton

📞 (705) 754-2739

🐦 @HHBrewing

🌐 haliburtonhighlandsbrewing.ca

🕐 Thu–Sun 12p.m.–6p.m.

Husband-and-wife team Michael and Jewelle Schiedel-Webb opened up Haliburton Highlands in 2014 at the beautiful Abbey Gardens, which uses the brewery's spent grains as compost to enrich the soil. Brewmaster Michael Schiedel-Webb trained at the Siebel Institute's World Brewing Academy in Chicago, and developed his skills by working for Shades of Pale Brewing in Utah and Rahr & Sons Brewing in Texas. Paired with Jewelle's twenty-plus years of management and operations experience, their first year in operation was a rousing success, showing that the demand for local beer is strong in Haliburton. So strong, in fact, that they had a traditional Mongolian yurt erected to expand their retail space. Further expansion is planned for the summer of 2016.

————

BLUELINE BLONDE is a fairly sweet beer with a distinct biscuity character and a quick finish (3). The **IRISH RED ALE** is a very dark ruby, featuring many of the same roasted malt qualities of a nut brown. The use of U.K. hops makes for a very understated and well-rounded hop character (3). The **ABBEY ALE** has the very low alcohol burn normally found in the style, but otherwise features notes of dried fruit, citrus, and banana with subtle notes of caramel (3). A strong local presence is evident in their **HONEY BROWN ALE**, which uses locally sourced honey to seamlessly blend sweetness with the roasted notes of the malt (4). The **RYE PORTER** is Belgian influenced and brings forth notes of dried fruit blended with chocolate and pepper (3.5). Finally, the **OATMEAL STOUT** pours very black with an almost berry-like note that makes way for cocoa notes and a very smooth finish due to the Ontario-grown oats featured in the brew (3.5).

THE HAMILTON BREWERY

9 117 Ferguson Avenue S, Hamilton

☎ (905) 962-8294

🐦 @hamiltonbrewery

🌐 thehamiltonbrewery.com

The goal of the Hamilton Brewery is eventually to establish a bricks-and-mortar facility in Hamilton itself, but for the time being their beer is brewed at Railway City in St. Thomas. In a town with a history of workingman's beers like President's Choice, Laker, and Lakeport, it makes sense that the company's first beer should be called Blue Collar Pale Ale. As Hamilton continues its transition from steel town to hipster bastion, it's unsurprising that the utility lagers of the past should be replaced by a craft pale ale.

———

BLUE COLLAR PALE ALE is a standard American take on the style, with Centennial pine coming through heavily over a lightly buttery, cracker body (2.5).

HIGH PARK BREWERY

 @HighParkBrewery

 highparkbrewery.com

High Park Brewery was launched in 2015 by four old hockey buddies wanting to form a locally focused brewery named after the area they all lived in. Currently contracting out of Grand River, they are planning on opening their own space in the High Park area in 2017.

————

Their initial offerings include the **ACROSS THE POND** ESB, with a distinct English influence, dry, thin mouthfeel, and slight biscuit character (2); the **OFF THE LEASH** IPA, which features a distinct taste of lime with a delicate caramel presence (1); and the **AGAINST THE GRAIN** lager, with a light mouthfeel, cereal notes, and a dry finish (3).

HIGH ROAD BREWING COMPANY

🐦 @HighRdBrews

🌐 www.highroadbrewing.com

Currently contract brewed out of Niagara College in Niagara-on-the-Lake, High Road Brewing is the project of Rob Doyle and Curtis Bentley, two veterans of the Ontario brewing industry. Both attended Heriot-Watt University's brewing program in Edinburgh. Doyle is currently a teaching brewer at Niagara College. Contract brewing seems to be a step toward a facility of their own — a prospect to be excited about given the quality of their first offering.

———

BRONAN is a Vermont-style IPA that takes advantage of the Alchemist's popular Conan yeast strain to produce bright orange Creamsicle and passion fruit throughout the aroma and palate (4.5).

HOCKLEY VALLEY BREWING COMPANY

 25 Centennial Road, Orangeville

 (519) 941-8887

 @Hockleybeer

 www.hockleybeer.ca

Mon–Fri 9a.m.–5p.m.

Since 2002 Hockley has been offering a limited selection of beers in English styles that reflect the training of brewer Andrew Kohnen. What is truly impressive is the inroads they have made in the market, not only in Ontario but in Manitoba and Alberta, with types of beer that are not currently in vogue: a sign that persistence and commitment to a model pays off. Since 2008, Hockley has been brewing slightly more mainstream beers under their Midland Beer Works label, which focuses on thematic elements related to Georgian Bay. In 2014, they announced a series of one-offs inspired by legends from the region.

———

HOCKLEY DARK is the brewery's most consistent and longest-serving offering. They describe it as being halfway between a northern English brown ale and a southern mild, which only means that it inhabits a realm between fruity, nutty toasted malt, and darker chocolate and licorice flavours (3.5). **HOCKLEY AMBER** depends a great deal more on the mid-range, with deep toasted cereal and caramel playing off against spicy, grassy hops (3). **HOCKLEY CLASSIC** is the most recent addition to the core lineup and lighter than the others; a lager with a saltine cracker body and light floral, apple aroma (2). **GEORGIAN BAY BEER** is a pale lager that fills the role of easygoing summer quaffer for a region-specific crowd. Its body is light cereal and a hint of corn with a light lemon hop character (2.5).

HOGSBACK BREWING COMPANY

☎ (613) 986-2337

🐦 @HogsBackBrewing

🌐 hogsback.ca

Named in reference to a prize-winning pig and a term historically used to describe a portion of the Rideau River that resembles the backbone of a hog, HogsBack opened in 2010 and contracts out to multiple breweries including Big Rig, Wellington, and Broadhead Brewery. They sell exclusively at the LCBO and the Beer Store.

———

Their **VINTAGE LAGER** is very European-influenced, with a distinct malt character featuring toffee notes with a slight earthy bitterness brought on by Saaz hops (2.5). The **ONTARIO PALE ALE** labels itself as an American pale ale, though it has much more of a sweet honey and malt note with little bitterness (2). HogsBack's winter seasonal beer is the punny **APORKALYPSE NOW**, a very carbonated stout with notes of chocolate, cherry, and, you guessed it, bacon (2). Real smoked bacon does go into this beer, so vegans and vegetarians beware.

ONTARIO CRAFT BREWERIES

HOGTOWN BREWERS

📞 (416) 453-7557

🐦 @HogtownBrewers

🌐 hogtownbrewers.ca

Trading on Toronto's late-nineteenth-century history as a supplier of pork to the British Empire, Hogtown is a contract brewery, currently produced out of Brick in Kitchener. Begun in 2012 with the input of the owners' rugby team, Hogtown quickly recruited Jay Cooke (previously of Paddock Wood and currently at District Brewing in Regina) for recipe design. Their porcine mascot has become a familiar sight on taps around the city of Toronto and goes by the name of Hogtown Hank.

———

The brewery's two offerings thus far have been **HOGTOWN ALE**, a light German hybrid ale, pleasantly grainy with a hint of floral noble hop and a light metallic sting in the finish (3), and **HOG WILD IPA**, which is not available at time of writing but should return in the near future (NR).

HOP CITY BREWING COMPANY

📞 (905) 855-7743

🐦 @HopCityBrewing

🌐 hopcity.com

While many think of Hop City as simply a subsidiary of Moosehead, the history of the brewery is surprisingly complex and contains significant craft pedigree. The brewery wasn't located in Brampton until 2007 and the Hop City brand didn't exist until 2009. Prior to the name change and relocation, the company had operated as Niagara Falls Brewing, famous for producing the first (and legendary) North American eisbock and the immensely popular Gritstone Premium Ale.

Head brewer Kevin Gray has been with the company since 1991, which makes Hop City's recent adaptability all the more impressive. The rebrand coincided with the launch of a new line of products emphasizing a colourful cartoon style and stylistically updated beers that show a brewery holding their own in a marketplace obsessed with novelty. Production has recently expanded past the 10,000-HL mark and several of their products are distributed in the United States.

ONTARIO CRAFT BREWERIES

The flagship brand, **BARKING SQUIRREL**, is an amber lager with a deep caramel body and a nose of dried fruit and wild grasses leading to a metallic bite on the finish (3). **LAWNCHAIR "CLASSIC" WEISSE** is mashed banana and pie spice on the nose with a spiky carbonation leading to the tang of wheat and a hint of yogurt on the finish (3.5). **8TH SIN BLACK LAGER** is a roasty schwarzbier that drifts roasted coffee and chocolate over the palate while a medium body rushes beneath toward a clean finish. It develops a touch of apple as it warms (4). **HOPBOT IPA** has a wide aroma of pineapple, grapefruit, and mango with an underlying caramel body that fades into a perfumy herbal finish (4).

HOUSE ALES

📍 587 Yonge Street, Toronto

📞 (416) 928-0008

🐦 @houseales

🌐 www.barvolo.com/house-ales

🕐 Mon–Wed 4p.m.–2a.m., Thu–Sun 2p.m.–2a.m.

House Ales is the in-house nanobrewery at Bar Volo, a craft beer bar that is one of the foundations of the Toronto beer scene and the most vocal proponent of beer served on cask since its original inception as a southern Italian restaurant in 1985. Under the supervision of proprietor Ralph Morana and his sons, Tomas and Julian, Volo is also behind boutique beer-import company Keep6 Imports, as well as being the organizers of Cask Days, the biggest cask beer festival in North America.

In the summer of 2010 a one-barrel pilot brewing system was set up in the popular beer bar's kitchen. Since then, House Ales have put out a large number of their own brews as well as collaborations with many famous breweries from both in and outside of Ontario. Currently at the helm of brewing is Ralph Morana himself, along with Dan Beaudoin, formerly of Boshkung Brewing Company.

ONTARIO CRAFT BREWERIES

—————

Of the many regular beers available on a rotating or seasonal basis in either cask or draught, **PUNTER'S GOLD**, a golden ale, has grassy aromas with lemon and biscuity malts (4). **MEZZA NOTTE** is an espresso milk stout with creamy chocolate and coffee notes in a smooth mouthfeel and a fruity, sweet finish (3.5). **BIG PAPA BROWN ALE** is nutty and smooth, with a fairly light mouthfeel (3.5). **CIVIL SERVANT** is a Belgian grisette that is the subject of special ingredient alterations, but the core beer itself is very delicate and lightly sweet, with hints of lemon and an earthy bitterness (4).

INDIE ALEHOUSE BREWING COMPANY

📍 2876 Dundas Street W, Toronto

📞 (416) 760-9691

🐦 @indiealehouse

🌐 www.indiealehouse.com

🕐 Mon 5p.m.–late, Tue–Sun 12p.m.–late

🛒 Mon 5p.m.–11p.m., Tue–Sat 12p.m.–11p.m., Sun 12p.m.–9p.m.

Opened in the autumn of 2012, the Junction's Indie Alehouse has become one of Toronto's most successful brewpubs over the course of its short existence. Owner Jason Fisher is one of the Ontario brewing industry's most vocal proponents for change to alcohol retailing, periodically becoming downright confrontational with government officials. Outspoken and unapologetic, this assertive character is also invested in the brewery, which specializes in larger-than-life flavours in their punchy ales.

The kitchen, under the direction of executive chef Todd Clarmo, has quickly gained a reputation for quality and generous portions, which seem to increase in size at the Indie's almost legendary beer dinners. Indie Alehouse produces

ONTARIO CRAFT BREWERIES

something like 1,500 barrels of beer a year at this point, thanks to an expansion of the brewery in 2014 that increased its size by 60 percent. Currently, they produce as many as fifty varieties of beer over the course of a year. The off-site barrel warehouse currently holds 120 barrels of various kinds, allowing brewer Jeff Broeders, an early graduate of Niagara College, plenty of room for experimentation.

———

BROKEN HIPSTER is a Belgian-style witbier with coriander and both sweet and bitter orange peel, and is the lightest of the regular lineup (3.5). **BREAKFAST PORTER** is sweetly chocolatey, practically Yoo-hoo with light roasty bitterness (3.5). **INSTIGATOR IPA** does a fantastic job of imitating grapefruit juice before slamming into a bitter wall (4). **BARNYARD BELGIAN IPA** is pleasantly spicy with orange and rye behind a lightly clovey Belgian yeast (3.5). **COCKPUNCHER DOUBLE IPA** is a massive dose of fruit salad with a sharply bitter impact that'll double you over (3.5). **ZOMBIE APOCALYPSE** is an imperial stout. The 2015 version has roasted malt, chocolate, and sweet dark fruit, but is dominated by molasses, almost taking on the character of a rum barrel despite never having been near one (4). **SUN KICKED ANEJO** is an example of the beers available through the Fates and Furies series, an imperial wit aged in tequila barrels with a sharp herbal nose and citric lemon sting that drops into an agave-sugared cereal finish (4).

INNOCENTE BREWING COMPANY

📍 283 Northfield Drive E, Unit 8, Waterloo

📞 (519) 725-1253

🐦 @Innocente_Brew

🌐 www.innocente.ca

🕐 Tours are available upon request. Please call ahead.

🛒 Mon–Wed 11a.m.–7p.m., Thu–Fri 11a.m.–9p.m.,
Sat–Sun 11a.m.–5p.m.

When Steve Innocente started contract brewing under the Innocente name in Scotland in 2013, his focus was on hop-forward ales, a genre that wasn't widely available in Scotland at the time. Innocente was living there while completing post-doctoral work on ale-yeast strains in cancer research. Upon returning home to Waterloo, Innocente opened a brewery of his own with the help of his brother David. His focus has since shifted from the bitter profile of those early ales to a more balanced portfolio featuring diverse styles that appeal to a wider audience.

———

The three core beers in the lineup are **FLING**, a take on a golden ale, with English and North American hops combining earthy, woody bitterness with citrus and toasted grain (3.5); **BYSTANDER**, an American pale ale with Galaxy hops, which express themselves as grapefruit and mango (3); and **CONSCIENCE IPA**, which amps up the bitterness further and adds Ella hops to the mix for a hint of melon (3).

PILS-SINNER is an updated take on a northern German pilsner using Waimea hops, with a leaf and tangerine note on the way to a crisp, bitter finish (4.5). **INN O'SLÀINTE** is an Irish red ale that leans squarely into toasted grain and caramel without becoming overly sweet (3.5). **CHARCOAL PORTER** is a light-bodied take on the style that nevertheless ventures just past roast into burnt-in smoky territory (4).

JUNCTION CRAFT BREWING

📍 90 Cawthra Avenue, Unit 101, Toronto

📞 (416) 766-1616

🐦 @junction_craft

🌐 junctioncraft.com

🕐 Thu–Fri 4p.m.–9p.m., Sat 11a.m.–9p.m., Sun 12p.m.–5p.m.

Based in the Toronto area it's named after, Junction Craft Brewing is the handiwork of Tom Paterson, who has notably opened several longstanding Toronto venues such as the Paddock, and brewer Doug Pengelly, who owns Saint Andre Brewing in Etobicoke, which was a regular presence on the taps at the fully restored 1940s jazz bar. The two hit it off and over time decided to go into business together.

After over a year of brewing under contract at Guelph's Wellington Brewery, Junction Craft finally opened up their brewery, taproom, and retail space on Cawthra Avenue in 2012. They have been a constant presence at festivals and on retail shelves ever since. Visitors to the brewery will be treated to imagery showcasing the area's history and can also visit next-door neighbour the Toronto Distillery Company for a taste of small-batch spirits.

Junction's primary strength lies in beers with a very English influence. Their initial offering and signature brew, **CONDUCTOR'S CRAFT ALE**, contains five malts and five hop varieties and is very malt-forward, with hints of stone fruit combined with an earthy bitterness in a slowly fading finish (3). The award-winning **BRAKEMAN'S SESSION ALE** has a distinctive biscuity malt presence with a light note of grapefruit (2.5). **LOCAL OPTION LAGER** has a very sweet aroma, with a significant amount of grain notes and a mild astringent finish (2). The star flavours of **STATIONMASTER'S STOUT** are without a doubt leather and dark-roasted coffee with a light wisp of cocoa (2). **ENGINEER'S IPA** is a West Coast IPA with mango and grapefruit leading the way to a very biscuity middle and a slightly honey-like aftertaste (2.5).

KENSINGTON BREWING COMPANY

📍 156 Augusta Avenue, Toronto

📞 (647) 648-7541

🐦 @drinkgoodbeer

🌐 www.kensingtonbrewingcompany.com

Kensington Brewing Company was started in 2011 by Kensington Market resident Brock Shepherd. Originally running it from a single desk at the back of his previous business, the now-closed Burger Bar, Shepherd collaborated with brewer Paul Dickey (Cheshire Valley) to create Kensington's flagship beer, Augusta Ale. From its debut at the Burger Bar, distribution of Augusta Ale has expanded, as has the range of beers offered by the brewery. They now have two other beers in their catalogue. While Kensington is currently brewing their beers at Cool Beer Brewing and Muskoka Brewery, a brewery of their own at 299 Augusta Avenue has been under construction for some time and is expected to open at some point in 2016.

――――

Kensington's beers are all named after aspects of Kensington Market's geography and history. Their flagship, **AUGUSTA ALE**, is named after the street that Burger Bar called home. It pours a hazy, sunset orange, with flavours of tangerine and a delicate malt note (4). Named for the fish markets of the area, **BALDWIN FISHEYE PA** has a toffee-like aroma with notes of citrus backed by a strong malt character (2.5). **FRUIT STAND WATERMELON WHEAT** is a clean-tasting beer brewed with kölsch yeast, featuring the unmistakable and pleasant aroma and taste of watermelon (2.5).

KICHESIPPI
BEER COMPANY

📍 866 Campbell Avenue, Ottawa

📞 (613) 728-7845

🐦 @kichesippibeer

🌐 www.kbeer.ca

🕐 Tours are available for groups of
up to fifteen. Please call ahead.

🛒 Mon–Wed 10a.m.–5p.m., Thu–Sat 10a.m.–6p.m.

While Kichesippi only began producing beer in April of 2010, the facility producing the beer has a longer history in the context of Ottawa's beer scene. Kichesippi's purchase of Heritage Brewing in late 2010 allowed it to make the jump from contracting out of the facility to owning it outright. While that deal did not initially include Perry Mason's popular Scotch Irish brands like Sgt. Major IPA and Stuart's Session Ale, Kichesippi was able to acquire them subsequently. Oddly, though, it has not produced them since. The brewery's vision was different than that of the brands that were previously produced out of the space, and the focus since has been on straightforward food-friendly styles of beer that are accessible to drinkers in all corners of the market. More recently,

Kichesippi has begun introducing smaller–batch, seasonal products to complement their staple offerings, and the addition of a new canning line and some plans for facility expansion suggest that they have been very popular. They also produce a retro-branded range of artisanal sodas under the Harvey and Vern's label.

———

1855 is an amber ale and the brewery's most popular year-round offering. It has a nutty body of toffee and toast that's well balanced by an appropriate bitterness and nearly ideal for pairing with pub fare (4). **NATURAL BLONDE** has a nose with a stone-fruit character and an earthy, peppery spice on the finish (3.5). **HELLER HIGHWATER** has a soft grain character with a gentle body and a light wildflower aroma, but verges on the sweet side for the style (3). **LOGGER PENNSYLVANIA PORTER** is a sort of American porter popularized by Yuengling, which uses a lager yeast. The result is a brown beer with a slightly peanutty, dark-caramel character reminiscent of Kerr's Molasses Kisses (3). **WUCHAK THROWBACK** is an IPA that uses the Cluster hop, which gives it a small citrus character dominated by blackcurrant in the aroma and spruce on the finish (3.5).

KILANNAN BREWING COMPANY

📍 103015 Grey Road 18, RR4, Owen Sound

📞 (226)909-2122

🐦 @KilannanBrewing

🌐 www.kilannanbrewing.ca

🛒 Mon–Wed 12p.m.–5p.m. Thu–Fri 10a.m.–5p.m., Sat 9:30a.m.–5p.m.

This three-year-old brewery near Georgian Bay boasts a Siebel Institute of Technology–educated brewer in the person of Spencer Wareham. The German portion of that program is evident in the brewery's core offerings: accessible, German-hybrid ales from Dusseldorf and Cologne on the Rhine. More recently, the brewery has begun to expand their offerings to include other styles, ones that more readily approach the expectations of the adventurous craft beer drinker. Kilannan is now brewing interesting one-offs with hops from New Zealand and branching out into more assertive styles of beer like IPAs and imperial stouts.

———

KÖLSCH is light-bodied and fruity with a white grape and wildflower aroma leading to a light, spicy bite on the finish

(3). **ALT** sticks close to the altbier style, with an earthy, topsoil aroma that leads into quite a mild body with caramel, dried fruit, and toasted nuts (3.5). **NEW ZEALAND RED ALE** plays light accents of passion fruit and pineapple against a deep biscuit and toffee background leading to a dry finish (3). **THE MEN WHO STARE AT OATS** is an oatmeal stout with hints of tobacco and leather playing around something vinous in a cola-dark body with hints of leafy bitterness (3).

KINGSTON BREWING COMPANY

📍 34 Clarence Street, Kingston

📞 (613) 542-4978

🌐 kingstonbrewing.ca

🕐 Daily 11a.m.–2a.m.

Founded in 1986, the Kingston Brewing Company was the second brewpub opened in Ontario and is currently the longest-lived. Housed in a nineteenth-century limestone building, the brewpub is a perennial Kingston hot spot, decorated in all manner of brewery memorabilia and especially festive at Christmas. The quality of the beer has had ups and downs over the years, but this is tied mainly to the popularity of the pub and the size of the on-site brewery; it has been hard to keep up with demand. For nine years (1992–2001), Dragon's Breath was produced by Hart Brewery in Carleton Place. It is currently served under the name Dragoon's Breath and produced by McAuslan in Montreal. The Whitetail Cream Ale is similarly produced off-site by the Muskoka Brewery.

DRAGOON'S BREATH PALE ALE is distinctly English in style, with a fruity flavour and pronounced bitterness (3.5). **WHITETAIL CREAM ALE** is clean for a cream ale, lightly fruity with pronounced notes of grain (3). Of the beers produced on-site, the most successful are the **FRAMBOISE ROYALE**, whose aggressive raspberry presence sits somewhere between Chambord and Swedish Berries (2), and the **DRAGON'S BREATH REAL ALE**, a malty cask-only offering with tea-like hops brewed on-site (2–3, depending on cask condition).

LAKE OF BAYS BREWING COMPANY

📍 2681 Muskoka Road, Unit 117, Baysville

📞 (705) 767-2313

🐦 @LB_Brewing

🌐 lakeofbaysbrewing.ca

🕐 Hours vary seasonally; check website for updates.

Very few stories begin, "At one time, my father found himself the owner of a commercial property in Baysville," but that's just how Darren Smith's goes. With his father's property, Darren's dream of opening a brewery was realized, and Lake of Bays Brewing Company was opened in 2010. Originally, Smith was the head brewer, but he later handed over operations to experienced Danish brewer Dan "Dunk" Unkerskov.

Aside from their year-round offerings, Lake of Bays is best known for their limited partnership beers, most notably with the NHL Alumni Association. Past beers in the Alumni series have included tributes to Jacques Plante, Darcy Tucker, and CuJo (Curtis Joseph).

———

The **TOP SHELF CLASSIC LAGER** is the year-round signature beer of the Alumni series. It is a rather light-bodied beer with a toasted malt backbone blended with very mild bitterness (2). **CROSSWIND PALE ALE** has a very strong biscuit-grain character with mild citrus and grassy notes (2.5). **SPARK HOUSE RED ALE** has warm toffee flavours accompanied by mild coffee in a subtle cocoa finish (2.5). **ROCK CUT BAYSVILLE LAGER** pours dark golden. With an overall bready flavour, there are grassy and candy-like properties that have also found their way in (2). **10 POINT INDIA PALE ALE** is an English-influenced IPA with a heavy caramel presence and a burst of grapefruit and pine (3).

LAKE OF THE WOODS BREWING COMPANY

📍 350 Second Street S, Kenora

📞 (807) 468-2337

🐦 @lowbrewco

🌐 lowbrewco.com

🕐 Mon–Wed 11a.m.–12a.m., Thu–Sat 11a.m.–1a.m.,
Sun 11a.m.–12a.m.

🛒 Daily 11a.m.–11p.m.

Lake of the Woods Brewing is a fine example of the way in which a determined brewer can help to revitalize a community. The signs of Kenora's industrial heritage are something that Lake of the Woods wears on its sleeve. Occupying a restored 1912 fire station that was gutted and rebuilt to purpose, the company brews beers named after a disused (ostensibly haunted) gold mine, a shuttered paper mill, and the firehouse itself. Owner Taras Manzie is helping to lead the tourism economy in the region by providing a 275-seat taproom, restaurant, and brewing facility that employs nearly one hundred people in the busy season during only its second year of operation. The taproom caters to wide-ranging tastes with specialty seasonal beers, a games room on the second floor, and a diverse selection of pub-grub favourites.

Lake of the Woods is poised for expansion into distilling and is currently playing with the idea of starting its own hop fields. While the long-term goal of exporting beer to the United States would require expansion from the current 10-HL brewhouse to an additional facility, the brewery does not suffer from a lack of ambition or ingenuity when it comes to problem-solving. Lake of the Woods has been operating at capacity for over a year and is currently working with Cool Beer Brewing in Etobicoke to produce additional volume for its flagship brew, Sultana Gold.

———

SULTANA GOLD is a North American–style blonde ale with an aroma of pear and unripe plum and a bushy bitterness in its light body (3). **PAPERMAKER PILSNER** is in the Czech-style with Saaz hops, spicy and aromatic (NR), while **FIREHOUSE** is toward the lighter end of the English nut-brown spectrum (NR). An example of the seasonal brews Lake of the Woods is currently producing, **FORGOTTEN LAKE** is a strong fruit beer, tart and lightly herbal. Brewed with wild blueberries, the fruit imparts a pinkish hue and the flavours of both berry and stem to the beer (3).

LAKE ON THE MOUNTAIN BREWING COMPANY

📍 264 County Road 7, Prince Edward County

📞 (613) 476-1321

🌐 lakeonthemountain.com/brewery

🕐 Open late April to late October.

Located just up the hill from the Glenora–Adolphustown ferry, the Lake on the Mountain Brewery is a part of a larger resort complex featuring two venues that serve their beers: the Inn, which resembles a rustic public house, and the Miller House Café, a light, open space that also contains a coffee bar. The significant strength of this extract brewery is its location; situated between the Bay of Quinte and Lake on the Mountain Provincial Park, the brewery has two of the best patios in the province of Ontario, both of which boast commanding views most publicans would kill for. Either would be an excellent lunch stop on a tour of Prince Edward County.

———

ONTARIO CRAFT BREWERIES

Several of the brewery's offerings are designed for mainstream accessibility. The **CREAM ALE** displays a fruity character with overtones of yeast but is otherwise fairly muted (1.5). The **LAGER**, while grassy also has a corn aroma (1.5). Better are brewer Ryan Kreutzwiser's more ambitious offerings. The relatively light-bodied **COFFEE PORTER** features freshly roasted beans from nearby County Coffee (3.5). The **ENGLISH ALE** possesses a distinct whiff of sulfurous matchstick character from the nearby limestone-heavy water source (2.5). The **SUMMER ALE** is well balanced, with a touch of candied lemon-drop sweetness to it (3).

LAKE WILCOX BREWING COMPANY

📍 1033 Edgeley Boulevard, Vaughan

📞 (647) 749-0489

🐦 @WilcoxBrewery

🌐 www.lakewilcoxbrewing.com

Behind Lake Wilcox Brewing Company are David De Ciantis and Ray Nicolini, who also own Lake Wilcox Canning, a canning facility that operates out of U-Brew facility the Brew Kettle of Richmond Hill. While currently brewing out of Railway City Brewing in St. Thomas, De Ciantis and Nicolini have plans to open a facility in their hometown of Richmond Hill.

———

Their first beer is the **WILCOX MAD QUACKER LAGER**, a Vienna-style amber with sweet caramel notes and a clean finish (2.5).

ONTARIO CRAFT BREWERIES

LEFT FIELD BREWERY

📍 36 Wagstaff Drive, Toronto

📞 (647) 346-5001

🐦 @LFBrewery

🌐 www.leftfieldbrewery.ca

🕐 Mon–Sun 12p.m.–9p.m. (Tours: Sat–Sun 3p.m.)

🛒 Mon–Sun 12p.m.–9p.m.

Situated in one of the few remaining industrial zones in the Greenwood-Coxwell corridor, Left Field Brewery is run by husband-and-wife baseball fans Mark and Mandie Murphy. Starting out as home-brewers, they soon moved to contracting out of Grand River Brewing and Barley Days Brewery before finally opening their own facility on Wagstaff Drive. The Murphys have developed a reputation in the beer community of Toronto as a local team that made it to the big leagues through a combination of talent and hard work. Since opening, the brewery has gained popularity as a community hub, with patrons from the neighbourhood and beyond congregating at the taproom to refill their growlers, sample new releases, and watch the game on the big screen. While Left Field intends to expand production at their facility, there are no immediate plans to expand distribution outside of Toronto.

———

With few exceptions, Left Field's beer names are based around their baseball theme. **EEPHUS OATMEAL BROWN ALE** takes its name from a kind of slow pitch. Left Field's first beer, it has cocoa and coffee notes and a creamy mouthfeel (4). **MARIS* PALE ALE** features hints of pine and a decent dry finish (3.5). Seasonals include the **GRANDSTAND HOPPY WHEAT**, which has distinct melon, orange peel, and pine notes (3.5), and **SUNLIGHT PARK SAISON**, made with grapefruit zest (4). Left Field also does a collaborative coffee porter, incorporating roasts from their neighbour Pilot Coffee Roasters. **BRICKS & MORTAR COFFEE PORTER**'s coffee notes are very well represented and not overbearing, with a slight hint of chocolate and dried-fruit sweetness at the end (4.5).

LIBERTY VILLAGE BREWING COMPANY

☎ (416) 577-7582
🐦 @LibertyVilBeer
🌐 libertyvillagebeer.com

Liberty Village Brewing Company is the creation of long-time friends Cassandra Campbell, Steve Combes, Kosta Viglatzis, and brewmaster Eric Emery, whose home-brewed beers inspired his friends to start a brewery in 2012. Their initial foray into large-scale brewing was at Junction Craft Brewing. They have since contracted out to Cool Beer Brewing in Etobicoke.

———

Their mainstays include the classic **504 PALE ALE**, named for the streetcar that serves their neighbourhood. It features a mild peach aroma with distinct lime and orange flavours that come together with a slight dry note, finishing well (4.5). The **BLACK BLESSING CHOCOLATE STOUT** has a distinct, creamy-chocolate tone with a touch of warming coffee flavours (3). The **GOSEBUSTER** is an excellent gateway beer to the gose style, with grapefruit notes, a delicate tartness, and a very subtle salt presence (3.5).

THE LION BREWERY RESTAURANT

📍 59 King Street N, Waterloo

📞 (519) 886-3350

🌐 www.huetherhotel.com

🕐 Mon–Fri 11a.m.–1a.m., Sat–Sun 10a.m.–1a.m.

Opened as a brewpub in 1987 by the Adlys family, the Lion Brewery at the Huether Hotel has to be seen to be believed. Although the beer is now brewed next door at the Gold Crown facility, which doubles as a brew-on-premises for area home brewers, the Lion Brewery's beers are served throughout the Huether Hotel complex.

The Lion Brewery Restaurant houses a cellar in which some of the first lager-style beer was ever brewed in Ontario, and a private dining room that had been part of the nineteenth-century brewery's maltings. Upstairs, the Speakeasy Billiards Room possesses a down-at-heel charm and a selection of vintage pinball and arcade machines. The compound also contains an upstairs bar called the Barley Works and a 280-seat outdoor patio for summer revelry. For an accurate sense of early brewing in Ontario, both in the nineteenth century and the 1980s, it is impossible to do better.

Although many beers are offered year-round, seasonal choices reflect highlights from the tastes of the last twenty years; the best offerings are in classic styles. **ADLYS ALE** is a straightforward full-bodied red ale with caramel and bready grain flavours, punctuated by a note of tart berry not unlike a jam roll (2.5). The **IPA** is British in style, with notes of blackcurrant and lemon and a balanced sweetness (3). **LION LAGER** is an amber lager, light on caramel with a distinct grassiness in the aroma and a reasonably bitter finish (3), while **WUERZBURGER** is lighter in malt character and more approachable to new converts (2.5).

LONDON BREWING CO-OPERATIVE

 623 Dundas Street, London

 @LondonBrewingca

 londonbrewing.ca

This small, London-based brewery is organized as a worker's co-operative. Operating since 2013, it is focused on brewing with local and organic ingredients. The co-op has been pouring their beers on a pop-up basis exclusively through the Root Cellar Organic Cafe, another co-operative business, which, along with food delivery service On The Move Organics, is partially owned by some of the owners of the brewery.

————

While the majority of the London Brewing Co-operative's beers are one-offs, an oft-brewed beer is the **LOCAL 117**, an amber ale made with ingredients from throughout the city and featuring a decent roasted-coffee profile matched with mild caramel sweetness (2.5).

LONGSLICE BREWERY

📍 259 Lansdowne Avenue, Toronto
📞 (647) 479-2469
🐦 @LongsliceBrews
🌐 www.longslice.com

Started in 2014, Longslice is a Toronto-based contract brewery currently producing beer out of the Cool facility in Etobicoke. The Peat brothers had success as home brewers during their high-school years and decided to start their own company after placing second in the IPA category of the Toronto Beer Week Homebrew Contest with their sole offering, Hopsta La Vista IPA. The beer has become relatively popular in bars across the GTA largely due to the variety of formats in which it's offered. As of late 2015, it is available in a number of LCBO locations.

———

HOPSTA LA VISTA is a hybrid of English- and American-style IPAs, malt-dominant with a wide range of hop characters, from a vegetal, somewhat earthy flavour to citrus and vanilla notes. The bitterness is relatively mild behind honeyed malts (3).

LOUIS CIFER
BREW WORKS

📍 417 Danforth Avenue, Toronto

📞 (647) 350-5087

🐦 @LouisCiferBW

🌐 www.louisciferbrewworks.com

🕐 Mon–Fri 11:30a.m.–2a.m., Sat–Sun 11a.m.–2a.m.

🛒 Mon–Fri 11:30a.m.–11p.m., Sat–Sun 11a.m.–11p.m.

Located on the Danforth between Chester and Pape subway stations, Louis Cifer has become a popular destination in a bustling neighbourhood full of young families due to its extensive pub menu and family-friendly atmosphere. Opened in 2014, the bar continues to retain a number of high-quality local craft beers on tap as well as a selection of their own house beers.

———

The **BLONDE ALE** contains a lot of roasted peanut flavour with a slight hint of mint at the end (1). The **COCONUT LEMONGRASS THAI-PA** was originally made for International Women's Day and contains coconut paste, giving a delicate hint of coconut meat at the finish of a beer that has a lot of tropical and citrus character (2.5). The **ESB (EXTRA SPECIAL BITTER)** is a good example of a typical northern English offering, with notes of fruit, caramel, and grain (3). The **GATES OF ALE IPA** contains distinct notes of tropical fruits such as pineapple and mango, ending with a slight hint of pine and a biscuity finish (3.5). The **HEFEWEIZEN**, however, is milder, with banana notes and lovely grain flavours. There is an overall earthy texture throughout (3). The **LAGER** has a mild biscuity grain character that becomes more prominent as it heads toward the end of the palate (2). The **STOUT** has a lot of coffee notes, with a rather light mouthfeel (2.5). The **WIT** predominantly highlights distinct banana and cloves, but also contains a welcome grassy bitterness and a slight sweet-berry flavour in the finish (3).

LOWERTOWN BREWERY

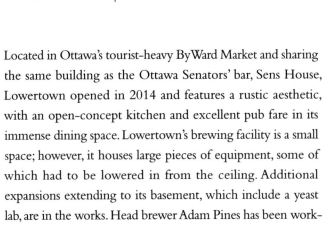

📍 73 York Street, Ottawa

📞 (613) 722–1454

🐦 @LowertownOttawa

🌐 www.lowertownbrewery.ca

🕐 Mon–Wed 11a.m.–1a.m., Thu–Fri 11a.m.–2a.m.,
Sat–Sun 9a.m.–10p.m.

Located in Ottawa's tourist-heavy ByWard Market and sharing the same building as the Ottawa Senators' bar, Sens House, Lowertown opened in 2014 and features a rustic aesthetic, with an open-concept kitchen and excellent pub fare in its immense dining space. Lowertown's brewing facility is a small space; however, it houses large pieces of equipment, some of which had to be lowered in from the ceiling. Additional expansions extending to its basement, which include a yeast lab, are in the works. Head brewer Adam Pines has been working hard to bring a "simple done well" approach to his beers, making them accessible to the tourists who frequent the area while also being of good enough quality to appeal to the locals.

———

The four core Lowertown offerings are the **LAGER**, which features a light mouthfeel with a pleasant biscuity character brought on by the German malts (3.5); the **DARK LAGER**, which pours a deep copper and has a molasses aroma with roasted-nut malt flavourings and a caramel sweetness (4); the **PALE ALE** is well balanced, with a distinct earthy hop character and biscuit presence that is rather inviting for newcomers to the style (4); lastly, the **RED FIFE** has a very toffee-like malty twirl levelled out with a slight dry finish (3.5).

MACKINNON BROTHERS BREWING

MACKINNON
BROTHERS
BREWING
Co.

📍 1915 County Road 22, Bath

📞 (613) 777-6277

🐦 @MacKinnonBrew

🌐 www.mackinnonbrewing.com

🕐 Tours available. For groups larger than five, the cost is $10.00 per head.

🛒 Summer: Wed–Sun 11a.m.–5p.m.
Winter: Thu–Sat 11a.m.–5p.m.

Located outside Bath, MacKinnon Brothers has the longest historical legacy of any brewery in Ontario despite being founded in 2014. The family has been on the farmland the brewery occupies since 1784. Between them, Ivan and Dan MacKinnon possess all of the skills needed to run a brewery. Ivan is a mechanical engineer, while Dan is a Heriot-Watt trained brewer. The time spent learning about beer in Scotland has created the happy result that their malt-driven beers are very like those their ancestors might have enjoyed in early Ontario. The brewery itself is ingenious in design and possesses one of the province's only subterranean cellars. In 2015, the brewery produced hops, wheat, and barley on its own land and held the first annual Back To The Farm Beer and Music Festival, which drew nearly one thousand people and is poised to become an important community tradition.

———

CROSSCUT CANADIAN ALE has a somewhat misleading name — it is in fact an amber lager, not a pale ale. With its slightly Grape-Nutty toasted grain flavour, it's very popular locally (2.5). **ORIGIN HEFEWEIZEN** has a clove-heavy aroma and leans toward malt dominance rather than wheaty tang. (2.5) **8 MAN ENGLISH PALE ALE** is modelled after northern English cask ales and features a significant toasted grain and toffee sweetness in balance with lightly dirty herbal bitterness (3.5). The highlight is **RED FOX**, the summer seasonal. Featuring Citra hops and coloured by beets, the aroma is of lemon and healthy beetroot sugar, though that is balanced on the palate by a drier finish than the other offerings (3.5).

MACLEAN'S ALES INC.

📍 52 14th Avenue, Hanover

📞 (519) 506-2537

🐦 @macleansales

🌐 macleansales.ca

🕐 Thu 4:30p.m.–7:30p.m. Tours are available
at other times by appointment.

🛒 Mon–Thu 11a.m.–4:30p.m.,
Fri 11a.m.–7:30p.m., Sat 11a.m.–4p.m.

Charles MacLean has been present through every stage of Ontario's brewing renaissance and is at least partially responsible for the early popularity of cask ale in the province. Breweries like Wellington and StoneHammer still display his influence in their recipes decades later. MacLean's Ales is the project he has chosen for the fourth decade of his career. For those familiar with his work, the range of products from the new brewery will not come as a shock. The specialization is in traditional English styles. The attraction here is the quality, subtlety, and balance that come from a long career of trial and error.

ONTARIO CRAFT BREWERIES

———

FARMHOUSE BLONDE, made with Ontario hops and barley, features a gentle biscuit character and a floral nose with light sweetness in a soft finish (4). The **PALE ALE** is lively and toffeeish with a distinct orange-pekoe hop aroma (3.5). **INDIA PALE ALE** breaks slightly from the English mould to feature pine and marmalade aromas and an assertive bitterness (3). **LUCK & CHARM OATMEAL STOUT** is a complex brew. Its smooth body displays notes of coffee, tobacco, licorice, and molasses (4). **ARMCHAIR SCOTCH ALE** is a boozy fireside sipper lodged deep in caramel with a small wildflower nose (3.5). **OLD ANGUS ALE** is a fruit-and-nut bar in a glass: raisin, plum, and dried stone fruit meet toasted cereal, chocolate, and toffee (4.5).

MAGNOTTA BREWERY

📍 271 Chrislea Road, Vaughan

📞 (905) 738-9463

🌐 www.magnotta.com/brewery

🕐 Tours available by contacting head office in advance through website.

🛒 Mon–Fri 9a.m.–9 p.m., Sat 8:30a.m.–6p.m., Sun 11a.m.–5p.m.

Founded in 1997 in a then recently expanded Magnotta facility in Vaughan, Magnotta Brewery is an offshoot of the main business at Magnotta: wine. The company rose to prominence selling grape juice to home winemakers under the Festa Juice name before becoming a winery in its own right. Over the years, the company's instinct with both its wine and its beer side has been to provide the highest quality product at very reasonable prices, an instinct that has garnered Magnotta's True North beers something of a cult following at the Beer Store. The brewing facility has a reputation for being one of the cleanest in the province, going as far as having positive-pressure filtered air pumped in to reduce the number of variables that might affect the beer in production.

Magnotta has not left behind its roots in the realm of home production. The Festa Juice label has been joined by Festa Brew, a high-quality pre-produced wort in a variety of styles for use by home brewers. In fact, Magnotta's various locations sell all the home-brewing equipment a novice brewer might need, at very reasonable prices.

———

BLONDE LAGER has a full mouthfeel with a sweet, Grape-Nut malt character and a wildflower and undergrowth hop aroma (3). **COPPER ALTBIER** leans toward the Dusseldorf version of the style, with a waft of composting leaves complementing deep-brown bready malt and light chocolate tones (3.5). The **CREAM ALE** is practically chestnutty in its toasted grain, with a mellow sweetness and a touch of leafy herb on the finish (3). The **STRONG ALE** is a full-on take on the English style. The malt is dark and contains deep toast, raisin, and caramel in addition to some light chocolate. The hops are twiggy and floral while the entire affair has a hint of golden syrup (3.5). The **INDIA PALE ALE** is properly English as well, with woody, orange-pekoe aromas and a hint of chrysanthemum (3.5).

MANANTLER CRAFT BREWING COMPANY

MANANTLER
CRAFT BREWING
20 Co. 14

📍 182 Wellington Street, Bowmanville

📞 (905) 697-9979

🐦 @manantler

🌐 www.manantler.com

🕐 Tours are available through a booking form on the website.

🛒 Mon–Wed 1p.m.–7p.m., Thu–Sat 11a.m.–11p.m., Sun 1p.m.–6p.m.

Since opening its doors in early 2015, Manantler has proven to be a pleasant surprise for the brewing scene in Bowmanville. The brewery houses a popular taproom with a speakeasy vibe that frequently acts as a live music venue. Manantler has produced a large number of different beers in its first year and while some appear more frequently than others, the appeal here is novelty. Their Lollihop series, for instance, uses single-hop pale ales to highlight different hop characters. Notable in all offerings, be they one-offs or collaborations, are the whimsical labels that highlight the brewery's fun-loving nature.

ROBERTA BLONDAR, one of Manantler's most frequent issues, is named for the Canadian astronaut, although the hops used are down-to-earth. The blonde ale possesses a subtle grapefruit aroma grounded by dirty, spicy bitterness in a lightly cereal-sweet body (3.5). **LIQUID SWORDS** is a massive American IPA that combines a number of different citrus characters. Grapefruit, tangerine, and blood orange vie for superiority above a sticky-sweet caramel body while retaining balance (4). **SEISMIC NARWHAL** is aptly named for its enormity. Resin, pine needles, tangelo, and pineapple combine in a practically overwhelming aroma. It has a hugely bitter body to match. Guaranteed to break the ice (4.5). **THE DARK PRINCE** is a black IPA that verges into stout territory. Deep roast and light, ashy smoke dominate the citrus hops and coffee-like bitterness (3.5).

MANITOULIN BREWING COMPANY

📍 43 Manitowaning Road, Highway 6, Little Current

🐦 @manitoulinbrew

🌐 www.manitoulinbrewing.co

🕐 Times vary. Check website for updates.

Inspired by the long lines in the craft beer tent at the Hillside music festival in Guelph, long-time friends Blair Hagman and Nishin Meawasige decided to bring this same love of beer to their home on Manitoulin Island. Located in Little Current off Highway 6, Hagman, Meawasige, and brewmaster Mark Lewis have worked together to create a brewery and a beer that is distinctly Manitoulin- and northern-Ontario focused.

———

This local focus is clearly seen in Manitoulin Brewing's branding, which makes use of the locally grown hawberry in its logo. The brewery's first beer, **SWING BRIDGE BLONDE ALE**, is a slightly bitter blonde with a dry aroma and pleasant notes of apricot in the flavour (3) and is named after the Little Current Swing Bridge, the iconic bridge that provides a gateway from the mainland to the island.

ONTARIO CRAFT BREWERIES

MASCOT BREWERY

MASCOT
—
BREWERY

📍 31 Mercer St, Toronto

📞 (416) 979-0131

🐦 @mascotbrewery

🌐 mascotbrewery.com

🕐 Tue–Fri 4p.m.–2a.m., Sat 12p.m.–2a.m., Sun 12p.m.–5p.m.

Mascot Brewery is the brewing space adjoined to entertainment district nightspot Odd Thomas. The multi-level bar, Bavarian-style beer garden, nightclub, and brewpub opened up in several phases starting in the spring of 2015, and is the work of long-time entertainment and dining industry veteran Aaron Prothro, previously the owner of noted nightclubs Nyood and F-Stop. While the beer selection includes a curated list of local beer, heading up the brewing of Mascot's own beers is long-time brewer Michael Duggan, who has taken over operations at Mascot's on-site brewing facility.

———

Mascot Brewing has two initial offerings. The **MASCOT HEFEWEIZEN** features a large presence of banana, both in aroma and taste, in an approachably light body with a crisp and delicately dry finish (3). The **MASCOT PILSNER** has a sweet, dry, biscuity grain note and a long finish (3).

MASH PADDLE BREWING COMPANY

📍 111 Sherwood Drive, Unit 3A, Brantford

📞 (289) 253-8157

🌐 mashpaddlebrewing.com

Mash Paddle is the creation of husband-and-wife team Teddy and Nicole Scholten and head brewer Matty Buzanko. Their beer made its debut at the Albino Rhino Beer Festival in Fort Erie. Finding their new home still under construction in the redeveloped former industrial site known as Artisan's Village, the Scholtens began releasing their beer to the public at select establishments in the late summer of 2015 before their retail space became open for business.

———

Their primary offering, **UNNAMED PALE ALE** is a full-on tropical assault, with distinctive melon, mango, and lemon notes and a subtle, biscuity finish (3.5).

MERCHANT ALE HOUSE

📍 98 St. Paul Street, St. Catharines

📞 (905) 984-4060

🐦 @merchantale

🌐 www.merchantalehouse.ca

🕐 Mon–Sun 11a.m.–2a.m.

Nestled on St. Paul Street in St. Catharines, Merchant Ale House opened its doors in 1999. Friends John Tiffin, Iain Watson, and James Vanderzanden wanted to bring the difference of house-made beer to a downtown restaurant scene that was starting to grow its vibrant nightlife. Since then, the "Merch" has been a favourite destination for families, friends, and students.

Murray Street Brewery, the official name of the brewing side of the pub, has gone from serving two house beers to eleven year-round, including a rotating seasonal offering as well as several quality guest taps. Food served is traditional pub fare, including nachos and an exceptional pulled pork sandwich. Especially of note, however, is the Merchant's atmosphere. The building itself is a beautifully restored historical structure, with much of the stone foundation and wooden flooring still intact.

The two original beers first poured at the Merchant are by far the most popular. The **OLD TIME HOCKEY ALE** is an amber ale with a slight hint of brown sugar (3) and the **BLONDE BOMBSHELL** has a floral aroma and a light, dry body with grassy and subtle apple notes (2).

Among the brewery's other offerings is the **DRUNKEN MONKEY OATMEAL STOUT**. It has a medium body and roasted-coffee notes complemented by a hint of cocoa (3). The **EXTRA SPECIAL BITTER** is actually bitter, featuring a nice aroma of molasses and distinct notes of English hops (1.5). The **MERCH LAGER**, made with German pilsner malt, is quite sweet and features a delicate, dry finish (2). Finally, the **IPA** is a representation of the West Coast style, with a fresh burst of citrus, tropical fruits, and a delicate hint of pine (3.5).

MILL STREET BREWERY

MILL STREET BREWHOUSE

📍 300 Midwest Road, Scarborough

📞 (416) 759-6565

🐦 @MillStreetBrew

🌐 millstreetbrewery.com

MILL STREET BREWPUB (OTTAWA)

📍 555 Wellington Street, Ottawa

📞 (613) 567-2337

🐦 @millstbrewpubot

🌐 millstreetbrewery.com/ottawa-brew-pub

🕐 Mon—Tue 11a.m.—10p.m., Wed 11a.m.—11p.m.,
Thu 11a.m.—12a.m., Fri—Sat 11a.m.—1a.m., Sun 10:30a.m.—11p.m.

MILL STREET BREWPUB (TORONTO)

📍 21 Tank House Lane

📞 (416) 681-0338

🐦 @millstbrewpubto

🌐 millstreetbrewery.com/toronto-brew-pub

🕐 Mon 11a.m.—10p.m., Tue—Wed 11a.m.—11p.m.,
Thu 11a.m.—12a.m., Fri—Sat 11a.m.—2a.m., Sun 10:30a.m.—10p.m.

BEER HALL AT MILL STREET BREWPUB

📍 21 Tank House Lane

📞 (416) 681-0338

🐦 @millstbeerhall

🌐 millstreetbrewery.com/toronto-beer-hall

🕐 Sun—Wed 12p.m.—9p.m., Thu 12p.m.—1a.m., Fri—Sat 12p.m.—1a.m.

Mill Street Brewery was founded in 2002 by Steve Abrams, Jeff Cooper, and Michael Duggan and set up shop at 55 Mill Street in Toronto's historical Distillery District. The area that housed the former Gooderham & Worts distillery has a rich history that dates to the 1830s and to this day stands as an example of the city's Victorian-era industry. In its first seven years, Mill Street won multiple awards, including Best Microbrewery in the Greater Toronto Area at the Golden Tap Awards from 2004 to 2008 and Canadian Brewery of the Year at the Canadian Brewing Awards from 2007 to 2009.

In 2005 Joel Manning was brought on as brewmaster, a position he has kept to this day. Manning originally got his start in 1986 as a trainee at Amsterdam Brewery, taking courses to expand his knowledge until his departure in 2004. His biggest task in the early years of Mill Street was overseeing the move of large-scale brewing to a much larger facility in Scarborough, while the original brewery location was converted into a brewpub.

ONTARIO CRAFT BREWERIES

Since then, Mill Street has become a national giant and one of the breweries where young brewers earn their stripes before moving on to another brewery or even starting their own. Further growth came in 2011 with the leasing of two additional locations: a historic grist mill located near Chaudière Falls in Ottawa, which became a brewpub; and a location at Pearson International Airport, which made Mill Street the first craft brewer to open shop in a Canadian airport. In 2013 the original location in the Distillery District saw an expansion in the form of a beer hall opening adjacent to the brewpub, which features a fully operational still that makes "bierschnaps," a spirit made with Mill Street's house beers.

In October 2015 Mill Street announced that it had been purchased by Labatt Brewing Company for an undisclosed amount, with a commitment of a $10 million investment that will help increase distribution to Quebec and expand brewing operations.

————

Mill Street makes many year-round beers that are available in stores and one offs available exclusively at its brewpub locations. The original offering from Mill Street, **ORIGINAL ORGANIC LAGER**, has a slightly sweet bready character to it, with a very subtle citrus note wrapped in rough, grainy mouthfeel (2.5). The **100TH MERIDIAN ORGANIC AMBER**

LAGER is the best of the lager offerings, bringing in notes of berries, dried fruit, and a hint of lemon with a mildly dry finish (3.5). **TANKHOUSE ALE** defines the Ontario pale ale style, with a slight toffee sweetness flowing nicely with notes of citrus and pine (4). **COBBLESTONE STOUT** is Toronto's answer to Guinness in that it is exclusively served on nitro in cans and on draught, giving it a smooth, creamy mouthfeel (4.5). Likewise, the **VANILLA PORTER** also has a creamy texture due to being served on draught or in cans on nitro, and its light mouthfeel with distinct vanilla notes makes it a good winter warmer (4.5). The **STOCK ALE** has a light body with a slight sweet lemon taste mixed with graham cracker and tied together with a crisp finish (3.5). The **BELGIAN WIT** is a fairly light-bodied beer with a touch of coriander and bready notes (3).

MOTOR CRAFT ALES

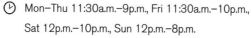

📍 888 Erie Street E, Windsor

📞 (519) 252-8004

🐦 @motorcraftales

🌐 thisismotor.com

🕐 Mon–Thu 11:30a.m.–9p.m., Fri 11:30a.m.–10p.m.,
   Sat 12p.m.–10p.m., Sun 12p.m.–8p.m.

🛒 Mon–Thu 11:30a.m.–9p.m., Fri 11:30a.m.–10p.m.,
   Sat 12p.m.–10p.m., Sun 12p.m.–8p.m.

Perhaps it's the proximity to Detroit or perhaps it's the flatness of Windsor's streets, which seem almost tailor-made for drag racing, but there's something of the home mechanic–DIY ethos about Motor. Part of the larger brand that includes Motor Burger (noted itself for having some of the best burgers in western Ontario), Motor Craft Ales is heavily invested with automotive symbolism. From the racing stripes and chalk-drawn schematics on the walls of Motor Burger to the piston-head tap handles and machined sample trays, down to the names of each brand, it's vastly successful thematically. At the moment, the entire brewing set-up is housed in the basement of Motor Burger, with fermentation taking place in glass carboys. It's a format that can prove somewhat limiting. An expansion of brewing facilities in another location is expected for 2016, which should continue the momentum the brewery has brought not only to its own products but to the brewing scene in Windsor.

———

C-HOP TOP IPA is built on a solid chassis of bitterness, accented with spruce, lemon, and a touch of blackcurrant (3). **MODEL A** is an amber ale that comes across in the body like apple butter on brown toast (2). **DRAGULA** is a slightly roasty schwarzbier, with licorice, chocolate, and a tarry whiff that finishes cleanly (3). **RIDER CREAM ALE** is a straight-ahead cream ale, lightly toasty with orchard fruit — really suited to pub fare (3.5). **FAST EDDY'S GOLD** is an apple core of an altbier, with peel and herb with a hint of earthy humus (2).

MUDDY YORK BREWING COMPANY

📍 22 Cranfield Road, Toronto

📞 (416) 619-7819

🐦 @mybrewingco

🌐 www.muddyyorkbrewing.com

🕐 Tue–Wed 11a.m.–4p.m., Thurs–Fri 11a.m.–7p.m., Sat 11a.m.–4p.m.

Muddy York Brewing Company is the first professional venture of multiple award–winning home brewer, BJCP-certified beer judge, and author of the blog *Hoptomology* Jeff Manol. Borrowing the moniker given to the settlement of York in the late 1700s on account of its unpaved streets, Muddy York has adopted historical elements in its branding and in its bottle shop. Located in Manol's second business, a steel-rule die shop in the East York area of Toronto, the brewery has achieved a reputation for helping the local brewing community and for being in high demand: the pop-up bottle shop frequently sells out in hours when it is open for business. It is worth contacting the brewery before making a visit to determine whether they have beer on hand.

———

During a period where IPAs were the standard introductory beer for a new brewery, Muddy York chose to offer a beautiful, traditional porter as its first beer. **MUDDY YORK PORTER** has a nice cocoa flavour, with subtle coffee notes and a smooth, marshmallow-like finish (4.5). **DIVING HORSE PALE ALE** features a nice kick of grapefruit and pine in the aroma and taste respectively, while fading out delicately in the finish (4). The **DERELICTION D.I.P.A.** offers a strong punch of pineapple and mango and some piney bitterness toward the end (3). Finally, and most impressively, is the **GASLIGHT HELLES**, with its light caramel and brown sugar flavours, delicate bitterness, and beautifully dry finish (4.5). Along with one-offs throughout the year, Muddy York Porter, Diving Horse Pale Ale, and Gaslight Helles will be brewed year-round, while the Dereliction Double IPA will be less frequently available.

MUSKOKA BREWERY

 1964 Muskoka Beach Road, Bracebridge

 (705) 646-1266

 @MuskokaBrewery

 muskokabrewery.com

🕐 Tours Fri–Sat at 12:30p.m., 1:30p.m., 2:30p.m.
Large groups please call ahead to book.

🛒 Mon–Thu 11a.m.–5p.m., Fri 11a.m.–6p.m., Sat 11a.m.–5p.m.

Folks with long memories might remember the brewery's original name of Muskoka Cottage Brewery. When it was opened under that name in 1996 by Gary McMullen and Kirk Evans, it quickly became a destination for visitors and locals of the town of Bracebridge. Many, however, will remember Muskoka more for its extensive rebranding effort in 2011, which opted for a more rustic and wood-cut look, with the original tagline, "The taste of cottage country," being replaced by "Venture off the beaten path." This rebranding followed on the tails of the release of Mad Tom IPA. Originally marketed as the first in the Cabin Fever series of one-offs, Mad Tom quickly replaced Muskoka's Cream Ale as its best-selling beer and helped set the scene for what would become the province's growing obsession with hop-forward beers.

In 2012 Muskoka grew out of its original location in downtown Bracebridge and made the move to a much larger facility, one definitely more "off the beaten path." The space allowed increased distribution of their beers as well as the ability to function as a contracting facility for other brewers.

_____

The signature **CREAM ALE** is a fantastic representation of the style, worthy of the best-seller title. It has a light caramel sweetness making way for hints of orange zest in a smooth mouthfeel and finishes on a dry note (4.5). **DETOUR** is one of the earliest beers in the province marketed as a session IPA and includes notes of melon, lemon sherbet, and pine, with an airy finish (4). **MAD TOM IPA** features distinct notes of grapefruit and pine with a touch of pepper at the tail end (4).

Muskoka also has a number of seasonal beers. **SUMMER-WEISSE** displays many of the common banana and clove characteristics of a hefeweizen, while also bringing in a fairly sweet honey note (3.5). **WINTER BEARD DOUBLE CHOCOLATE CRANBERRY STOUT** is commonly sold in bottles that have been aging in the brewery's cellar for fourteen months. Expect to find heavy cocoa notes in there, with very little in the way of cranberry (3). The **HARVEST ALE** is an American pale ale that combines sweet toffee with earthy hop bitterness that makes it an appropriate beer for the fall season (4).

NEUSTADT SPRINGS BREWERY

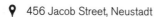

📍 456 Jacob Street, Neustadt

📞 (519) 799-5790

🐦 @NeustadtBeer

🌐 neustadtsprings.com

🕐 Tours are available during the summer for $7.00 by advance booking. Group tours are available by special arrangement.

🛒 Daily 10a.m.–6p.m.

One of the few success stories of the second wave of Ontario's brewing renaissance, Neustadt Springs Brewery was founded by Val and Andrew Stimpson. Transplants from Lancashire, England, the pair had worked there as licensees for Daniel Thwaites PLC, a brewery that thrives on tradition. This must have had an impact, as they chose to situate their own brewery in Neustadt, Ontario's picturesque Crystal Springs Brewery, originally founded in 1859. When Neustadt launched in 1997, it was so popular locally that the first batch of beer sold out in five hours.

The range of beers that they offer tends to adhere not only to traditional English styles but also to the lower alcohol templates of that pub culture. This does make Neustadt's offerings somewhat niche in terms of the current craze for experimentation with new hop varietals but no less impressive in terms of quality or international recognition. Several of the couple's products have routinely made a strong showing in the U.S. Open Beer Championship, and the brewery holds the distinction of being Ontario's most internationally awarded brewer.

———

10W30 is a complex English mild, though it has a slightly exaggerated strength. Tasting notes are of pear, dark-bread rusk, dusty cocoa, woody hops, and dried fruit before a medium-length roasty finish (3.5). **MILL GAP BITTER** is a sessionable pint with a pronounced bready malt and fruity, tea-like hop character shining through (4). **SCOTTISH PALE ALE** is a sweeter, deeply malty number with a mellow, woody hop character, suitable for pairing as a chaser with whisky (3.5). **BIG DOG BEAUJOLAIS PORTER** replaces 3 percent of its volume with Pelee Island wine in order to emulate the sour, vinous character of traditional London-style porters (3.5). The **LAGER** is brewed in a northern-European style, meaning that the bitterness is somewhat light, leaning toward floral and metallic (3), while **SOUR KRAUT** is a raspberry-flavoured light lager — tart yet moderately subtle (3). **456 MARZEN LAGER** is a richly malty Oktoberfest-style beer, bready and nutty with earthy hops and a small whiff of smoke balancing out the finish (3.5).

NEW LIMBURG BREWING COMPANY

📍 2353 Nixon Road, Simcoe
📞 (519) 426-2323
🐦 @NewLimburg
🌐 newlimburg.com
🕐 Daily 1p.m.–9p.m.
🛒 Daily 1p.m.–11p.m.

Located in a decommissioned elementary school near Simcoe, New Limburg is a unique story in the Ontario brewing landscape. The Geven family, who own the brewery, are transplants from Holland by way of Limbourg, Belgium. As a result of Jo Geven's nostalgia for the beers of Wallonia, the majority of the beers brewed by son Mischa at New Limburg are in Belgian styles. The ingredients used are traditionally Belgian, with the brewery manufacturing its own candi sugar on-site. Initial pilot batches have given way to a larger, 2-BBL system that is just barely keeping up with local demand. With a significant amount of room for expansion and a more-or-less untapped niche in the market, New Limburg is one to watch.

THE ONTARIO CRAFT BEER GUIDE

BELGIAN BLOND is a brightly carbonated take on the style. Fairly high in alcohol, it has an aroma of poached pear and peppery spice through its sweet, grainy body (4). **PETIT BLOND** is in the table-beer style, although incorporating American hops in the form of Crystal and Cascade. There is a light lemon-drop character, bolstered by lightly peppery spice and a mildly grainy body with significant effervescence (4). **BELGIAN DUBBEL** takes advantage of the in-house sugar production to create a profile of raisin, molasses, and raw cane sugar amid a nutty grain character with hints of licorice and bittersweet chocolate (3.5). **BLACK SHEEP MILK STOUT** is full of cocoa, light-roast coffee, cigar smoke, and vanilla, with a lightly creamy body (3).

NEW ONTARIO BREWING COMPANY

📍 1881 Cassels Street, North Bay

📞 (705) 707-1659

🐦 @NewOntarioBrew

🌐 newontariobrewing.com

🕐 Sun–Mon 11a.m.–9p.m., Tue–Sat 11a.m.–11p.m.

New Ontario Brewing Company is the first brewery to open in North Bay since the original brewery of the same name began selling beer in 1907. Opened in the summer of 2015, the brewery is an active member of the community, sponsoring local events. Their taproom acts as a local watering hole where folks of all ages sit, sip, and chat with one another. The trio who runs New Ontario Brewing Company, cellarman and operations manager Dan Delorme, along with long-time friends and military comrades front-of-house and business manager Ron Clancy, and brewmaster Mike Harrison, have been doing their bit in bringing good beer to northern Ontario.

———

Their initial selection includes the **BEAR RUNNER BLONDE**, which has a touch of biscuity sweetness followed with a subtle, earthy dryness in the middle leading toward a steady, drifting finish (3.5). **FRISKY PETE'S ESB**, named in honour of the chipmunk that lives under the brewery, has beautiful, warming roasted-toffee notes, and a slightly spicy, bitter aftertaste (3), and the **IPA**, an English-style brew with an American twist, provides a unique and impressive balance between the bready malt backbone and the prominent flavour of mango (4).

NIAGARA BREWING COMPANY

📍 4915-A Clifton Hill, Niagara Falls

📞 (905) 374-4444

🐦 @NiagaraBrewCo

🌐 niagarabrewingcompany.com

🕐 Mon–Thu 12p.m.–10p.m., Fri–Sat 12p.m.–12a.m.,
   Sun 12p.m.–10p.m.

Fronting directly on Clifton Hill, this brewery is a brand new addition to the street of fun and a somewhat surprising one. One might not have high expectations of a brewery neighbouring two wax museums, but the Niagara Brewing Company caters to the parents taking (or possibly sending) their children to those attractions. Staffed by long-time industry veteran Gord Slater and relative newcomer Megan Konstantonis, the brewery is open-concept, providing visitors with an inside look at the function of a brewhouse from their tables. The food menu is tight and focused, featuring local ingredients where possible and including spectacular cheese and charcuterie boards. A spacious patio to the side of the brewery provides some respite from the bustling main drag.

For the most part, the offerings on tap are straightforward representations of popular styles. **WHITE CANOE** is a light and refreshing American wheat, focusing on the wheaty tang the ingredient provides (3.5). **NIAGARA PREMIUM LAGER** is soft bodied, leaning toward being a Munich helles with a light, clean grain sweetness and a hint of citrus (3). **AMBER EH!** is a toasty caramel amber ale with a spicy hop bite (3.5), while **HONEYMOON PEACH RADLER** does exactly what it's meant to: bring peach nectar to the party in a light-bodied summer quaffer (3). **BEERDEVIL IPA** is a throwback to early craft IPAs, with caramel malts slightly overwhelming the bitterness, leaving a sweet finish (2.5). The **DARK LAGER** has an upfront aroma of espresso and a roasty medium-full body that disappears into a clean finish (4).

NIAGARA COLLEGE TEACHING BREWERY

📍 135 Taylor Road, Niagara-on-the-Lake

📞 (905) 641-2252 x 4099

🐦 @NCTBrewery

🌐 firstdraft.ca

🛒 Summer: daily 10a.m.–6p.m.
   Winter: Mon–Fri 11a.m.–5p.m., Sat 10a.m.–5p.m., Sun 11a.m.–5p.m.

The NCTB is likely the most influential brewery in Ontario at the moment given that its primary product is not beer but graduating brewers. The teaching brewery, ably headed since 2010 by Jon Downing (himself with a brewing pedigree stretching back to the opening of Ontario's first brewpub in 1985), is manned by students with varying levels of experience and ability. As the goal of the program is to transform students into professionals with hands-on brewing experience, the quality of the standard beers can differ slightly from batch to batch. The real highlight here is the ability to taste the over one hundred styles of beer designed by the students each year before they are employed by breweries across the province, and to taste those designed by Downing himself.

———

The core offerings here are **FIRST DRAFT LAGER**, a highly accessible pale lager with a grassy, citrus nose (2.5) and **FIRST DRAFT ALE**, with a light, sweet, grainy character and an orchard-fruit aroma (2.5). The Brewmaster series includes the **WHEAT**, which leans toward spicy clove and nutmeg in character (3), the **STRONG ALE**, full of nuts and toffee on the palate (3.5), and the nearly overwhelming **STOUT** with significant chocolate and espresso character (3.5). Their most commercially successful beer thus far has been **1812 BUTLER'S BITTER**, which balances toasted malt with subtle floral aromas (3.5).

NIAGARA OAST HOUSE BREWERS

📍 2017 Niagara Stone Road,
Niagara-on-the-Lake

📞 (289) 868-9627

🐦 @OastHouseBeer

🌐 oasthousebrewers.ca

🕐 Public tours and tastings Sat–Sun 11:30a.m. and 3:30p.m.
Patio open on summer evenings.

🛒 Mon–Thu 10a.m.–5p.m., Fri 10a.m.–11p.m., Sat–Sun 10a.m.–6p.m.

Situated among vineyards on the way into the village of Niagara-on-the-Lake, Niagara Oast House is an instance of geography dictating the character of a brewery. The brewery, housed in a bright red barn, crafts beers in the Belgian style, and captures the farm-to-table ethos that the Niagara Peninsula has come to embody in recent years. An expansion of the brewery in 2014 created more fermentation space and room for barrel aging. An immaculate taproom clad in barn board, and a special-event space for live music and the occasional wedding reception were also added at this time. The brewery will be expanding its patio, making it an ideal beery lunch stop on the way through wine country.

Year-round offerings include **SAISON**, a spritzy, bottle-conditioned affair with a bright, lemon-drop character and a slighty soapy, herbal accent. It has improved vastly since its introduction (4). **BIERE DE GARDE** features a loamy, earthy approach with dried berry and fruit notes in the mid-palate (3.5). **BARN RAISER** is a hybrid pale ale with citrus, orchard fruit, and lychee and a full, toasted malt mouthfeel (3.5).

Occasional specialties include the standout quaffer **OOST INDIE BIER**, a rare interpretation of a Dutch koyt with an aroma of steel-cut oatmeal and a lightly fruity herbal character (4); **BIERE DE MARS**, which runs sweet and sour, with dried fruits and vanilla playing off a souring grain character with touches of vanilla and yogurt on the way to a tart finish (3); and **KONNICHIWA PEACHES**, a firm and fruity oak-aged hefeweizen that uses locally grown peaches to fantastic effect (4).

NICKEL BROOK BREWING COMPANY

NICKEL BROOK
TRADE **BREWING** MARK
Cº

📍 864 Drury Lane, Burlington

📞 (905) 681-2739

🐦 @NickelBrookBeer

🌐 www.nickelbrook.com

🕐 Mon–Tue 11a.m.–6p.m., Wed–Fri 11a.m.–9p.m., Sat 9a.m.–5p.m., Sun 12p.m.–4p.m.

Nickel Brook originally came into existence in 2005, intending to be an impressive addition to Better Bitters Brewing Company, a brew-on-premises business that brothers John and Peter Romano have been operating since 1991. Named after John's children, Nicholas and Brooke, the brewery began thriving on its own almost immediately, with several award-winning beers hitting the market.

Popular success for Nickel Brook began in early 2010, when Ryan Morrow became brewmaster after spending four years climbing the ranks. Since then, Morrow has been providing unique and often critically celebrated beers to the public. This embrace of innovation is highlighted by a rebranding effort implemented to more accurately reflect Nickel Brook's modern approach to brewing.

As of 2015 much of Nickel Brook's volume is produced by Morrow, who does double duty as brewer for Collective Arts, at Arts & Science Brewing in Hamilton. The original Burlington location will continue production, though chances are good that it will be used primarily to make sour beers.

———

The **GREEN APPLE PILSNER** features a distinct aroma and the taste of, surprise, sweet apple along with a grain character that gives an almost apple-skin flavour in terms of bitterness (2.5). **CAUSE & EFFECT BLONDE** contains a lot of citrus, backed up with hints of honey and flowers (3). **NAUGHTY NEIGHBOUR** is an American pale ale with a crisp and refreshing mouthfeel, and grapefruit zest, orange, and honey notes (4). **HEADSTOCK** is a rather high ABV IPA at 7%, containing flavours of mango, lychee, orange, and pine, with a slight caramel flavour (4.5). **LE PAYSAN SAISON** has a lot of lemon, papaya, and sweet malts, with notes of coriander and pepper (4). **EQUILIBRIUM ESB** has a lot of sweet bready notes and toasted malts with a citrusy bitterness toward the end (3.5). **BOLSHEVIK BASTARD** is the original of several beers in the Bastard series of imperial stouts, with lots of roasted coffee, chocolate, and a slight ashy note (4).

Finally, along with beer Nickel Brook also makes a respectable non-alcoholic root beer. **BABBLING BROOKE'S ROOT BEER** has flavours of licorice, star anise, cinnamon, and vanilla.

NITA BEER COMPANY

📍 190 Colonnade Road, Unit 17, Ottawa

📞 (613) 688-2337

🐦 @nitabeerco

🌐 nitabeer.com

🛒 Wed–Fri 11:30a.m.–7p.m., Sat 11a.m.–5p.m.

Situated in a Nepean industrial park, the Nita Beer Company is named for its founder and chief beer officer, Andy Nita. Nita began production in January of 2015 and is already looking to expand. The brewery is a DIY affair with most of the work done by the seven investors in the business, all of whom come from technical professions. The event space at the front of the building is clad in barnboard from a structure they personally demolished.

———

The lineup of beers on offer from Nita is structured around ski trail difficulty ratings from bunny slope to off-piste. **TEN12** is a lightly floral, slightly sweet blonde ale, accessible to mainstream beer drinkers (2.5). **PERFECTUM** is a dry stout that takes on a heavy, dark-roast character to complement its thick, chewy body (2.5). **EL HEFE** is a lightly tangy hefeweizen, with accents of banana, vanilla, and matchstick (3). **OPA** is a heavily herbal take on the IPA that is slightly overbalanced by malt sweetness (3). **PUCKER** is an extremely literal take on the English bitter. At 100 IBU, it could reasonably be charged with assault on the palate (1.5).

NORTHUMBERLAND HILLS BREWERY

📍 1024 Division Street, Cobourg

📞 (289) 435-2004

🐦 @TheNHBbrewpot

🌐 www.nhb.beer

🛒 Wed–Sat 12p.m.–6p.m.

Located close to the 401 in Cobourg, Northumberland Hills is the result of fifteen years of home-brewing on the part of brewer and co-owner Rick Bailey. Taking inspiration from Whitby's 5 Paddles, this nanobrewery has aimed not for a flagship brand but for a variety of styles over the course of its first year of operation. The brewery exudes a DIY ethos, from its carefully organized and scrupulously clean brewhouse to its repurposed flat-bottomed wine fermenters. Northumberland Hills may lay claim to the province's coolest delivery vehicle with its recently repurposed El Camino.

———

The beer for sale at their retail store changes frequently, but these brands are reliably available. **P.S. I LUV YOU**, a blonde ale that started life as a single malt (pilsner), single hop (Saaz)

beer, but which has evolved into a floral and spicy example of the style (3). **COOLER BY THE LAKE** is a clever, fruity, and lightly peppery take on a hybrid ale in the style of a Mexican amber lager (3). **SUPER CONTINTENTAL** is a malty take on the Ontario pale ale with pronounced notes of chocolate and roast (3).

NORTHWINDS BREWHOUSE & EATERY

📍 499 First Street (Highway 26), Collingwood

📞 (705) 293-6666

🐦 @Northwindsbeer

🌐 northwindsbrewhouse.com

🕐 Mon–Tue 12p.m.–10p.m., Wed–Sat 12p.m.–late, Sun 12p.m.–10p.m.

🛒 Daily 12p.m.–10p.m.

Collingwood's first brewpub, Northwinds, has chosen to produce an array of rotating beers rather than focus on a single flagship brew for the retail market. The kitchen cooks up high-quality pub fare, sourcing many of its ingredients from local vendors in the Georgian Bay area. Brewer Andrew Bartle, a graduate of the first year of the Niagara College brewing program, has directed his efforts toward flavourful, accessible offerings aimed at providing enjoyment to both the novice and seasoned beer drinker. Offering as many as sixteen varieties at once, on tap and through their bottle shop, Northwinds has become a Collingwood mainstay since its opening day in 2014.

OLD BALDY is an American farmhouse ale, gently grainy but perked up in the middle by orange peel and a rye bite; it finishes dry (3.5). **JUNKYARD CAT** is a hoppy lager, dry-hopped with Cascade and Simcoe for a citrus and pine character throughout (3). **SWAMP FLY SOUR ALE** cleverly matches kettle-souring *lactobacillus* with haskap berries, creating a gently tart beer not unlike a Berliner weisse (4). **ROUTE 26 AMERICAN BROWN ALE** is full of hazelnutty roast with brown malt and coffee making up the balance of flavour (3.5). **MILK RUN STOUT** uses coffee from Collingwood's Ashanti to complement the cocoa, vanilla, and deep roast in its cream-smooth body (3.5).

OLD CREDIT BREWING COMPANY

📍 6 Queen Street W, Mississauga

📞 (905) 271-9888

🌐 www.oldcreditbrewing.com

🛒 Mon 1p.m.–7p.m., Tue–Sat 10a.m.–9p.m., Sun 12p.m.–5p.m.

Founded in 1994, Old Credit is situated in Mississauga next to the mouth of the Credit River and owes its nautical theme to the presence of nearby Snug Harbour. It occupies the original site of Conner's, one of the first-wave craft breweries. The original brewmaster, Orrin Besco, had been a Molson employee for fifteen years before he helped establish Old Credit. He formulated the recipes, which have not changed substantially these last two decades. The brewery employs an interesting technique after fermentation. Beer is held for eight weeks of maturation at -3.5° Celsius, a process which they refer to as "ice-aging."

––––

PALE PILSNER has a malt and honey aroma with a light floral hop and a corny mid-palate that leads to slight bitterness (2).

AMBER ALE is Grape-Nut and granola throughout its light body, with a slight herbal tang on the finish (2). **HOLIDAY HONEY** is in the honey-brown style and has a floral aroma with a thin body and hints of chocolate and toasted bread that disappear on the finish (2.5).

OLD FLAME BREWING COMPANY

 135 Perry Street, Port Perry

 (289) 485-2739

 @OldFlameBrewery

 oldflamebrewingco.ca

 Tours Tue–Fri 12p.m., 2p.m., 4p.m., Sat 2p.m., 4p.m., Sun 12p.m.

 Mon 11a.m.–6p.m., Tue–Sat 11a.m.–9p.m., Sun 11a.m.–6p.m.

Located a mere block from Lake Scugog, Old Flame has helped Port Perry reclaim some of its heritage. The 130-year-old building that houses the brewery was originally the Ontario Carriage Works, but more recently spent a significant amount of time as an LCBO outlet. The 2013 renovations have restored the building's original brick facade featuring carriage windows. The brewery has a 15-HL brewhouse manned by Niagara College graduate Scott Pautler and a brewery store that's open seven days a week. Featuring a thematic motif of lost romantic love, Old Flame is about drinking to remember rather than drinking to forget.

The year-round selections from Old Flame are all lower-alcohol-style lagers, while the Brewer's Discretion series allows for experimentation in other directions. **BLONDE** is a helles-style lager with a soft grain mouthfeel, a whiff of sulphur, and a vinous, herbal hop character that ends abruptly (3). **RED** is a candy-apple-coloured Vienna lager that leans malt-heavy for the style, with notes of toffee, raisin, and chocolate complementing a slightly coppery hop bite (3). **BRUNETTE** is the star of the show with toasted grain and bittersweet chocolate riding the roundness of a creamy mouthfeel (4).

OLD TOMORROW

📞 (416) 792-6553

🐦 @OldTomorrowBeer

🌐 www.oldtomorrow.com

Founded by the Toronto-based mother-and-son team Pat and Ian MacDonald and assisted by consulting brewer Jamie Mistry, Old Tomorrow is a contract brand that leans heavily on Canadian history for its appeal — their bottles are emblazoned with the silhouette of John A. Macdonald. Old Tomorrow was initially brewed at Cool Beer Brewing in Etobicoke but production has subsequently shifted to Big Rig in Ottawa.

———

The core beer is billed as a Canadian pale ale and features a small amount of spicy character from the Canadian rye that is used as part of the grist. **OLD TOMORROW** has a soap and pepper aroma with a spicy citrus mid-palate and a dry finish (3). Their second beer, **MONTY'S GOLDEN RYED ALE**, a collaboration with Amazing Race Canada host and Olympian Jon Montgomery, takes on the flavour of rye whisky and oak. Rye spice and orange zest are highlights on the nose but are encased on the palate by the deep woody character, lingering after the swallow (3.5).

THE OLDE STONE BREWING COMPANY

📍 380 George Street N, Peterborough

📞 (705) 745-0495

🐦 @OldeStoneBrew

🌐 oldestone.ca

🕐 Mon 11:30a.m.–12a.m., Tue–Sat 11:30a.m.–1a.m., Sun 12p.m.–12a.m.

Founded in 1996, the Olde Stone Brewery actually caters to two separate on-premise restaurants: the Olde Stone Brewpub, which specializes in typical pub fare, and Hot Belly Mama's, a Cajun-inspired restaurant. Until 2015, the brewer was Doug Warren, who started with Upper Canada in Toronto, but the duty has been assumed by Aaron O'Neil, who was previously the assistant brewer. What has not changed are the recipes brewed in the basement of the building, all of which use whole cone hops.

The brewpub reflects Peterborough's Irish heritage and displays a tasteful, minimalist appearance of dark wood, exposed brick, and high ceilings, without garish branding. A cozy, elevated snug in the middle of the room provides a quiet

ONTARIO CRAFT BREWERIES

space for small groups. The kitchen makes the majority of the food items from scratch, including house-made beer pickles and stout mustard. Seasonal beers are brewed at the brewer's discretion and the cask rotates depending on what's available.

———

RED FIFE is an American wheat beer that uses Red Fife wheat (originally developed as a crop near Peterborough) as a specialty ingredient. Its aroma resembles nothing so much as a wheat cracker with a heavy dash of black pepper. The body is light, dry, and refreshing (4). **PICKWICK'S BEST BITTER** is a biscuity, cookieish take on a Yorkshire bitter with an earthy, spicy hop aroma and appropriate lightly buttery mouthfeel (4). **WILDE OLDE ALE** has a light coffee aroma with a touch of raisin and plum brightened up by mild pine bitterness (3). **OR DUBH** is a dry Irish stout served on a nitro tap. The whole cone hops are noticeable here, lending a round spiciness to the body, which is full of coffee, chocolate, and lightly smoky roast (4). **PEPPERMINT PORTER**, the seasonal at time of writing, has a subtle, muddled mint-leaf character that plays well with the lightly fruity, vinous body (3.5).

ONTARIO BEER COMPANY

 @OntarioBeerCo

Initially a partnership between Toronto brewers Michael Duggan and Brad Clifford, Ontario Beer Company is committed to the idea of making beer exclusively with ingredients grown in the province of Ontario. Brewed at Cool in Etobicoke, the beers have never quite lived up to their one-hundred-mile branding, but this is largely due to the fact that the adoption of agricultural practice has not grown as quickly as the ambition of brewers. The beers have proved instrumental in exposing Ontario's hops and barley to consumers and brewers alike, and in introducing the idea that Ontario has the possibility of producing these ingredients in larger quantity in the future.

———

100 MILE LAGER has a taste that is practically honey-nut cereal in terms of malt sweetness, with a character of clover, wildflower, and stone fruit in the aroma (2.5). **100 MILE ALE** has deep toffee malts, practically singed around the edges, with a sprig of shrubby vegetation and a touch of resin (2.5).

ONTARIO CRAFT BREWERIES

ORANGE SNAIL BREWERS

📍 295 Alliance Road, Unit 16, Milton

📞 (289) 270-1680

🐦 @OrangeSnailBrew

🌐 orangesnailbrewers.ca

🛒 Wed 12p.m.–6p.m., Thu–Fri 12p.m.–9p.m.,
Sat 11a.m.–6 p.m., Sun 12p.m.–4p.m.

Located in a small industrial unit, and visible due to the words CRAFT BEER chalked in foot-high letters on the wall outside the taproom, Orange Snail is the first brewery based near Milton in over a hundred years. The brewers are mindful not only of their heritage but of their place in the community. Black-and-white pictures of the previous brewery are featured on the walls of the gift shop, and all of the beers in their regular lineup are named for landmarks and personages from the Milton area. Currently, they are working with a 3-BBL system and fermenting in plastic equipment in temperature-controlled cold rooms; however, demand for their beer locally suggests that they will shortly be forced to look into a larger facility.

IRON PIG PALE ALE is moderately sweet with a combination of Hallertau and Cascade hops that create a pithy, refreshing orange and spice character (3). **RATTLE 'N' NEMO,** named for two local conservation areas, is halfway between an amber ale and an Irish red ale. The balance and depth of chocolate and toffee-malt notes with piney Cascade shows good judgment (3.5). **16 JASPER IPA** is an American-style IPA that begins with a Douglas fir sting in the aroma and follows on with a lightly fruity minerality before crashing into a wall of berry bitterness (3.5).

OUTLAW BREW COMPANY

📍 196 High Street, Southampton

📞 (519) 797-1515

🐦 @outlawbrew

🌐 www.facebook.com/
Outlaw-Brew-Co-668129646562470

🕐 Hours vary seasonally. Check website for details.

Outlaw Brew Company opened the doors to their country-themed brewery, bar, and restaurant in the summer of 2014, offering spirits and wine alongside their beers, with country-style eats and a stage for live performances. Brewmaster Andy D. Preston, a fifteen-year veteran of Molson Coors and two-time winner of the Iron Brewer competition, originally contracted out Outlaw's beers from Niagara College until their own facility was up and running in 2015.

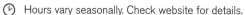

Outlaw's **21 LAGERED ALE** has a very light mouthfeel, with a large cereal-grain presence and a subtle candy swirl (1.5). **2MOONJUNCTION BLUEBEERY WHEAT** is a very dry wheat beer with a subtle note of blueberry in the aroma and hints of banana in the flavour (2). **BRONCO COPPER ALE** delivers a very evident roasted malt character with an astringent note at the back of the throat ending with a candy sweetness (1.5).

OUTSPOKEN BREWING

📍 350 Queen Street E, Sault Ste. Marie

📞 (705) 206-2858

🐦 @OutSpokenBrew

🌐 www.outspokenbrewing.com

🛒 Tue, Thu, Fri 4p.m.–9p.m., Sat 1p.m.–6p.m.

Opened in 2014, OutSpoken Brewing is the first operating brewery in Sault Ste. Marie since the famous Northern Breweries closed in 2006. For over two years, partners Vaughn Alexander and Graham Atkinson have been cutting through red tape and restoring the eighty-year-old building's original elements, creating a rustic, historical feel. Their opening is one of several examples of the rise of good beer in northern Ontario.

———

OutSpoken's flagship is **RABBIT'S FOOT IPA**. This warming ale has a spicy tangerine and pine bitterness blending with rich caramel (3). A notable seasonal is **FIRESTOKER PUMPKIN SPICE ALE** for autumn. Naturally, pumpkin pie spices provide the main flavour here. The brew has a dry mouthfeel and a somewhat clean finish (2.5).

PEPPERWOOD BISTRO & BREW HOUSE

BREWERY & CATERING

📍 1455 Lakeshore Road, Burlington

📞 (905) 333-6999

🐦 @pepperwoodgroup

🌐 pepperwood.on.ca

🕐 Mon–Thu 11:30a.m.–11p.m., Fri 11:30a.m.–1a.m.,
Sat 10:30a.m.–1a.m., Sun 10:30a.m.–10p.m.

On its opening in 2000, the Pepperwood Bistro's original focus was the selection of beers conceived and brewed in-house by Paul Dickey before he left in 2009 to start Cheshire Valley. Along with its beers, the bistro also developed a fine dining atmosphere offering a selection of tantalizing dishes and a brunch experience that has made the establishment famous city-wide. After a long hiatus, Pepperwood has once again put its focus on its house beers, using its on-site facility to brew and making slight adjustments to the recipes while still retaining the original concept of Paul Dickey's beers.

——

ONTARIO CRAFT BREWERIES

MONKEY BROWN NUTTY BROWN ALE has a deceptively thin mouthfeel when compared to the intense roasted grain character the aroma advertises (3). **PEPPERWOOD PALE ALE** is a very well-balanced beer, featuring lovely hints of mango, pineapple, and lemon zest, with a roasted malt profile evening out in a dry finish (3). The **PEPPERWOOD CREAM ALE** has a candy-like aroma that makes way for a creamy sweet mouthfeel with a slight earthy bitter finish (2.5), and the **ESB** is fairly representative of the style, with a decent malt backbone and a subtle bitter presence at the end (3). Finally, the **FRAMBOISE** showcases raspberry notes, even finishing off with the fruit's characteristic dryness (3).

PERTH BREWERY

📍 121 Dufferin Street, Highway 7, Perth

📞 (613) 264-1087

🐦 @PerthBrewery

🌐 perthbrewery.ca

🕐 Mon–Fri 9a.m.–6p.m., Sat 9a.m.–5p.m.,
Sun 12p.m.–4p.m.

Started in 1993 during the brew-on-premises craze that gripped the province, the Perth Brewery made the transition to brewing commercially in late 2013. It is for this reason that the facility still allows customers to package their own beer in cans and wine in bottles. The more important story here is the size and speed of the transition they have made. During the summer, the busiest season in the beer industry, the brewery has twenty full-time employees. Their 15-BBL brewhouse has allowed them to up their volume significantly, and new fermenters installed in the spring of 2015. A canning line added even more recently has helped increase the consistency and variety of their brews. The taproom has also been remodelled with a twenty-five-foot granite bar, allowing visitors to sample their wares in a more comfortable environment.

ONTARIO CRAFT BREWERIES

OH CANADA MAPLE ALE comes across as banana pecan pancakes drenched in syrup both in aroma and on the palate (2.5). **BONFIRE BLACK LAGER** has a waft of smoke across the nose followed by dark rye bread, bitter chocolate, and a dry, lightly tannic, roasty finish in the throat (3.5). **EASY AMBER** is robustly malty with sherry and roasted notes creeping in around the edges of a smooth body (3). **EURO PILSNER** is a good example of the style, with a properly sharp grass-and-bark herbal bitterness supported by a lightly sweet mid-palate (3.5). **CASCADER INVADER** has pine, orange peel, and dank, Nugget-hopped pine resin over a lightly slick caramel body (3). **BUDBUSTER IPA** is massively bitter at 100 IBU, with spruce needles dominating the bitter spike of flavour, overpowering slightly the deep caramalts and outlasting the roast on the finish (3.5). **OATMEAL STOUT** is an interesting take on the style, with pear-nectar aroma buried in the middle of dark chocolate and nutty grain (3).

PITSCHFORK BREWING COMPANY

 @Pitschfork

🌐 www.pitschforkbrewing.com

Founded in 2015, Pitschfork is a contract brewery headquartered in midtown Toronto, but brewing out of the Stratford Brewing Company. Out of the gate, owner Mike Schroeter is attempting to emulate the drinkability of the dry, crisp pilsners of the Rhineland-Palatinate, Bitburger being a prime example.

———

PITSCH PERFECT PILSNER is a northern German–style pilsner with a slightly soapy, reed-and-flower hop aroma, deep cereal grains, and a somewhat metallic note on the soft palate at the finish (2.5).

THE PUBLICAN HOUSE BREWERY

📍 300 Charlotte Street, Peterborough

📞 (705) 874-5743

🐦 @PublicanHouse

🌐 www.thepublicanhouse.com

🕐 Mon–Thu 11a.m.–11p.m., Fri–Sat 10a.m.–11p.m.,
Sun 11a.m.–11p.m.

🛒 Mon–Thu 11a.m.–11p.m., Fri–Sat 10a.m.–11p.m.,
Sun 11a.m.–11p.m.

Founded in 2009, Publican House helped to fill the void left in Peterborough's local brewing scene by the purchase of Kawartha Lakes Brewing by Amsterdam Brewing in 2003. Impressively, the brewery has made an impact across the province. It gained an almost immediate presence in Toronto pubs upon opening, but owes a great deal of its success to local consumption and cottagers. Publican House has been constantly expanding since its inception. The original space housed a brewery and a retail store which has subsequently moved into the storefront next door. Further expansion in 2016 will take annual production to just under 4,000 HL annually and include plans to convert the Peterborough Arms next door into a brewpub. Currently, the retail store sells cans and growlers. There is a tasting room, and an outdoor beer garden in pleasant weather.

———

PUBLICAN HOUSE ALE is a take on a kölsch, with meadow grasses in the aroma, a light-bodied corny grain character, and a reedy, bitter finish (3). **SQUARE NAIL PALE ALE** is a quality example of a West Coast pale ale, with pine and citrus over a light toffee malt body (4). **HENRY'S IRISH ALE,** named for nineteenth-century Peterborough brewer Henry Calcutt, is ruby in colour with a sweet, toasty-malt character and very low bitterness, moreish and popular locally (3).

RADICAL ROAD BREWING

 1177 Queen Street E, Toronto

 @RadicalRoadBrew

When Jon Hodd and Simon Da Costa, two brewers from Black Oak Brewing, announced plans to start their own label, many anticipated the usual motions for a new beer venture. In most cases a brewery's first beer is something like a pale ale, but that proved to be small beans for Da Costa and Hodd. Soon after their announcement, the back room of Black Oak found itself awash in Speyside Scotch whisky barrels for Radical Road's opening brew to age for seventy-one days.

———

To make their 2013 grand debut to the public stand out further, Hodd and Da Costa spared no expense to ensure that the resulting beer, a 9.1% alcohol barrel-aged and bottle-conditioned wee heavy style named **CANNY MAN** featured a lavish bottle design including patterned tissue wrapping and a well-designed label hanging from the neck. Later that year, the arrival of their second offering, **THE WAYWARD SON**, a 7.5% Belgian-style golden ale aged in Ontario Pinot Noir barrels, was released exclusively to the LCBO and highlighted Radical Road's ethos of "bigger is better."

After a prolonged hiatus, Da Costa and Hodd announced in January 2016 that later in the year they would be operating out of their own facility, a brewery and taproom located, rather suitably, inside a former wine-making shop in Toronto.

RAILWAY CITY BREWING COMPANY

📍 130 Edward Street, St. Thomas

📞 (519) 631-1881

🐦 @Railwaycity

🌐 www.railwaycitybrewing.com

🕐 Tours Mon–Wed 4p.m.–5p.m.,
Thu–Fri 4p.m.–6p.m., Sat 12p.m.–5p.m., Sun 12p.m.–3 p.m.

🛒 Mon–Wed 11a.m.–8p.m., Thu–Fri 11a.m.–9p.m.,
Sat 11a.m.–8p.m., Sun 11a.m.–5p.m.

Founded in 2008, Railway City borrows its identity from the legacy of St. Thomas as an important rail junction in the development of the province in the nineteenth century. This even affects the name of their IPA, Dead Elephant, which commemorates the unfortunate collision between a locomotive and P.T. Barnum's star attraction, Jumbo.

The brewery has expanded significantly in recent years and now features a 20-HL brewhouse in a new location five times the size of the original site. It has become so much larger that it now has the capacity to produce brands for contract brewers and has begun to grow its presence in the Beer Store.

CANADA SOUTHERN DRAFT is a small-brewery take on a gateway light lager, driven mostly by a light grain body and lightly grassy hops — appropriate for hot summer days (2). **IRON SPIKE BLONDE** is more robustly flavoured, with a light, crackery barley body and peppery, floral sting, making it a good example of a blonde ale (3). **IRON SPIKE AMBER** is a lightly fruity amber ale, leaning more English than Belgian, with a caramel mid-range and a soft carbonation (2.5). **BLACK COAL STOUT** may go so far as to over-pronounce its roast character, actually leaning into charcoal territory and creating a gap between its deep cindered-coffee flavour and the alcohol burn (2). **DEAD ELEPHANT** has dank resin, apricot, and grassy characters jousting for dominance in the aroma; underpinning that is a restrained malt body (3).

———

Less frequent offerings include **THE WITTY TRAVELLER**, a witbier that uses orange peel, coriander, white pepper, and Belgian yeast strains to create a refreshing summer quencher (3.5); and **CRANBERRY FESTIVE LAGER**, a light-bodied lager with a hint of Craisin in the mid-palate (2.5).

RAINHARD BREWING COMPANY

 100 Symes Road, Toronto

 @RainhardBrewing

 rainhardbrewing.com

 Fri 4p.m.–9p.m., Sat 12p.m.–8p.m.,
Sun 12p.m.–4p.m.

Tucked away in a 1940s industrial building in the Stockyards neighbourhood near St. Clair and Keele, Rainhard Brewing is one of a number of promising Toronto breweries founded in 2015. Brewer Jordan Rainhard spent the better part of a decade as a home brewer before deciding to take on the challenge of opening his own brewery. Rainhard specializes in North American styles, but his experience in home-brewing has led to the use of relatively uncommon malt varieties (Honey, Special W) and outside-the-box hopping techniques that will help set his beers apart from the rest of the market. Although the brewery began with 700 BBL of annual production in the summer of 2015, it is already struggling to keep up with demand and expansion in the near future seems likely.

———

The core lineup includes the lightly funky farmhouse ale **TRUE GRIT**, which features crackery wheat, lemon, and pepper (3.5); the biscuit-, orange-, and lemon-accented **DAYWALKER SESSION IPA** (3.5); **ARMED 'N CITRA NORTH AMERICAN PALE ALE**, whose name is derived from the Magnum and Citra hops used in its brewing, and which has a robust aroma of grapefruit and apricot (3.5); and **LAZY BONES**, a familiar and comforting American IPA with a light, sweet body and tropical fruit aroma overlying a Douglas fir bitterness (4). A periodic offering, their Russian imperial stout, **HEARTS COLLIDE**, allows for experimentation. The first batch featured cold-brew coffee from Propeller Coffee Company, which complements the cherry, chocolate, and raisin in the aroma and body (3.5).

RAMBLIN' ROAD BREWERY FARM

📍 2970 Swimming Pool Road, La Salette

📞 (519) 582-1444

🐦 @RamblinRoadBeer

🌐 www.ramblinroad.ca

🕐 Mon–Wed 10a.m.–4p.m.,

🛒 Thurs–Sat 10a.m.–5p.m., Sun 12p.m.–4p.m.

Ramblin' Road bills itself as Ontario's first and only brewery farm. It is also the location of Picard Peanuts, where owner John Picard has been producing peanuts as well as kettle chips and confectionery products for over thirty years. In 2007, seeing the potential in recently thriving agricultural tourism in southern Ontario, he planted over seven varieties of hops in the fertile land of the farm outside La Salette in Norfolk County. The brewers draw their own spring water from the land.

Ramblin' Road has six beers available. The three originals include **COUNTRY LAGER**, which is dry and crisp, with a colour that resembles orange blossom honey (2.5); **COUNTRY**

THE ONTARIO CRAFT BEER GUIDE

PILSNER, which has decent head retention and a pronounced grain character ending with a dry finish (3.5); and the **COUNTRY CREAM ALE**, which is a fantastic representation of the style, showcasing the characteristics of the grains well and providing a very smooth drink (4.5). Other beers include the **PUREBRED RED ALE**, which has a strong bready and toasted malt backbone accompanied by a toffee-like note in the finish (2.5); **IPA UNLEASHED**, which incorporates a rich, malty depth with strong grapefruit notes (2.5); and most interestingly, the **DAKOTA PALE ALE (DPA)**, which is beer that has washed the Dakota Pearl potatoes that Picard's uses to make their Extreme Style Kettle Chips in its beer-bathed flavour. It pours a nice golden colour with a smooth, potato note that adds a creamy mouthfeel (3). Unsurprisingly, it pairs very well with the kettle chips it helped create.

REDLINE BREWHOUSE

📍 431 Bayview Drive, Units 8 & 9, Barrie

📞 (705) 881-9988

🐦 @RLBrewhouse

🌐 www.redlinebrewhouse.com

🕐 Sun–Wed 11a.m.–10p.m., Thurs–Sat 11a.m.–11p.m.

Redline Brewhouse, a family-owned pub and brewhouse, can best be described as a fully realized dream. After decades of living the corporate life, Doug Williams made the change to starting his own heavy-equipment sales and rental house, but he and his wife, Kari, often found themselves daydreaming about starting a brewery and bar, which they nicknamed "Our Bar." After some encouragement from their son, Devon, they set to work creating a space.

Redline focuses on serving locally grown food; the beer is made by award-winning brewer Sebastian "Seb" MacIntosh, who most notably won the Cask Days IPA Challenge in 2013. Staying true to what they'd dreamed of for "Our Bar," Doug and Kari have made sure that the letter R is prominent in all of Redline's branding, and the name of the brewery itself is a testament to the Williams family line.

Redline's offerings include a variety of beers. The **5:01 GOLDEN ALE** has a refreshing mouthfeel, with peppery, orange sweetness, and a dry, biscuity finish (3.5). **CLUTCH AMERICAN PALE ALE** has a beautiful orange and grapefruit aroma that flows on to the palate, followed by a jab of pine (4). **SPEED WOBBLE AMERICAN STRONG ALE** pours a dark ruby colour and features a decent balance of sweet, bready malts, roasted grains, and hints of dark fruit and pine (3.5).

REFINED FOOL BREWING

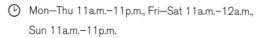

 137 Davis Street, Sarnia

 (519) 704-1335

 @refinedfool

 www.refinedfool.com

 Mon–Thu 11a.m.–11p.m., Fri–Sat 11a.m.–12a.m., Sun 11a.m.–11p.m.

Daily 11a.m.–11p.m.

Prior to Refined Fool's advent in 2014 there had not been a brewery in Sarnia for at least eighty years and even that brewery was designed to surreptitiously provide beer to Michigan. Refined Fool is more focused on bringing craft beer to Lambton County and is one of very few breweries in Ontario that operates in a co-op ownership structure. It is the result of a group of ten friends coming together to realize their goal of opening a nanobrewery. Growth has been rapid. The brewery's lively taproom features a patio in summer and has begun to host live music. Occasional beer dinners are very well attended, with mouth-watering recipes to pair with their beers listed on their website. The playful branding, featuring a top hat and colourful stripes, renders their beer visually distinct.

The range of offerings is impressive considering the relatively small size of the brewhouse. **TROLL TOLL** is an upscale cream ale with a full mouthfeel and orchard fruit aroma (3.5). **THE LAST OF THE WARM BOHEMIANS** is a surprisingly faithful recreation of a Czech pilsner, with a spicy hop bite and clean finish (4). **POUCH ENVY**, an Australian pale ale, is very gently bitter, presenting most of its tropical fruit character in the aroma (3). **NOBLE OAF** is an effervescent rye saison with a light, spicy body and a peppery finish (3.5). **ANTIQUE PEEPSHOW** is a straightforward Pacific Northwest pine and orange IPA (3), and its big brother, double IPA **SHORT PIER, LONG WALK** packs a punch like a pine cudgel (3.5). Perhaps the most impressive offering is **YOU ARE LAZY, SUSAN**, a rosemary gose with a light salt, bright citrus, and oily herbal aroma that leaves a lingering rosemary puff after the swallow (4.5).

ROYAL CITY BREWING COMPANY

📍 199 Victoria Road S, Unit C8, Guelph

📞 (888) 485-2739

🐦 @RoyalCityBrew

🌐 www.royalcitybrew.ca

🕐 Tues–Wed 12p.m.–7p.m., Thurs–Fri 12p.m.–9p.m., Sat 11a.m.–9p.m., Sun 12p.m.–5p.m.

Royal City is the project of Russell Bateman and brewmaster Cameron Fryer, two long-time friends and home brewers, both of whom have a passion for beer and an optimistic outlook in regards to the thriving scene in Guelph. Fryer is a self-professed beer geek, having first found his love of craft beer while drinking brews from Wellington Brewery during his time as a student at the University of Guelph. He gained further experience in the employ of Great Lakes Brewery in Etobicoke. After honing their skills by focusing on three core beers, they finally opened their space on Victoria Road in early summer 2014.

———

In the time since it opened, Royal City has added five beers to its core lineup. The **DRY HOPPED PALE ALE** has distinct notes of citrus and pine while being backed by a subtle malt character (NR). **SUFFOLK ST. SESSION ALE** is a special bitter with distinctive honey and caramel notes followed by a moderate earthy hop presence (4). The **HIBISCUS SAISON** has a sweetly floral aroma that makes its way into the taste, ending with a dash of peppercorn in the finish (4). **SMOKED HONEY** is a brown ale that features leather and tobacco notes accompanied by a subtle note of local honey, all tied together with a coffee finish (3). **100 STEPS STOUT** pairs well with graphic novels (if the bottle label is anything to go by) and contains a smoky note blended well with light-roast coffee and a ping of molasses (3).

SAINT ANDRE

Started in August of 1999 by Doug Pengelly, Saint Andre was one of Ontario's earlier experiments in contract brewing. Launched at Toronto's Festival of Beer when it was still hosted by Fort York, the brewery's beer was originally brewed in Guelph at F&M Brewery before a transition to Cool Beer Brewing in Etobicoke was made in the first decade of this century. Deliveries were initially made by Pengelly himself in a Citroën 2CV truck, which turned heads around the city, but have since been taken over by Cool.

———

Although the owner's attention has been focused largely on Junction Craft Brewing (in which he is a partner), the Saint Andre brand persists among a cult audience on a limited number of taps around the city and in several Toronto Beer Store locations. **SAINT ANDRE VIENNA LAGER** has a light, sweet malt body with biscuit accents and a pleasing grassy, peppery bitterness (3.5).

SAWDUST CITY BREWING COMPANY

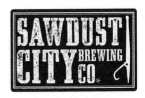

📍 397 Muskoka Road N, Gravenhurst

📞 (705) 681-1100

🐦 @sawdustcitybeer

🌐 www.sawdustcitybrewing.com

🕐 Mon–Sun 11a.m.–11p.m.

🛒 Mon–Sun 9a.m.–11p.m.

Sawdust City is a testament to the phrase "patience is a virtue," as it took over three years of battling red tape and overcoming logistical problems to go from brewing their beer out of Etobicoke's Black Oak to realizing their dream of running a brewery, saloon, and retail space. Now the dream is a reality, and all of it is housed in what was once a Canadian Tire in Gravenhurst. The spacious location has become a central destination in the community, being the chosen spot for parties, concerts, game nights, and gatherings for locals and tourists alike.

Much of Sawdust's success lies with its two colourful brewers, Sam Corbeil, a student of VLB in Berlin and former instructor at Niagara College's Brewmaster and Brewery

Operations Management program, and Aaron Spinney, Niagara College graduate and established brewer. Together, their skill and creativity have developed some award-winning beers that have made the province, and northern Ontario, all the better.

———

Many of Sawdust City's beers are named after aspects of life in Gravenhurst, though the connection is often subtle. **GATEWAY KÖLSCH**, named for the town's nickname as the gateway to Muskoka, pours a clear golden wheat colour and has a crisp mouthfeel featuring notes of cereal, light honey, and citrus (4.5). **OL'WOODY ALT** pours a rich copper and has lovely, bready malt notes that round out nicely with a dry finish and has and slight roasted grain note (3.5). **GOLDEN BEACH AMERICAN PALE ALE** is a brightly flavoured beer, with notes of pineapple, passion fruit, mango, and lemon dancing around together with a slight grain note to make up a refreshingly light body (5). **LONE PINE WEST COAST IPA** is the beer that effectively put the brewery in the mind of the public. A very hop-forward beer — expect notes of grapefruit and pine, with a touch of malt quietly hiding (4). **SKINNY DIPPIN' OATMEAL STOUT** is a smooth oatmeal stout featuring notes of black coffee, chocolate, and a plum-like sweetness that ends on a nice bitter note (3.5).

Sawdust City also brews several interesting seasonal beers. The cheekily named **LONG, DARK VOYAGE TO URANUS** is an imperial stout with a sweet aroma that has cocoa and espresso flavours with an alcohol burn that makes its way to the end (4). **THE PRINCESS WEARS GIRLPANTS** is a hoppy, Belgian-inspired golden ale that combines grapefruit and lemon notes with a sweetness that masks the 9% alcohol content well (3.5). A variation of that beer, **PRINCESS & GIRLPANTS MEET THE O.D.B.**, is a golden ale that has been aged in Gamay barrels for two months, adding a very dry, wooden note with distinct tart flavours (4).

SHILLOW BEER COMPANY

 @ShillowBeer

www.shillowbeer.com

Founded in 2014 by Ben and Jamie Shillow, the real strength of this contract brewery is the amount of experience brought to the table by the husband and wife team. Ben Shillow spent four years as a sommelier at Toronto's Oliver and Bonacini group of restaurants, while Jamie Shillow gained experience at Bar Volo and beerbistro prior to attending Niagara College's brewing program. While their first beer was exclusive to the beerbistro, they expanded into the LCBO with a second offering in late 2015.

———

SASS ON THE SIDE is an American brown ale with a lightly sweet body that is reminiscent of a chocolate chip cookie, with biscuit and cocoa notes (3). **BITTER WAITRESS** is an assertive black IPA that runs from spruce branch down to the pine-tar roast of an export stout (3.5).

SIDE LAUNCH BREWING COMPANY

📍 200 Mountain Road, Unit 1, Collingwood

📞 (705) 293-5511

🐦 @sidelaunch

🌐 www.sidelaunchbrewing.com

🛒 Mon–Wed 12p.m.–6p.m., Thu–Fri 12p.m.–7p.m.,
Sat 10a.m.–6p.m., Sun 12p.m.–5 p.m.

Despite the fact that Side Launch entered the market in May of 2014, many of the beers on offer have been on the market since the early 1990s. Brewer Michael Hancock was the prime mover and shaker behind Denison's Brewing Company in downtown Toronto. The quality at Denison's was never in doubt; Prince Luitpold of Bavaria was one of its principal investors. In fact, the quality of Denison's range of beers was such that despite the brewery being shuttered in 2003, the beer remained in high demand in Toronto and gained a cult reputation internationally. For a not-insignificant period of time, Denison's Weissbier enjoyed the position of the highest-rated wheat beer in the world. Despite this, the brand bounced around as a contracted product from Mill Street to Black Oak to Cool.

The genius of Side Launch is to have provided an excellent brewer with a platform to bring his products to market. If the ubiquity of Side Launch's tap handles is any indication, it is a strategy that has paid off. The brewery already has plans to expand both the capacity of its Collingwood facility and the lineup of beers it will have as standard at retail.

———

WHEAT is a fine example of a hefeweizen, which manages to balance three different yeast esters (banana, clove, and bubble gum) with a creamy mouthfeel and effervescent carbonation on the way to a tangy wheat finish (4.5). **DARK LAGER** lives in a malt mid-range where there's chocolate, but without its rich intensity; dark, dried fruit without assertive sweetness; and nutty grain verging on woodiness. A fine choice paired with barbecue (4.5). **MOUNTAIN LAGER** may be billed as a simple lager, but it's actually Ontario's finest example of a Munich helles. The soft mouthfeel and lightly bready cereal is balanced perfectly by spicy, herbal hops, creating a drinking experience that is at once both quenching and moreish (5). **PALE ALE** is on the maltier side of the American pale ale spectrum, displaying a typically English mild caramel influence to balance the resinous, citrus hop character (4).

SILVERSMITH BREWING

📍 1523 Niagara Stone Road, Niagara-on-the-Lake

📞 (905) 468-8447

🐦 @SilversmithBrew

🌐 www.silversmithbrewing.com

🕐 Tours are available for $20.00 per person. Please book in advance.

🛒 Mon—Wed 10a.m.—9p.m., Thu—Sat 10a.m.—11p.m.,
Sun 10a.m.—9 p.m.

Opened in 2011, Silversmith Brewing was an early figure in the current explosion of small-town breweries in Ontario. Located in an ivy-covered hundred-year-old church on Niagara Stone Road, Silversmith Brewing's home is deceptively small and picturesque. In fact, brewing is actually carried out in an extension just off the taproom, the bar of which dominates the converted nave. Communal seating, frequent live entertainment, and a food menu curated and prepared by the Tide and Vine Oyster House mean that there is no less a congregation than there was before the conversion. The result of the clever incorporation of the original building's features in its new incarnation is a restful space not unlike a traditional English pub.

It is something that has become equally popular with locals and tourist groups.

———

BLACK LAGER is a schwarzbier and the brewery's specialty. The espresso-roast character is rounded out on the palate by a touch of brown sugar sweetness and a waft of tarry smoke (4). **BAVARIAN BREAKFAST WHEAT** is a banana-and-graham-cracker affair and rather like a banoffee pie in a glass (3). **HILL 145 GOLDEN ALE** is suggestive of orchard fruit, its apple and peach character lingering over sweet malt (2.5), while **DAM BUSTER ENGLISH PALE ALE** leans into ESB territory, with a touch of dank woodiness to go along with light stone fruit and nutty malt (3).

SLEEPING GIANT BREWING COMPANY

📍 946 Cobalt Crescent, Thunder Bay

📞 (807) 344-5225

🐦 @sleepgiantbrew

🌐 sleepinggiantbrewing.ca

🛒 Mon–Wed 11a.m.– 6p.m., Thu–Fri 11a.m.–7p.m.,
Sat 10a.m.–6p.m.

Perhaps the fastest to succeed of northern Ontario's breweries, Sleeping Giant was founded in 2012 by two couples who wanted to bring better beer to the area. While the ownership structure has changed during the brewery's short lifespan, the path of expansion has clearly been a good one. Taking advantage of social media interest and providing education via its own chapter of Barley's Angels (a collective of female beer enthusiasts), Sleeping Giant has managed to build its own audience in a place where there was interest in craft beer, but also uncertainty about its acceptance. The addition in early 2015 of an in-house canning line and a line of beer-cured beef jerky suggests Sleeping Giant is ready to take on all comers.

Stylistically, Sleeping Giant is heavily geared toward North American flavour profiles. **NORTHERN LOGGER** is ostensibly a kölsch, but the grassy burst of bitterness in the mid-palate after the honeyed barley nose suggests it's big for the style (3). **360 PALE ALE** is juicy clementine, with basil and bay leaf over supportive English-style caramel malts (3.5). **BEAVER DUCK** American pale ale has a gigantic Centennial-hops pine nose that bridges to a restrained, crackery body through Amarillo tangerine. It's somewhat unbalanced, but the aroma makes it irresistible (4). **HOPPET IPA** has some juicy fruit aroma on the nose that becomes medicinal on the palate due to overwhelming bitterness (2.5). **SKULL ROCK STOUT** has a roasty cocoa nose that fades into a dry, fruity, slightly vinous finish, not entirely unlike a milk chocolate–covered raisin (3.5).

SMITHAVENS BREWING COMPANY

📍 687 Rye Street, Unit 6, Peterborough

📞 (705) 743-4747

🐦 @SmithavensBrew

🌐 www.smithavensbrewing.ca

🕐 Thu 11a.m.–6:30p.m., Fri 11a.m.–8p.m., Sat 11a.m.–7p.m.

🛒 Mon–Wed 10a.m.–5:30p.m., Thu 10a.m.–6:30p.m.,
Fri 10a.m.–8 p.m., Sat 10a.m.–7p.m.

Located on the site of the old Kawartha Lakes Brewery (which was moved to Toronto after being purchased by Amsterdam in 2003), Smithavens, founded in 2014 under the name Smithworks, is the most recent addition to Peterborough's brewing scene. Trained in Germany, brewer Graham Smith works in traditional European styles in order to set his brewery apart from the crowd. Special attention is given to authentic brewing techniques, which means that the wheat beers are produced in a special room with open fermenters and that all of the beers from the brewery are bottle-conditioned for carbonation. The brewery's taproom and tank-view rooms both borrow heavily from the German

Alpine style, emulating the wooden beam structure of a hunting lodge in a tasteful and understated way. Plans are already underway to expand the volume of the brewery to allow for additional production.

––––––

DUNKELWEIZEN has the aroma of moist banana bread and a flavour of dark malts cutting through wheat, trailing a touch of ripe cherry and cherry-stone (3.5). **HEFEWEIZEN** develops an extremely creamy texture behind an aroma of clove and mashed banana, with a refreshing wheat tang (4). **KELLERBIER** is an unfiltered pale lager with a full bready malt presence and a heavier than usual lime and thyme bite (3.5). **AMBER SOLACE** is somewhere between a festbier and a Vienna-style lager — its sweet, almost candied malt has a light bitter sting that redemptively plays through the finish (3). **BLONDE**, the only ale Smithavens produces, is 7.5% but hides it well behind an aroma of black pepper and orange peel (3.5).

SPEARHEAD BREWING COMPANY

📞 (416) 907-6952

🐦 @SpearheadBeer

🌐 www.spearheadbeer.com

Founded in 2011, Spearhead was one of the first in a series of contract breweries that have become increasingly popular in Ontario. It was also one of the first to brew out of Cool in the Toronto suburb of Etobicoke on a regular basis. Unlike other breweries in the category, Spearhead uses the services of a talented brewer. Ex–Labatt brewer Tomas Schmidt (also of Toboggan Brewing Company) frequently develops experimental and one-off batches that are available on tap if not at retail. Spearhead's beers are noted for their inclusion of whimsical ingredients and geographic inspiration, making a sample flight something like a world cruise. Spearhead is also unusual in that it maintains a large staff, who ensure that its beer is available across the province and represented at festivals.

———

HAWAIIAN STYLE PALE ALE was the first offering from the brewery, introduced in 2011. It uses pineapple juice to emphasize the tropical fruit and citrus character that comes through on the aroma (3.5). **BIG KAHUNA** is Hawaiian's bigger brother, again using pineapple juice for a tropical blast, but this time in the service of a 100-IBU imperial IPA (3.5). **BELGIAN STYLE STOUT** fills the chocolatey, roasty body of an American-style stout with demerara sugar, coriander, and orange peel and then caps it off with Belgian ale yeast, somewhat overcomplicating matters (2.5). **MOROCCAN BROWN ALE** is brewed with figs, dates, raisins, and cinnamon, all of which reinforce the dried fruit and malt character that comes through in a brown ale, but also creates a very sweet finish (3). **INDIA WHITE ALE** is a combination of German hefeweizen with mango and orange juice, revelling in its flavours of exotic fruit salad and spice (3.5). **SAM ROBERTS BAND SESSION ALE** is a hybrid English/American pale ale with bready, caramel malts and hops that veer toward herbs and iron (2.5).

SPLIT RAIL BREWING COMPANY

MANITOULIN ISLAND

SPLIT RAIL
BREWING CO

📍 31 Water Street, Gore Bay

📞 (705) 370-8284

🐦 @SplitRailBrew

🌐 splitrailmanitoulin.com

🕐 Hours vary. Check website for updated information.

Having officially launched in the summer of 2015, Split Rail is a small operation with big ambitions of putting Manitoulin Island on the map as a beer destination. The brewery had already achieved renown before it opened, however. In early 2014, owners Eleanor Charlton and Andy (Andrea) Smith launched a successful crowdfunding campaign to help cover a portion of the costs involved in starting up a brewery on Manitoulin Island. This not only helped raise funds for the brewery, it also helped raise its profile. The crowdfunding campaign helped to make real a dream that had existed since 2009. Eventually, they developed a recipe, which they refined in a garage facility with brewmaster Glenn Fobes (formerly of Lakeport Brewing).

ONTARIO CRAFT BREWERIES

Split Rail's **AMBER ALE** is all toasted toffee in its flavour, with a cream-like mouthfeel and a delicate citrus note at the end wrapped in a smooth finish (3). The **WHEAT** features the classic banana and clove notes associated with the style, but has an interestingly tart, berry-like flavour toward the end that makes it stand out (3). The **LAGER** is a clear and crisp beer with a mild malt character and explicit floral and citrus notes (NR).

SQUARE TIMBER BREWING COMPANY

📍 800 Woito Station Road, Pembroke

📞 (613) 312-9474

🐦 @squaretimber

🌐 www.squaretimber.com

🛒 Fri 3p.m.–6p.m., Sat 1p.m.–4p.m.

Located in the Ottawa Valley, Square Timber was founded by Marc Bru, an avid home brewer with a family history in the beer industry. Bru has also been an active member of his local community and in helping to promote the rise of craft beer in the valley, having co-hosted the first-ever Ottawa Valley Craft Beer Festival in the autumn of 2015. His brewery, named for the square-timber industry that was instrumental in making the Ottawa Valley what it is today, officially opened its doors in the fall of 2014. The small taproom is open two days a week.

————

TIMBER CRIB PALE ALE is an American pale ale with notes of caramel and a distinctive floral hop note (NR). **BIG PINE**

IPA presents heavy pine notes followed by jammy fruit sweetness (NR). **DEACON SEAT HEFEWEIZEN** features the classic notes of banana and clove familiar in the style (NR). **CAMBOOSE DOUBLE IPA** has a large citrus character with a strong malt backbone that carries into the end (NR).

STACK BREWING

📍 1350 Kelly Lake Road, Sudbury

📞 (705) 586-7822

🐦 @StackBrewing

🌐 stackbrewing.ca

🛒 Mon—Wed 11a.m.–7p.m.,
Thu—Sat 11a.m.–8p.m.,
Sun 11a.m.–3p.m.

Sudbury's first craft brewery, Stack has enjoyed a large amount of success locally since starting in July of 2013. Its beer proved so popular in northern Ontario that, with the help of the Northern Ontario Entrepreneur Program, it was able to increase production by 1,500 percent after only three months of operation. Stack has become a significant part of the community, hosting fundraisers for breast cancer research and "beer and yoga" events. The brewery is extremely transparent about the difficulties it has faced in its growth, with anniversary ales named for the challenges faced that year.

———

SATURDAY NIGHT is a cereal-driven, lightly fruity cream ale representative of the style, but without much complexity (2.5). **IMPACT ALTBIER** is a lighter take on the style, with earthy malt and brown bread surrounded by toffee and chocolate (4). **SHATTER CONE** IPA presents scrubland conifer and a touch of sage above a slightly browned caramel and vaguely dusty malt character (3). **STACK '72** brings candy, grapefruit, and pine to a 9% imperial IPA and manages to balance the bitterness admirably (3). **VALLEY GIRL** is an American wheat beer with a pronounced citrus, berry, and hay aroma and a tart, dry finish (3.5).

Stack has begun to branch out from typical stylistic choices with beers like **PANACHE**, an American pale ale brewed with oats and aged in cedar, imparting a full mouthfeel and a round woodiness (3.5). **VANILLA CHAI** is a restrained take on a spiced brown ale with notes of gingerbread, cinnamon, and vanilla, all the better for its subtlety (4). **TRADEMARK INFRINGEMENT**, brewed for their second anniversary, was a take on a gose, with a citric acidity and a sour, wheaty bite (3.5).

STEAM WHISTLE BREWING

📍 The Roundhouse, 255 Bremner
Boulevard, Toronto

📞 (416) 362-2337

🐦 @steamwhistle

🌐 steamwhistle.ca

🕐 Tours run every thirty minutes Mon–Sat 11:30a.m.–5p.m.,
Sun 11:30a.m.–4p.m. For groups of ten or more
please book in advance.

🛒 Mon–Sat 11a.m.–6p.m., Sun 11a.m.–5p.m.

When Frank Heaps's Upper Canada Brewing Company was acquired by Sleeman in the late 1990s, Steam Whistle Brewing was an unintended consequence. Steam Whistle was founded in 2000 by Greg Taylor, Cam Heaps, and Greg Cromwell, all of whom had been fired by Upper Canada after the takeover. Having learned the problems that can result from over-diversification during their days at Upper Canada, the owners of Steam Whistle made a pact to do things differently. As a result, Steam Whistle operates under the motto "Do one thing really, really well."

While Steam Whistle continues to produce a single beer out of the Bremner Boulevard roundhouse, many of its accomplishments in recent years have to do with its responsible ecological choices. The brewery runs on renewable energy and uses bottles with significantly longer lifespans than the industry standard. Steam Whistle has managed to flawlessly combine this green ethos with an instantly recognizable 1950s aesthetic. As a result, it has long occupied a position as an ambassador for craft beer in Ontario.

———

STEAM WHISTLE PREMIUM PILSNER is a Czech-style pilsner with a pleasingly grassy aroma and a lightly grainy malt character (3). For maximum enjoyment, it is best drunk as fresh as possible. During the brewery tour, which is one of the best brewery tours on offer to the public in Ontario, if you're lucky, you may be able to try the **UNFILTERED PILSNER**, which has an enhanced hop aroma and a slight doughy yeastiness (4).

STONE CITY ALES

CRAFT BREWERY + TAP ROOM

- 📍 275 Princess Street, Kingston
- 📞 (613) 542-4222
- 🐦 @stonecityales
- 🌐 stonecityales.com
- 🕐 Mon–Wed 11a.m.–11p.m.,
  Thu–Sat 11a.m.–12a.m.,
  Sun 11a.m.–11p.m.
- 🛒 Daily 11a.m.–11p.m.

Located in downtown Kingston, Stone City Ales has managed to develop a significant following in its first year of operation. While the majority of the space at the Princess Street locale operates as a brewery, the building also houses a bright, open taproom that features a thoughtful and reasonably priced food menu and vintage vinyl on the turntable. Stone City managed to brew twenty-four separate one-off batches in its first year of operation. Despite this, it has not at any time lost focus on its core brands. The bottle shop mostly features growlers, but some specialty one-offs are sold by the bottle. Taking into account the calibre of the breweries it has collaborated with and the number of awards it has won, it is almost a certainty that Stone City Ales was the best new brewery in Ontario in 2014.

ONTARIO CRAFT BREWERIES

WINDWARD BELGIAN WHEAT features camomile, grains of paradise, and orange peel, which support a pleasantly smooth, wheaty body and a freshly squeezed orange juice character (4). **12 STAR SESSION ALE** is a completely balanced pale ale with an orange zest aroma that includes a hint of chalkiness somewhat akin to orange pith (4). **UNCHARTED IPA** presents aromas of grapefruit and peach balanced by lightly sweet caramel malt throughout (4), while **SHIPS IN THE NIGHT OATMEAL STOUT** has gentle, dry leafy hops poking through nutty chocolate and coffee roastiness (4.5). **NELLIE-JEAN,** a Pinot-Noir-barrel-aged farmhouse ale, shows its barreling chops with effervescent notes of peach, apricot, and vinous fruit in front of a long oak finish (4).

STONEHAMMER BREWING

📍 355 Elmira Road N, Unit 135, Guelph

📞 (519) 824-1194

🐦 @StoneHammerBeer

🌐 www.stonehammer.ca

🕑 Tours are available Saturdays at 12:30p.m., 2p.m., and 3:30p.m., call to book.

🛒 Mon—Wed 10a.m.—5p.m., Thu—Fri 10a.m.—6 p.m., Sat 12p.m.—5p.m.

Founded in 1995 by Rick Fortnum and Charles MacLean, F&M Brewery was a late casualty of the Ontario craft beer market contraction of the mid-1990s. Reopened in 1997, the branding became somewhat confused as a result of the introduction of the StoneHammer brands. Despite the presence of a widely respected and universally beloved brewer, George Eagleson, the brewery had languished over the years.

Jump forward to 2015. The brewery's new owners, Phil and Lesley Woodhouse, have reinvigorated the business. The F&M name has been dropped completely in favour of StoneHammer and the packaging has shifted entirely to tallboy cans. The staff has been retained and the brewery is now frequently producing one-offs, allowing for some creativity.

———

StoneHammer's lineup includes **LIGHT**, which features a healthy cereal character with light floral notes and a hint of banana from the yeast esters (2.5). **PILSNER** leans toward toasted grain, with a fresh minty and grassy hop character (3.5). The darker beers benefit from caramelization from the direct-fired kettle. The **PALE** is a toasty, sweet interpretation of early West Coast pine and citrus pale ales (3). The **DARK ALE** is toffee in a glass with hints of dried berries as it warms through (4). The **OATMEAL COFFEE STOUT** uses coffee from local roasters Planet Bean to great effect. While full bodied, the roast never overtakes the cocoa and tobacco notes on the palate (4).

STOUFFVILLE BREWING COMPANY

 1802 Spruce Hill Road, Pickering

 (416) 453-6120

🐦 @sbcbeerco

🌐 www.sbc.beer

Started in October of 2012 by Bill Perrie and Jim Williamson, both long-time beer industry veterans, Stouffville began selling its beer in August of 2013. The initial product was contract brewed at Wellington Brewery and designed by Paul Dickey. Plans have been proceeding for some time, however, for them to open their own location in downtown Stouffville, although the search for physical premises continues. Stouffville is notable for being one of very few contract-brewed beers to have launched its product directly into the Beer Store rather than the LCBO — a tactic that seems to be paying off due to their can's Euro-styled branding.

———

RED FALCON ALE is an Irish red with a sweetish grain and toffee aroma leading to a small amount of grassy hopping, which ends in a lightly roasty, dry finish (3).

STRATFORD BREWING COMPANY

STRATFORD
BREWING COMPANY

📍 114 Erie Street, Stratford

📞 (519) 273-6691

🐦 @stratfordbrew

🌐 stratfordbrewing.com

Founded in 2004 by Joseph Tuer, the Stratford Brewing Company occupies an unassuming repurposed auto-mechanic shop near the market square. Dedicated largely to brewing lager-style beers for the Ontario market, Stratford has had some success selling its products at the LCBO, and its pilsner currently represents one of the best values in the category. Its beers are best enjoyed fresh in one of Stratford's many bars and restaurants.

———

COMMON is a take on a pre-Prohibition California common, a hybrid-style lager fermented at higher temperatures. The toasted grain and roasted nutty-malt character is complemented by an aroma with a touch of pear and grassy, floral hops in a rather smooth body (3.5). The **PILSNER**'s aroma is that of saddle soap and meadow grasses. The body is, perhaps, slightly heavy for the Czech style that it purports to emulate (2).

STRATHROY BREWING COMPANY

 62 Albert Street, Strathroy

 (226) 238-1815

 @StrathroyBrewCo

 www.strathroybrewingcompany.ca

 Wed–Fri 12p.m.–6p.m., Sat 11a.m.–4p.m.

Opened by brothers Alex and Matt Martin in 2014, Strathroy Brewing is based in a former flour mill that has been converted to purpose by Alex, an experienced home brewer.

———

Strathroy's core brand is their **1812 INDEPENDENCE PALE ALE**, a bottle-conditioned product that uses two yeasts and is named for the historic American incursion into the province of Ontario (NR). The brewery produces a number of other varieties on a rotational basis. All of these are seemingly inspired by details pertaining to the War of 1812, which is fitting considering the fact that so many of its battles took place in and around Strathroy.

ONTARIO CRAFT BREWERIES

SWEETGRASS BREWING COMPANY

 @sweetgrassbeer

 www.facebook.com/sweetgrass.brewing

Founded in 2013, Sweetgrass Brewing is a Toronto brewery started by the owners of the Auld Spot Pub on the Danforth. At the moment, its single brand is brewed at Wellington Brewery in Guelph, but that has not stopped Sweetgrass from becoming involved in other projects. As part of the Local 7 group of pubs, Sweetgrass has acted as the brewery of record (with guest brewmaster Sam Corbeil) for a series of beers for Session Toronto Craft Beer Festival, including a lemon-verbena saison and a gose. Additionally, it seems that Sweetgrass is looking to expand from contract to bricks and mortar. A curtailed attempt at launching a brewpub in Toronto has given way to speculation about a Prince Edward County location at some point in the next few years.

———

Stylistically, Sweetgrass's single year-round **GOLDEN ALE** offering is something of a cuckoo's egg. Billed as a German golden ale (a style for which there is little precedent), it's a light, noticeably sweet beer, with a touch of herbal grass and mint that has a coating mouthfeel and a sticky finish (2).

SYNDICATE RESTAURANT AND BREWERY

🌐 www.syndicaterestaurant.ca

SYNDICATE GRIMSBY

📍 13 Mountain Street, Grimsby

📞 (289) 447-1122

🕐 Mon–Thu 11:30a.m.–10p.m., Fri–Sat 11:30a.m.–11p.m., Sun 11:30a.m.–10p.m.

SYNDICATE NIAGARA FALLS

📍 6863 Lundy's Lane, Niagara Falls

📞 (289) 477-1022

🕐 Daily 11:30a.m.–11p.m.

🛒 Daily 11:30a.m.–11p.m.

SYNDICATE ST. CATHARINES

📍 332 Ontario Street, St. Catharines

📞 (905) 228-3199

🕐 Daily 11:30a.m.–11:30p.m.

The initial location of the Syndicate restaurant has a storied brewing history in Niagara Falls. The Lundy's Lane location was at one time home to Niagara Falls Brewing, before the brewery was purchased by Moosehead. Filling the void after that was Niagara's Best, which itself moved to Niagara Falls in 2009. While the Niagara's Best brands still exist (and are still available at a small number of Beer Store locations), the brewery location became the Syndicate brewpub in 2010, adopting a Prohibition-era, Mafioso-themed branding with a twist. Focusing on a food menu that includes simplified bistro fare with locally sourced ingredients and an accessible three-course, prix fixe menu, the Syndicate has now expanded operations to three locations including St. Catharines and Grimsby, all of which pour beer from their home brewery, Niagara's Best. Since the same family owns Taps on Queen in Niagara Falls, it is common to see their beer on tap at all of the locations.

NIAGARA'S BEST BLONDE is a straightforward blonde ale, with a medium body, tasting of light grain and hay, and a little grassy, noble hop in the aroma (2). **LOGGER LAGER** is a thin, lightly bready pale lager designed for mass appeal, with a hint of orchard fruit and a simple, restrained bitterness (2.5).

TAPS ON QUEEN BREWHOUSE & GRILL

📍 4680 Queen Street, Niagara Falls

📞 (289) 477-1010

🐦 @TapsOnQueen

🌐 tapsbeer.ca

🕐 Daily 12p.m.–1a.m.

🛒 Daily 12p.m.–11p.m.

Although Taps On Queen began brewing in 2004, it has since changed locations, leaving behind its original premises in Niagara-on-the-Lake for its current home on Queen Street in Niagara Falls. The brewpub operates in a bright yellow converted garage, which houses a large, open brewhouse and bar area with ample seating. In the summer, a large and well-appointed patio provides a relaxed venue for lounging in the sun. Throughout the year the bar features live music twice a week and nightly food specials. Taps has become very popular locally; its special Growler Club provides members the opportunity to try new small-batch projects and interact with the brewers.

TAPS MILD ALE has a light caramel and toffee body with simple grain notes and mild hay-like hops that barely poke through (2.5). **WITT** has a significant amount of citrus and floral character coming from the coriander and orange peel — brightly lemony and good for hot weather (3.5). **CHARLESTON LAGER** is straightforward with a very light hop presence in the aroma and a somewhat doughy middle (2.5). **SINISTER SAM'S INSANE IPA** does not quite require a straitjacket; grapefruit, lemon, and bright orange peel show significantly, overbalancing the malt core (2.5). **RED CREAM ALE** is smooth and fruity and somewhat oversweet (2). Taps also serves Niagara's Best beers due to their shared ownership.

THORNBURY BEVERAGE COMPANY

📍 5645 King Road, Nobleton

📞 (905) 859-5464

🐦 @thornburybevco

🌐 www.thornbury.co

If the range of products offered by the Thornbury Beverage Company seems familiar, there's a very good reason for that. Following Provincial Beverages of Canada's acquisition of Thornbury Cider in 2011, cider exploded in the Canadian market. Thornbury became Provincial Beverages' best-selling brand, displacing the previously popular King Brewery beers and severely undercutting the introduction of the Barn Door Beverage Company brands in 2014. The decision to axe King, a brand that had been successful and heavily decorated in competition since 2002, might best be described as unconventional and courageous. That said, the King beers are still available under the Thornbury label.

In some ways, the consolidation solves problems. In the modern era of craft beer, it can be difficult for a brewery to keep the attention of consumers with its flagship brands, regardless of quality. The King-branded lagers may have been too iconic to permit seasonal experiments, while Barn Door's continuing exploration of more esoteric seasonal beers eventually may have needed a counterpoint in its own core product. One hopes that the Thornbury branding will result in some stability and the chance to experiment.

———

PICKUP TRUCK PILSNER has decreased in spiciness in recent years, now possessing a more floral hop profile and Chex Mix cereal body that lacks some of the assertive pepper of the Czech style (3). **DARK HORSE LAGER** toys with the palate, dark malt and roast notes dancing around the outside of a sweet grain core with an effervescent body (3.5). **JUBILEE AMBER LAGER** has toasted bready malt with a hint of brown sugar and touch of vinous fruit (3). **BLUE MOUNTAIN LAGER** is a newer beer; in the German helles style, it complements a full cereal body with hints of thyme, mint, and long grasses (4).

THE 3 BREWERS

 @3brasseursca

 les3brasseurs.ca

THE 3 BREWERS KANATA

📍 565 Kanata Avenue, Kanata

📞 (613) 380-8190

🕐 Mon—Wed 11:30a.m.—12a.m., Thu 11:30a.m.—1a.m.,
Fri—Sat 11:30a.m.—2a.m., Sun 11:30a.m.—12a.m.

THE 3 BREWERS HEARTLAND

📍 5860 Mavis Road, Mississauga

📞 (289) 643-1888

🕐 Mon—Wed 11a.m.—12a.m., Thu 11a.m.—1a.m.,
Fri—Sat 11a.m.—2a.m., Sun 11a.m.—12a.m.

THE 3 BREWERS OAKVILLE

📍 2041 Winston Park Drive, Oakville

📞 (289) 813-2239

🕐 Mon—Wed 11:30a.m.—12a.m., Thu 11:30a.m.—1a.m.,
Fri—Sat 11:30a.m.—2 a.m., Sun 11:30a.m.—12a.m.

THE 3 BREWERS SPARKS

📍 240 Sparks Street, Ottawa

📞 (613) 380-8140

🕐 Mon—Wed 11a.m.—12a.m., Thu 11a.m.—1a.m.,
Fri—Sat 11a.m.—2a.m., Sun 11a.m.—12a.m.

THE 3 BREWERS RICHMOND HILL

📍 125 York Boulevard, Richmond Hill

📞 (289) 637-2637

🕐 Daily 11a.m.—2a.m.

THE 3 BREWERS ADELAIDE

📍 120 Adelaide Street W, Unit 100, Toronto

📞 (647) 689-2898

🕐 Mon—Wed 11a.m.—12a.m., Thu—Fri 11a.m.—1 a.m., Sat 11a.m.—1a.m.

THE 3 BREWERS YONGE STREET

📍 275 Yonge Street, Toronto

📞 (647) 347-6286

🕐 Mon—Wed 11:30a.m.—12a.m., Thu 11:30a.m.—1a.m.,
Fri—Sat 11:30a.m.—2a.m., Sun 11:30a.m.—12 a.m.

The 3 Brewers chain of brewpubs was started in France in 1985. Perhaps due to the commonality in language, the chain succeeded in Quebec in the first decade of the twenty-first century. The expansion into Ontario has been more rapid than anyone would have predicted when the first location opened at Yonge and Dundas in 2009. Now with seven locations spread across Ontario, the chain succeeds by bringing a level of standardization to its brewing and a focus on healthy portions of Alsatian and German food at very reasonable prices. How many pub menus feature cassoulet and flammekuchen?

——

The core lineup of beers share a house character due to the spicy character of the proprietary yeast strain. The **BLONDE** is a touch full bodied for the style, with floral and peppery notes (2.5), while the **AMBER** touches simply on caramel and brown sugar in aroma and body (2). The North American–style **BROWN** ale is remarkably complex with notes of toasted grain, chocolate, and molasses (3). The more contemporary offerings are more successful. The **IPA** is heavy on citrus and tropical fruit and packs a solid bitterness (3).

The main attraction is the neighbourhood beers, each tied to a specific location. At Yonge and Dundas, the choice is **TEMPERANCE WILLIE**, a Mosaic-hopped session IPA commemorating William Horace Temple, a local prohibitionist (3).

Additionally, brewers at the different locations compete frequently for the prestige of creating a seasonal offering to be brewed across the chain, resulting at the time of writing in a textbook **BLACK IPA** (3.5).

TOBERMORY BREWING CO. & GRILL

📍 28 Bay Street, Tobermory

📞 (519) 596-8181

🐦 @tobermorybrew

🌐 www.tobermorybrewingco.ca

🕐 Wed–Sat 12p.m.–9p.m., Sun 10a.m.–9p.m.

🛒 Wed–Sat 12p.m.–9p.m., Sun 10a.m.–9p.m.

Overlooking the harbour in the small community at the northern tip of the Bruce Peninsula, Tobermory Brewing is the work of husband and wife Matt and Kristin Buckley, who also own the Crowsnest Pub located less than a minute's walk away. Tobermory's brewmaster is Niagara College's brewmaster program grad Morag Kloeze, who drove up to the Tub shortly after writing her final exam just in time for the opening on the May 24 weekend in 2015. Overlooking the food side of Tobermory is executive chef Robert Larochelle, who takes a one-hundred-mile market approach to his ingredients, underlining the importance of fresh and local.

———

While Kloeze will be producing a number of one-offs and experimentations, there are two mainstays currently on offer year-round. The **BRUCE TRAIL BLONDE ALE** features an underlying spice note with tropical fruits and citrus (NR), and the **FATHOM FIVE PORTER** is a medium-bodied beer with roasted chocolate flavours rounded out with caramel and plum notes (NR).

TOBOGGAN BREWING COMPANY

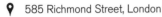

📍 585 Richmond Street, London

📞 (519) 433-2337

🐦 @TobogganBrewery

🌐 www.tobogganbrewing.com

🕐 Mon–Thu 11a.m.–11p.m., Fri–Sat 11a.m.–2a.m., Sun 11a.m.–11p.m.

🛒 Daily 11a.m.–11p.m.

Located in the space that used to house popular student bar Jim Bob Ray's, Toboggan is a well-appointed modern brewpub, one that seems poised to cater to a wider audience in London's downtown core. The wood-accented dining room is large and comfortable, subtly tied together by the massive sled that acts as ceiling and lighting feature. The contemporary pub menu has something for everyone, with vegetarian and gluten-free options featured alongside house-smoked meats and topping-heavy customizable pizzas. In summer, a large outdoor patio allows patrons to work on their tans while hoisting a pint.

The brewpub has proved so popular that months after opening, it is already nearing its capacity. This may be accounted for in equal parts by the talent of brewer Tomas Schmidt and the great enthusiasm for the place among London's craft beer drinkers. Screens behind the bar display the taplist, which features beers from a number of breweries from around the province in addition to the brewery's own beers.

———

KOLSCH has a pleasing floral aroma and a grainy body, finishing slightly sweeter than traditional takes on the style (3). **BLONDE ALE** borrows heavily from its heritage, deriving the majority of its character from earthy, forest-floor European hops (2.5). **POMEGRANATE WHEAT** allows the fruit to come through as an overtone on top of the tangy body, layering tart on tart (3). **AMERICAN PALE ALE** goes for the classic Cascade hop profile of pine over caramelized body and does it well (3.5). **IPA** finishes sweet and the malt character edges out accents of pomelo and grapefruit (2.5). **STOUT** is the highlight of the list, with gentle woodiness dominated by light-roast coffee and cream, not unlike a velvety coffee truffle (4).

TOGETHER WE'RE BITTER CO-OPERATIVE BREWING

📍 300 Mill Street, Unit 1, Kitchener

📞 (519) 746-9468

🐦 @twbpub

🌐 brewing.coop

🕐 Wed–Sat 11a.m.–9p.m., Sun 11a.m.–5p.m.

Also known as TWB for short, Together We're Bitter is a multi-stakeholder co-operative brewery with six worker-owners each having a say in how the brewery is operated. The brewpub opened in Kitchener in early 2016 thanks to a combination of the owners' own contributions and a crowdfunding campaign focused on helping the brewery purchase a fermenter for more experimental brews. TWB's primary focus is on creating a vibrant community by becoming a central hub in Kitchener.

———

TWB's beers include but are not limited to the **AMERICAN BROWN ALE**, which has a light mouthfeel and a delicate presence of the expected roasted toffee and caramel while finishing things off with a punch of mango (2.5). The **OKTOBERFEST** is a seasonal beer, with a light to medium mouthfeel and a jab of bitterness at the midway point that leads to a gentle, grainy finish leaving a satisfying impression (3.5).

TOOTH AND NAIL BREWING COMPANY

📍 3 Irving Avenue, Ottawa

📞 (613) 695-4677

🐦 @toothnailbeer

🌐 toothandnailbeer.com

🕐 Tue–Wed 4p.m.–11p.m., Thu 4p.m.–12a.m., Fri 4p.m.–1a.m.,
Sat 2p.m.–1a.m., Sun 2p.m.–6p.m.

🛒 Tue–Sat 12p.m.–11p.m., Sun 12p.m.–6p.m.

Opened in September of 2015 in Ottawa's Hintonburg neighbourhood, Tooth and Nail is the first brewing project from husband-and-wife team Matt Tweedy and Dayna Guy. Both are professionals in their own right. Tweedy has spent the last six years brewing in various locales around North America, including King Brewery and Beau's in Ontario. Guy worked as bar manager for nearly a decade at Toronto's beer-bistro, an influential beer destination. Tooth and Nail benefits from their collection of skills, experience, and context of international beers; the result is a brewery producing high-quality, complex offerings out of the gate.

STAMINA is a Belgian-style session ale somewhere between a wit and a patersbier, using the recently developed Mandarina Bavaria hop, which gives it a tangerine character throughout (4). **TENACITY** is an English–American hybrid pale ale with a white grape and citrus aroma. Toasted malt sweetness leads to a short, shrubby finish (4). **RABBLE-ROUSER** IPA uses El Dorado and Azzaca hops and derives its peach, ground-cherry, and mango character from them. There is a persistence of fruit that helps to lessen somewhat the bitter finish (4). **VIM AND VIGOR** is a bracing pilsner in the current American craft style, with assertive, peppery mown-hay and wildflower aromas and a stinging mouthfeel (5). The stout, **FORTITUDE**, is in the sweeter American style and enfolds dark-roast coffee and chocolate notes in its creamy body (4).

TRACKS BREW PUB

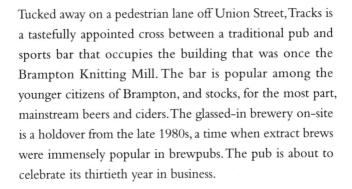

📍 60 Queen Street E, Brampton

📞 (905) 453-3063

🐦 @tracksbrewpub

🌐 www.tracksbrewpub.com

🕐 Sun–Thu 11a.m.–11p.m., Fri–Sat 11a.m.–1a.m.

Tucked away on a pedestrian lane off Union Street, Tracks is a tastefully appointed cross between a traditional pub and sports bar that occupies the building that was once the Brampton Knitting Mill. The bar is popular among the younger citizens of Brampton, and stocks, for the most part, mainstream beers and ciders. The glassed-in brewery on-site is a holdover from the late 1980s, a time when extract brews were immensely popular in brewpubs. The pub is about to celebrate its thirtieth year in business.

———

The house beer on offer at Tracks currently is its take on an ESB and designed specifically for the system. Very mild dark fruit and a whisper of roast underpin a very light body, leaving a faint impression of copper and cucumber (1.5).

ONTARIO CRAFT BREWERIES

347

THE TRAFALGAR CLUB

TRAFALGAR
ales & meads

📍 1156 Speers Road, Oakville

📞 (905) 337-0133

🐦 @Trafalgar_Club

🌐 thetrafalgarclub.com

🛒 Daily 10a.m.–6p.m.

Founded during the last gasp of the first wave of Ontario's brewing renaissance, Trafalgar has proved to be one of the most durable of Ontario's breweries since. An initial site in Oakville, founded in 1993, and the Old Mill Brewery in Elora, established in 1997, were eventually consolidated on the current site in 2003.

Trafalgar has rightly suffered in the estimation of beer enthusiasts over the last decade due to severe inconsistencies in packaging, but vast improvement has been made since the renovation of its facility in 2014 and a rebranding as the Trafalgar Club. Production has shifted to include a line of flavoured moonshines and continues to include a small selection of meads for those Vikings among us. The most impressive part of its lineup, the Black Label series, is only available at the brewery (for the time being) and is worth the trip to Oakville.

Their **IRISH BROWN ALE** is thin bodied with a bite of sherry. The mid-palate tastes of cocoa and dried fruit and it finishes ever so slightly sour (1.5). The Black Label series includes **BIG HEFE**, a banana-heavy American-style wheat beer leaning toward the sweeter end of the spectrum (3). **WEE BEASTIE** is a caramel-heavy Scotch ale with dark fruit and toasted grain notes (3.5). **SCHWARTZY XPRESSO** is a vanilla-and-coffee infused milk stout that sits like chocolate cream on the tongue (4). **SHIFTER** is a heavily dry-hopped IPA with hints of lemon, melon, and grass (3.5).

Trafalgar has a **GINGER BEER** and a **MEAD BRAGGOT** available year-round for those of you who wish to channel their inner Viking.

TRIPLE BOGEY BREWING & GOLF COMPANY

 4 Kew Beach Avenue, Toronto

📞 (416) 844-7702

🐦 @triplebogey

🌐 www.triplebogey.com

As evidenced by the name of the company, the primary thrust of Triple Bogey was to appeal to those golfers contemplating a quick pause for refreshment on the way to the back nine. Contracted out of Great Lakes Brewery in the Toronto suburb of Etobicoke, Triple Bogey is simply interested in selling beer to thirsty duffers who are focused on not slicing the ball into the rough. In 2015, Triple Bogey launched a second brand called Hurry Hard, which will no doubt find its way into curling clubs across the province. While the company is primarily focused on marketing rather than brewing, one must admit that they are at least very successful at it.

———

TRIPLE BOGEY LAGER tastes of light cereal, with a hint of green apple and a barely detectable noble hop character (2). **HURRY HARD** is a clean, lightly bready Vienna lager (3).

TUQUE DE BROUE

 @tuquedebroue
 www.tuquedebroue.ca

Named after classic Canadian headwear and alluding to the importance of a beer's head, Tuque de Broue was founded by former Canadian wine seller Nicolas Malboeuf, who was inspired to enter the craft beer world upon hearing his wine-making friends say, "It takes a lot of good beer to make great wine." While Tuque de Broue currently contracts out to Big Rig Brewery in Ottawa, Malboeuf is planning to open the doors of his own establishment in 2017.

———

The first and so far only offering from the brewery is **TUQUE DORÉE CANADIAN PALE ALE**. It presents a decent head, golden colour, and very sweet bread and grain characteristics, with very little bitterness (2).

ONTARIO CRAFT BREWERIES

UNION JACK BREWING COMPANY

📍 9 Queen Street E, Sault Ste. Marie

📞 (705) 575-8991

🐦 @brewingjack

🕐 Mon–Thu 12p.m.–6p.m., Fri–Sat 12p.m.–8p.m.

Right next door to the well-known Ernie's Coffee Shop on Queen Street in Sault Ste. Marie, Union Jack Brewing Company has been open for business since May of 2015. It is run by two brothers, Jeff and Jordan Jack, who both work in the medical profession when not making beer for the good people of the Soo and breathing new life into the city's west end. While its beers are primarily sold in bars and restaurants in and around the area, growlers and tastings of head brewer Jeff's offerings can be found within the brewery itself.

———

Offerings from Union Jack include the **ALGOMA PALE ALE**, which pours a golden honey colour and contains hints of ginger and cereal (1.5), and **RAPID RIVER CREAM ALE**, which is, overall, a very dry beer, with hints of lightly spiced grain in the finish (2).

WALKERVILLE BREWERY

📍 525 Argyle Road, Windsor

📞 (519) 254-6067

🐦 @WalkervilleBrew

🌐 walkervillebrewery.com

🕐 Tours are available Saturdays at 12:30p.m., 3:30p.m., and 5p.m. Tours are available for groups of fifteen or more by advance appointment.

🛒 Mon—Wed 11a.m.–6p.m., Thu 11a.m.–7p.m., Fri 11a.m.–9p.m., Sat 11a.m.–7p.m., Sun 11a.m.–6p.m.

Located in the Walkerville neighbourhood of Windsor, this brewery borrows from the pedigree of two previous incarnations under the Walkerville name. The first, distiller Hiram Walker's own brewery, was founded in 1890 and survived until 1956. The next, a second-wave brewery was ahead of its time and survived from 1998 until 2007, garnering a number of accolades. The current version is housed in a repurposed tank-storage warehouse that was itself originally part of Hiram Walker's distilling empire.

Walkerville differentiates itself from a number of recently founded breweries in that it is set up to produce both ales and lagers rather than focusing solely on quicker-to-turn-over ales. The brewery is also able to produce specialty barrel-aged beers thanks to its relationship with the adjacent Hiram Walker plant — a relationship that ensures the brewery ready access to aged oak barrels.

Walkerville prides itself on being a neighbourhood brewery and has a spacious taproom that has become popular for events locally. Their recent expansion into the LCBO stands them in good stead for the near future and the facility will provide space for expansion should their 4,000-HL capacity prove insufficient.

———

HONEST LAGER is a light-bodied, bready, Oktoberfest-style beer that ranks among the best brewery flagships in the province, with a spicy, late-palate bitter pop that fades into a clean finish (4.5). **LOOPHOLE ALE** is a crystal-clear, filtered, kölsch-style beer, whose fruity character leans toward peach with a black pepper sting (4). **GERONIMO IPA** possesses restrained bitterness with a grapefruit character leaning toward blood orange (3.5). **AMPELMÄNN DUNKEL** has mostly nutty grain through the body with a hint of spice from the yeast (3). **WATERFRONT WIT** is a light summery affair flavoured with organic Florida-orange peel (3.5). **EASY STOUT** is a flavourful milk stout with coffee character — specifically cream and two sugars (3.5).

WALLER ST. BREWING

📍 14 Waller Street, Ottawa

📞 (613) 860-1515

🐦 @WallerStBrewing

🌐 www.wallerst.ca

🛒 Thu 4p.m.–8p.m., Fri–Sat 1p.m.–10p.m.

Opened in August 2015 in the basement of the Lunenburg Pub, an 1868 Ottawa heritage building, Waller St. Brewing's image is inspired by the romanticism of the Prohibition era. The brewery is very much the product of its founders' dreams; indeed, much of the brewing equipment was designed by brewmaster and co-founder Marc-Andre Chainey himself, pulling from his background in engineering.

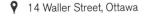

Waller St.'s offerings include the **BOOTLEG BLONDE**, with a refreshingly thin mouthfeel, distinct grain characteristics, and a finish that gives off the taste of lemon zest (3). The quite smooth **MOONLIGHT PORTER** offers intense roasted-coffee flavours and a lingering finish (3), and the **SPEAKEASY RED**, a dry-hopped, red rye session IPA has a lot of sweet corn notes accompanied by passion fruit and lychee (2.5).

WELLINGTON BREWERY

 950 Woodlawn Road W, Guelph

📞 (519) 837-2337

🐦 @WellingtonBrew

🌐 wellingtonbrewery.ca

🕐 The brewery hosts guided samplings
on Saturdays between 1p.m. and 4p.m.

🛒 Mon–Wed 9a.m.–6p.m., Thu–Fri 9a.m.–8p.m.,
Sat 10a.m.–8p.m., Sun 11a.m.–6p.m.

Founded in 1985, Wellington occupies the spot of Ontario's oldest independent microbrewery, and its character highlights the gist of the early brewing renaissance in Ontario. The beers that Wellington brews are English in style and influenced by time the brewers spent in England — then one of the only remaining bastions of diversity in brewing left. Given that history, the brewery's early adoption of cask-conditioned ales makes perfect sense. Less successful was the initial plastic retail packaging, which may also be put down to English influence.

Thirty years later, Wellington has been expanding its volume and diversifying both its own portfolio and its business practices. A not inconsiderable part of its business is made up of producing contract brands for other breweries.

That said, the core lineup remains nearly identical to the way it was during the 1980s. Wellington is one of a very few breweries in Ontario that has a house yeast character, a traditionally English strain that imparts a light savouriness not unlike brewer's yeast (think Marmite) across its entire range. It is a flavour profile that lends itself to service on cask and you should enjoy their beer from that source if possible.

———

ARKELL BEST BITTER is lightly coppery in body with an almost cruciferous bitterness, and is mildly tea-like with a hint of caramel (3.5). **SPECIAL PALE ALE** has a somewhat deeper caramel flavour and the impression of orange pekoe and a hint of vanilla on the finish (3). **COUNTY DARK** forges ahead into nutty crystal malts with hints of raisin, licorice, and chocolate (3.5). **IMPERIAL RUSSIAN STOUT** is a well of complexity, with leather and peat smoke emerging from the bittersweet depths of its roasty body (4.5). **TRAILHEAD** is the brewery's take on a Vienna lager and for many years the best value in the Beer Store's discount section: a light, doughy, caramel body with gentle noble-hop accents (3). **FRESH OFF THE WIRE** is a good example of the brewery's newly found range. A wet hop beer made with Centennial hops, it eschews the tea-like character of older offerings, aiming rather to emulate the marmalade on the toast next to it (4).

WHIPRSNAPR BREWING COMPANY

📍 14 Bexley Place, Unit 106, Nepean

📞 (613) 596-9882

🐦 @whiprsnaprbrew

🌐 www.whiprsnaprbrewingco.com

🕐 Wed–Fri 12p.m.–8p.m., Sat 12p.m.–6p.m., Sun 12p.m.–4p.m.

Located in Bells Corners, a suburb of Ottawa, Whiprsnapr is one of the more ambitious breweries in the Ottawa craft beer scene. In its first year of operation, the brewery graduated from a nanobrew-sized, 1.5-BBL set-up to a 20-BBL brewhouse. The first six months on the small system were spent in recipe development, allowing brewer Ian McMartin to experiment with possibilities.

This experimentation truly separates Whiprsnapr from the rest of the market. Its tendency is not to abide by conventional stylistic distinctions or guidelines. Rather than emulating beers from particular regions, the focus seems to be on a recipe-development and marketing process that appears largely autobiographical. This results in interesting products, some of which are more successful than others. Rather than attempting to slot each beer into a pre-existing style for ratings, we have used the brewery's descriptions.

———

ROOT OF EVIL is a pre-Prohibition lager with a whiff of matchstick on the nose and a lightly peachy corn aroma. Reminiscent of Vermont-smoked ham, the beer has a surprisingly crisp finish (2.5). **CAROL ANNE** is an Irish blonde ale, hopped like a flower bed, full bodied and full of honey (3). **OK LAH!** is a cream ale flavoured with ginger and coriander, producing a certain amount of zippy citrus and aromatic fresh ginger in a light, refreshing body. Drink it, steam mussels with it, or pair it with pad Thai (3.5). **BLACK SUNSHINE** is a black lager; aged with whisky-soaked oak chips, it tastes deeply roasty with a full, creamy mouthfeel and a drying, woody core (3.5). **F'N'L** is a British IPA with a limey nose that settles into a full-bodied, nutty, cookieish bed of malt with a lingering hedgerow and blackcurrant finish (2.5). **INUKSHUK** is a "Canadian IPA," with a nose of pine, kiwi, and lime, and a full, bitter finish (3).

WHITEWATER BREWING COMPANY

📍 22 Fletcher Road, Foresters Falls

📞 (613) 582-7227

🐦 @WhitewaterBrew

🌐 whitewaterbeer.ca

🕐 Summer: Mon–Thu 10a.m.–6p.m., Fri 10a.m.–8p.m., Sat 12p.m.–8p.m., Sun 12p.m.–6p.m.

Inspired by their adventures on the mighty Ottawa River, professional whitewater rafting guides Chris Thompson, Chris Thompson (yes, there are two of them), and James Innes started the brewery in 2013. After a year during which the brewery experienced considerable growth, the founders decided to expand by opening a three-thousand-square-foot brewpub near popular tourist destination Wilderness Tours Rafting in Foresters Falls, opening seven days a week during the peak summer months. While larger-scale brewing operations for bars and the LCBO are handled through Big Rig Brewery in Ottawa, Whitewater still provides brewpub patrons with regular and seasonal beers brewed in-house.

CLASS V is a standard North American IPA, with caramel notes accompanied by hints of orange peel and grapefruit zest (3.5). **FARMER'S DAUGHTER** is a very malt-forward blonde ale that features cereal-grain notes followed up with flavours of honey and lemon (2). **WHISTLING PADDLER** is an English-style pale ale that includes toffee and citrus character with a grassy bitterness (3). **MIDNIGHT STOUT** is a very sessionable offering, with cocoa and brown sugar coming together with a smooth mouthfeel brought in by oatmeal (NR).

WILD CARD BREWING COMPANY

 (613) 394-1010
 @wildcardbeer
 wildcardbrewco.com
 Check website for updates.

Wild Card is a new development in Trenton's small brewing scene. The brewery displaces Gateway Brewing (itself opened in 2011), which has become the name for the brew-on-premises business in the unit next door. Owned by Nathan and Zack Card, and located just across the Trent River from the Fraser Park Marina, Wild Card is named for the boat the Card family owned during Nathan and Zack's childhood. The brewery's branding is largely inspired by card games, specifically poker.

The range of beer on offer at Wild Card has diversified somewhat since the handover from Gateway Brewing, with more complex flavours and specialty ingredients being used. Fermentation still takes place in the type of equipment that one might find in a brew-on-premises facility, but this is likely to change in the near future with upgrades and expansion in the offing.

ACE OF DIAMONDS is a raspberry-accented saison that elongates the Belgian yeast character with a tart fruit presence and the gentle bitterness of berry seeds (3.5). **BLONDE BARISTA** is ostensibly a blonde stout but uses coffee and lactose to produce a beer that tastes like a combination between a hoppy pale ale and a Tim Hortons double-double (3.5). **ESCAPE VELOCITY** is a single-hopped pale ale made with Galaxy hops, meaning it's like a glassful of pineapple and passion fruit but with a relatively subdued pop (3). **THE FLOP** is a blonde ale with a sweetly malty nose, accented by drying herbs and cracked leather with a touch of apple toward the swallow (2). **QUEEN OF HEARTS**, a chocolate-raspberry milk stout, is a bitter chocolate-raspberry truffle with just a waft of smokiness (2.5). **RIDE THE BRAKE** is the brewery's India pale ale, a hybrid of the English and American styles, using mostly West Coast hops to promote an orange-peel and mango-pulp aroma with a lurking pine bitterness (3).

WILLIAM STREET BEER COMPANY

 412 William Street, Cobourg

 (905) 377-9090

 @CobourgBeer

🌐 www.williamstreetbeer.com

🛒 Wed–Fri 12p.m.–6p.m., Sat 10a.m.–5p.m.

Founded in April of 2014, William Street is a promising outfit located in a disused garage near downtown Cobourg. The first brewery in Cobourg in over a century, it has jumped directly into the modern era, with owner Sean Walpole preferring to sell his beers in tall cans with winning graphic designs, and growlers for local consumption. The first year was a very successful one and demand for the brewery's product routinely began to outstrip supply.

———

The year-round offering, **CLIFF TOP PALE ALE**, fits comfortably into the hybrid category, gaining a rugged, earthy dirtiness from Perle hops supplementing the Cascade pine and citrus (3). **WHITE SAIL WHEAT** is a clove-heavy hefeweizen running to the darker, sweeter end of the style (2.5). The massively inventive **ORANGE CREAM CYCLE** almost manages to replicate the profile of the Creamsicle ice-cream novelty through its use of vanilla bean, orange zest, flaked corn, and lactose (2.5).

WOODHOUSE BREWING COMPANY

 @woodhousebeer

 www.woodhousebrewing.com

Founded in 2014, the Woodhouse Brewing Company is the first independent venture from Graham Woodhouse, an ex-Labatt employee who decided to test the waters of the craft market. The initial offering from Woodhouse Brewing is a lager, developed in collaboration with Charles MacLean and currently brewed in the Toronto suburb of Etobicoke at Cool Beer Brewing. When possible, the beer includes Ontario-grown hops in the recipe, but due to limited volumes, their availability is sometimes an issue.

———

WOODHOUSE LAGER is an amber lager leaning toward the Vienna style, and features significant crystal malt fruitiness and a lightly floral hop aroma (3).

BRACEBRIDGE

GRIFFIN GASTROPUB

- 9 Chancery Lane, Bracebridge
- (705) 646-0438
- @griffingastro
- www.thegriffinpub.ca

Run by Curt Dunlop and Jed Corbeil, who are in charge of Toronto's annual Session craft beer festival, the Griffin features twelve rotating taps, among which Sawdust City is a regular pour.

BURLINGTON

RIB EYE JACK'S ALE HOUSE

📍 4045 Harvester Road, Burlington

📞 (905) 633-9929

🐦 @RibeyeJacks

🌐 www.ribeyejacksalehouse.com

Rib Eye Jack's has a healthy taplist featuring a number of Ontario beers on draught and a bottle list longer than your arm. Macro beers seem to be priced at a premium and require you to order from the "Beginner's List." Nice.

Rib Eye Jack's has recently opened a new location in Mississauga. Located at 6531 Mississauga Road (905-820-6300), it features the same ambience, menu, and beer selection as the original Burlington location.

CAMBRIDGE

BEERTOWN PUBLIC HOUSE

📍 561 Hespeler Road, Unit 1-A, Cambridge

📞 (519) 629-0288

🐦 @beertownph

🌐 www.beertown.ca

This three-location chain of pubs features a mix of Ontario craft products, imports, and macro beers. The modern decor and eclectic menu of pub food and bistro fare make for a good destination for those new to craft beers or for craft beer drinkers with friends who haven't made the switch yet.

FONTHILL

IGGY'S PUB AND GRUB

📍 115 Highway 20 E, Fonthill

📞 (905) 892-6667

🐦 @Iggyspub

🌐 www.iggyspub.com

With its large selection of frequently updated craft beers listed in bright colours on a chalkboard, Iggy's is a favourite of the brewmaster students from Niagara College. If that's not a ringing endorsement, I'm not sure what would be. The menu focuses on bringing farm-to-table cuisine to a traditional pub menu.

GUELPH

BAKER STREET STATION

📍 76 Baker Street, Guelph

📞 (519) 265-7960

🐦 @BakerStStation

🌐 www.bakerstreetstation.ca

This relatively young pub's menu features a number of truly interesting fusion items in addition to a series of frequently rotating brewery-dedicated taps. The second-floor balcony patio is a real draw in summer. Try the duck and waffles.

WOOLWICH ARROW

📍 176 Woolwich Street, Guelph

📞 (519) 836-2875

🐦 @WoolwichArrow

🌐 www.woolwicharrow.ca

A legendary Guelph pub, the Wooly is a great place to try beers from the Guelph and Kitchener-Waterloo region. It also periodically hosts interesting tap takeovers from out-of-town breweries.

HAMILTON

AUGUSTA'S WINKING JUDGE

- 25 Augusta Street, Hamilton
- (905) 524-5626
- @winkingjudge
- www.winkingjudge.com

The Winking Judge is a holdover from the first wave of micro-breweries in Ontario and feels not unlike an English front room. The selection of beers on offer is wholly made up of Ontario craft brews, with the majority coming from Hamilton or nearby.

THE SHIP

- 23 Augusta Street, Hamilton
- (905) 526-0792
- @ShipTwits
- www.theship.ca

The Ship features a well-curated thirteen-tap lineup of craft beers and ciders in addition to a limited number of cans. The late-night-eats menu makes it a natural choice for an evening out on the lash in Hamilton.

KINGSTON

THE ALIBI

 293 Princess Street, Kingston

📞 (613) 767-1312

🐦 @alibikingston

The Alibi is the sister pub of the Brooklyn. By way of contrast, the Alibi has a more relaxed atmosphere, suited to trivia nights. With beers from east and west of Kingston, it might have one of the most diverse tap lineups in the province, geographically speaking. The Alibi also hosts occasional interesting tap takeovers.

THE BROOKLYN

📍 14 Garrett Street, Kingston

🐦 @brooklynktown

 www.brooklynktown.com

The Brooklyn features a taplist best encapsulated by its motto, "No crap on tap." It features American selections as well as Ontario craft beers. The pub also functions as a live-music venue and on some nights has a busy dance floor.

RED HOUSE

📍 369 King Street E, Kingston

📞 (613) 767-2558

🐦 @RedHouseKtown

🌐 www.redhousekingston.com

Red House has a small number of craft taps available, but the selection is rock solid. In terms of food, the variety might be best categorized as down-home bistro.

KITCHENER

THE BENT ELBOW

📍 2880 King Street E, Unit E, Kitchener

📞 (519) 208-0202

🐦 @haroldkroeker

🌐 www.thebentelbow.ca

The Bent Elbow features thirty-nine taps, the vast majority of which pour Ontario craft beer. While the rest of the selections are from other countries, they're still really good. The pub menu has a daily burger that changes according to the chef's whim.

LONDON

MILOS' CRAFT BEER EMPORIUM

- 420 Talbot Street N, London
- (519) 601-4447
- @PubMilos
- www.pubmilos.com

Featuring a selection of Ontario craft beers and the house's Beer Lab products, Milos' is a real favourite in London, and Milos himself is one of the few remaining examples of a real publican.

MORRISSEY HOUSE

- 359-361 Dundas Street, London
- (519) 204-9220
- @morrisseyhouse
- themorrisseyhouse.wordpress.com

The Morrissey House features seventeen taps of Ontario craft beer and cider. The converted mansion provides an interesting ambience and there is a pleasant patio with a courtyard feel in the summer.

POACHER'S ARMS

📍 171 Queens Avenue, London

📞 (519) 432-7888

🐦 @Poachers_Arms

🌐 www.poachersarms.ca

The Poacher's Arms is just starting to diversify into craft beer, but provides a number of options both on tap and in bottles.

MISSISSAUGA

THE CROOKED CUE

📍 75 Lakeshore Road E, Mississauga

📞 (905) 271-7665

🐦 @crookedcue

🌐 www.crookedcue.ca

The Crooked Cue is a great place to play pool and enjoy an Ontario craft beer. The Mississauga location is one of the few places where you can find Old Credit's beers on tap. Why not enjoy one or two on the patio?

NEWMARKET

HUNGRY BREW HOPS PUBLIC HOUSE & EATERY

📍 211 Main Street S, Newmarket

📞 (905) 235-8277

🐦 @hungrybrewhops

🌐 www.hungrybrewhops.com

A destination on Newmarket's main street, Hungry Brew Hops boasts thirty-two taps, which include a number of Ontario choices along with quality international selections. The impressive beer list and the contemporary menu can be enjoyed in a bar area with a unique rustic, industrial feel. The authors recommend the pork rinds.

NIAGARA-ON-THE-LAKE

THE GARRISON HOUSE

📍 111C Unit 2 Garrison Village Drive, Niagara-on-the-Lake

📞 (905) 468-4000

🐦 @tghnotl

🌐 www.thegarrisonhouse.ca

A gastro-style tavern, the Garrison House has six taps with Ontario beer. The real attraction here is chef David Watt's menu, which features his take on modern Canadian pub fare, including a fun black lager beer-a-misu for dessert.

THE OLDE ANGEL INN

📍 224 Regent Street, Niagara-on-the-Lake

📞 (905) 468-3411

🐦 @oldeangelinn

🌐 www.angel-inn.com

Standing since 1789, the main draw of the Olde Angel Inn is the ambience. Its cozy rooms with low ceiling beams make the pub a nice place to enjoy a craft beer and a ploughman's lunch.

NORTH BAY

THE RAVEN AND REPUBLIC

📍 246 1st Avenue W, North Bay

📞 (705) 478-6110

🐦 @RavenandRepubli

🌐 www.ravenandrepublic.ca

The Raven and Republic has sixteen taps focused on local breweries and serves upscale pub food. As well as offering delicious beer and great food, the pub hosts a beer-101 course taught by the owner on the first Wednesday and Thursday of each month. Delicious, but also educational.

OSHAWA

BUSTER RHINO'S SOUTHERN BBQ

📍 28 King Street E, Oshawa

📞 (905) 436-6986 ext. 3

🐦 @busterrhinosbbq

🌐 www.busterrhinos.com

Buster Rhino's features completely legit Southern BBQ, chicken and waffles, an extensive selection of craft beers, and a whisky menu longer than many grade school primers. It now has a second Oshawa location at 30 Taunton Road E, Unit 6 (905-436-6986 ext. 2), as well as one in Whitby at 2001 Thickson Road S (905-436-6986 ext. 1).

OTTAWA

ARROW & LOON PUB & RESTAURANT

- 99 Fifth Avenue, Ottawa
- (613) 237-0448
- @ArrowAndLoon
- www.arrowandloon.com

Originally a part of the Neighbourhood Pub Group, the Arrow and Loon continues to supply Ontario-made beer and local foods to the people of Ottawa. The authors heartily recommend the bison chili.

BROTHER'S BEER BISTRO

- 366 Dalhousie Street, Ottawa
- (613) 695-6300
- @brosbeerbistro
- www.brothersbeerbistro.ca

Located in the ByWard Market, Brother's features a selection of European beers in addition to the local brewery choices that are exploding onto the Ottawa scene. The cheese and charcuterie boards offer fantastic selections.

CHESHIRE CAT

📍 2193 Richardson Side Road, Carp

📞 (613) 831-2183

🐦 @cheshirecatpub

🌐 www.cheshirecatpub.com

Rising like a phoenix from the ashes (having suffered a catastrophic fire in recent memory) is this Ontario craft beer institution that features continually rotating taps and casks. Absolutely everyone is glad to have it back.

PUB ITALIA

📍 434½ Preston Street, Ottawa

📞 (613) 232-2326

🐦 @pubitalia

🌐 www.pubitalia.ca

An Italian restaurant combined with an Irish pub, Pub Italia is a beer bar that provides an excellent selection of craft and imports, and offers customers the opportunity to order them in a 38-ounce "Holy Grail pint," a Pub Italia exclusive. The can and bottle list is extensive.

WELLINGTON GASTROPUB

📍 1325 Wellington Street W, Ottawa

📞 (613) 729-1315

🐦 @thegastropub

🌐 www.thewellingtongastropub.com

One of only three pubs on the list to have begun brewing out of their own location, the Wellington specializes in bistro fare. The brewery is temporarily on hiatus but will rebrand as Stalwart.

SUDBURY

HARDROCK 42

📍 117 Elm Street, Sudbury

📞 (705) 586-3303

🐦 @hardrock42G

🌐 www.hardrock42.com

Featuring a wide range of craft beers from both inside and outside Ontario, this gastropub also boasts a selection of poutines and more gourmet burgers than you can shake a patty at.

LAUGHING BUDDHA

📍 194 Elgin Street, Sudbury

📞 (705) 673-2112

🐦 @buddhasudbury

🌐 www.laughingbuddhasudbury.com

In addition to a carefully chosen list of Ontario beers in cans and bottles, Laughing Buddha has beer from all over the world. It may be the only pub in the world with a sandwich named after the star of the 1970s Canadian TV series *The Hilarious House of Frightenstein*.

TORONTO

BAR HOP

📍 391 King Street W, Toronto

📞 (647) 352-7476

🐦 @barhopbar

🌐 www.barhoptoronto.com

Since opening in 2012, Bar Hop has established itself as one of Toronto's can't-miss beer destinations. Expect a comprehensive bottle and tap selection along with unique food offerings and a commendable spirits list.

BAR HOP BREWCO

📍 137 Peter Street, Toronto

📞 (647) 348-1137

🐦 @barhopbar

🌐 www.barhoptoronto.com

Bar Hop Brewco is Bar Hop's second location. Taking up two floors, it has over thirty-six beers on tap, exquisite food by chef Mark Cutrara, and its own brewing facility.

BAR VOLO

📍 587 Yonge Street, Toronto

📞 (416) 928-0008

🐦 @barVolo

🌐 www.barvolo.com

A pub that has proved instrumental in pushing the Ontario beer scene out of its complacency, Bar Volo features over thirty taps, as many as six casks at a time, and a selection of bottles it imports under its Keep6 label.

BEERBISTRO

📍 18 King Street E, Toronto

📞 (416) 861-9872

🐦 @beerbistroTO

🌐 www.beerbistro.com

Started by chef Brian Morin and beer writer Stephen Beaumont, beerbistro remains a sundown destination for the Bay Street crowd. While the bottle selection may have lost a step since a change in ownership, the taps are still well-curated and include the house beer from Shillow Beer Company. The Belgian frites are a favourite of the clientele.

CASTRO'S LOUNGE

📍 2116E Queen Street E, Toronto

📞 (416) 699-8272

🐦 @CastrosLounge

🌐 www.castroslounge.com

Castro's Lounge features a selection of Ontario craft beers on tap, from the cask, in bottles, and in cans. The menu is vegetarian and vegan friendly. The decor is of the Communist-Socialist persuasion in this cozy little pub.

THE CEILI COTTAGE

📍 1301 Queen Street E, Toronto

📞 (416) 406-1301

🐦 @TheCeiliCottage

🌐 www.ceilicottage.com

As properly Irish a pub as one can fit into a modified garage, the Ceili features oysters and daily dinner specials in addition to a selection of Ontario beers and a whisky selection worthy of Brendan Behan.

THE CRAFT BRASSERIE AND GRILLE

📍 107 Atlantic Avenue, Toronto

📞 (416) 535-2337

🐦 @thecraftliberty

🌐 www.thecraftbrasserie.com

Catering to the Liberty Village condo crowd, the Craft features over 100 different taps, many of which feature Ontario craft brews. The eclectic menu includes upscale takes on pub classics and interesting bistro fare.

THE LOOSE MOOSE

📍 146 Front Street W, Toronto

📞 (416) 977-8840

🐦 @LooseMooseTO

🌐 www.theloosemoose.ca

The Loose Moose features something for everyone, with a significant number of craft beers on offer in addition to macro lagers for the sports crowd in downtown Toronto.

MORGAN'S ON THE DANFORTH

📍 1282 Danforth Avenue, Toronto

📞 (416) 461-3020

🐦 @morgansonthedan

🌐 www.morgansonthedanforth.com

Morgan's has a small but dependable selection of Ontario beers, with rotating taps and an interesting bottle selection. The kitchen boasts chef Anne Sorrenti, who won *Chopped Canada* in 2015. The authors' standard recommendation is the Hoisin chicken wings.

THE ONLY CAFE

📍 972 Danforth Avenue, Toronto

📞 (416) 463-7843

🐦 @TheOnlyCafe

🌐 www.theonlycafe.com

The Only's frequently rotating taps and seventies' rec room feel make it a comfortable hangout on the Danforth. Bonuses include the spacious patio, seasonal beer festivals, a decent music selection, and the fact that it's within stumbling distance to Donlands subway station.

THE QUEEN AND BEAVER PUBLIC HOUSE

📍 35 Elm Street, Toronto

📞 (647) 347-2712

🐦 @QueenBeaverPub

🌐 www.queenandbeaverpub.ca

The Queen and Beaver serves pub fare of the extremely old school. British fare includes an excellent lamb curry, devilled kidneys, and mushrooms and Stilton on toast. A good place to catch Ontario ales on cask.

THE REBEL HOUSE

📍 1068 Yonge Street, Toronto

📞 (416) 927-0704

🐦 @rebelhouse_ca

🌐 www.rebelhouse.ca

A Rosedale institution, the Rebel House isn't just for the rich folks. Its selection of beers is also quite inclusive. On tap is a well-curated selection from Ontario brewers with bricks-and-mortar facilities. There is also a limited selection of cans. In summer, the patio is an excellent hideaway from the real world.

THE RHINO

📍 1249 Queen Street W, Toronto

📞 (416) 535-8089

🐦 @TheRhinoBar

🌐 www.therhinobartoronto.com

The Rhino is a Parkdale institution. It features a great selection of Ontario craft beers and ciders on tap in addition to an interesting cellar. The patio is an excellent place to people-watch in summer.

STOUT IRISH PUB

📍 221 Carlton Street, Toronto

📞 (647) 344-7676

🐦 @stoutirishpubTO

🌐 www.stoutirishpub.ca

Situated in Cabbagetown, Stout has all the trappings of a traditional Irish pub but a vastly better beer list, made up of both standards and seasonal taps. In summer, the alley patio is a popular spot for a beer in the shade.

TALL BOYS

📍 838 Bloor Street W, Toronto

📞 (416) 535-7486

🐦 @tallboysbar

🌐 www.tallboyscraft.com

Tall Boys likely features the largest number of Ontario craft beers available in a single location. While the taps rotate periodically, the real attraction here is the vast number of different canned beers, many of which aren't available anywhere else in the GTA.

TEQUILA BOOKWORM

📍 512 Queen Street W, Toronto

📞 (416) 504-2334

🐦 @tequilabookworm

🌐 www.tequilabookworm.com

Tequila Bookworm is a popular destination for those seeking Ontario-made beer and cider. Its "upshtairs" event space, used to host tap takeovers and allow breweries to show off their new products, is an added attraction and is available for private bookings. A patio on the second floor at the rear is a quiet sanctuary from bustling Queen Street.

WISE BAR

📍 1007 Bloor Street W, Toronto

📞 (416) 519-3139

🐦 @WiseBarToronto

🌐 www.wisebar.ca

With a masterfully curated beer list, courtesy of owner Tamara Wise, Wise Bar is a small and relaxed hangout. Along with its impressive drinks menu, Wise Bar also has simple, unpretentious snacks for grazing. There's something for everyone to enjoy.

WVRST

📍 609 King Street W, Toronto

📞 (416) 703-7775

🐦 @wvrstbeerhall

🌐 www.wvrst.com

Specializing in duck-fat fries and a variety of sausages from different parts of the world, Wvrst is a good place for communal dining and stein hoisting. Their cellaring program will eventually produce interesting results. From the sausage menu, the authors recommend the Boerewors.

WATERLOO

KICKOFF SPORTS BAR AND CAFE

📍 170 University Avenue W, Waterloo

📞 (519) 888-9699

🐦 @kickoffwaterloo

Supporting a diverse lineup of beer from across the province and across its borders, Kickoff is a laid-back sports bar with great beer. A perfect place to watch the footie and probably also the football.

WINDSOR

THE BARREL HOUSE DRAUGHT CO. & GRILL

📍 3199 Sandwich Street, Windsor

📞 (519) 977-5334

🐦 @BHWindsor

🌐 www.facebook.com/barrelhousedraughtco/

The Barrel House serves a variety of Ontario beers on tap and is a contender for the hotly contested title of best burger in Windsor.

RINO'S KITCHEN & ALE HOUSE

📍 131 Elliott Street W, Windsor

📞 (519) 962-8843

🐦 @rinoskitchen

🌐 www.rinoskitchen.com

Located in a converted one-hundred-year-old house, Rino's carries only Ontario and Quebec beers, and the menu is dedicated to showcasing Essex County on a farm-to-table basis.

ROCK BOTTOM BAR & GRILL

📍 3236 Sandwich Street, Windsor

📞 (519) 258-7553

🐦 @RBwindsor

🌐 www.rockbottom.ca

Rock Bottom has Windsor's best selection of Ontario beers on tap (thirty-one) and a total lack of pretense. It is the kind of bar in which peanut shells crunch underfoot — a refreshing change in an age of often unnecessary refinements.

GLOSSARY

ACETALDEHYDE   An organic compound that presents as a flaw in beer above certain concentrations and is notable for its pungent green-apple aroma. Typically a sign of young beer that has been rushed through production.

AMERICAN FARMHOUSE ALE   A North American derivation of the Belgian saison style of beer. Typically made with some percentage of wheat and fermented with a Belgian yeast strain, and frequently finished with Brettanomyces for a dry mouthfeel.

AMERICAN IPA   An invention of the North American brewing renaissance, American IPA borrows the structure of the heavily hopped India pale ale from England and substitutes American hop varieties for English ones. The beer is usually quite bitter (between 40 and 70 IBU) and features notes of pine and citrus from C-hop varieties.

AMERICAN WHEAT BEER   American wheat beers are defined largely by the inclusion of wheat in their grist rather than the yeast esters prevalent in their German counterparts. The American version is frequently filtered, resulting in a light-coloured, clear beer with more hop than yeast character.

ALT (BIER)   A hybrid style of beer from Dusseldorf that is fermented with ale yeast and then conditioned as though it were a lager. Typically coloured between amber and chestnut, alts tend to be earthy in character and lean toward malt dominance.

BARREL (BBL)   One of two commonly used brewery volume measurements. In America, a barrel represents 31.5 U.S. gallons, which is approximately 119 litres of beer.

BITTER   Referring to a range of styles of English beers from the early decades of the twentieth century, *bitter* is something of a catch-all term for lower-alcohol English ales served on cask and featuring biscuit malts and mild hop bitterness.

BLONDE ALE   A light ale, typically offered by breweries as an alternative to a pale lager. Although lightness in body and in flavour is of primary concern, the blonde ale can be a good showcase for fruit and hop flavours.

BOCK   Properly a family of lager styles that has its origin in the town of Einbeck in northern Germany, bocks tend to enjoy a complex, malty character, although their primary commonality is their above-average strength. Since *bock* means *ram* in German, labels are frequently festooned with goats.

BOTTLE CONDITIONING   Instead of being bottled at the desired carbonation level, beer is packaged in bottles with a small amount of unfermented wort or priming sugar and left to carbonate naturally. This is popular in Belgian styles and may include a number of different yeast strains.

BRETTANOMYCES   A strain of wild yeast most commonly found on the skin of fruit. The specific strain *bruxellensis* is a defining characteristic of sour beers made in Brussels. Brettanomyces typically dries out beers by eating sugars other yeast strains can't. Frequently used descriptors of the resultant aroma include "horse blanket," "sheep pen," and the more general "funky."

BREWHOUSE A general term for the equipment used in the first half of the brewing process, including but not limited to the mash tun, lauter tun, and kettle.

BREWMASTER Properly, a professional designation afforded to the most senior member of staff at a large brewery after years of experience have been gained. Commonly, whoever is doing the brewing at a brewery.

BREWPUB Typically a restaurant that has its own in-house brewery and largely features its own beers on tap. Usually brewpubs sell their beers only on their own premises, but there are exceptions.

BROWN ALE Full-strength English ales that tend toward deep caramel and malt character; predictably coloured. American versions retain the colour but frequently have a cleaner yeast profile and substitute American hop varieties.

BUTYRIC ACID In beer, an off-flavour. At low concentrations it may present as vaguely cheesy, reminiscent of Parmesan. At high concentrations it is similar to baby vomit and therefore to be avoided.

CAMPAIGN FOR REAL ALE (CAMRA) An English consumer-advocacy group concerned about the dwindling diversity of traditional beers on draught.

CANDI SUGAR A specialty invert sugar typically used in stronger Belgian-style beers. The simple sugars (fructose and glucose) are more easily digestible by yeast and result in a quick and characteristic boost in alcohol.

CREAM ALE A North American hybrid-style beer that is fermented like an ale but conditioned like a lager. Developed as a response to the popularity of pale lagers, cream ale may contain adjuncts for lightness of body.

GLOSSARY

CZECH PILSNER   The originator and most hop-forward version of the pilsner style, Czech pilsner tends to feature Saaz hops and a low level of diacetyl among its notable characteristics. Pilsner Urquell is a prime example.

DIACETYL   A flavour compound in beer that is typically noted as a brewing flaw. At low levels it may help define a style, such as Czech pilsner or some English ales. At high concentrations it is detectable as butterscotch or imitation-butter flavouring and creates an unpleasant, slick mouthfeel.

DIMETHYL SULPHIDE   A brewing flaw that typically presents as cooked or canned vegetables. In home-brewing it is frequently the result of an insufficiently vigorous boil or a covered kettle.

DOUBLE IPA   An outsized version of the American IPA, double IPA tends to be higher in alcohol and bitterness, frequently surpassing the human threshold for detection (110 IBU). Vibrant hop aromas define the style.

DRY HOPPING   A technique whereby fermented beer is dosed with hops in order to produce a more vibrant aroma in the finished beer.

EXPORT STOUT   Historically, a version of stout brewed for international markets that is stronger and sweeter than usual in order to survive transport.

FESTBIER   A modern version of the traditional marzen style usually served at Oktoberfest celebrations in Germany. This lager is typically just above 5% alcohol and is characterized by heavier malt sweetness than a typical lager.

GOLDEN ALE   Typically, golden ale refers to a style of beer developed in England in the 1980s as a response to the prevalence of lagers in the market. Often includes North American hop varieties in some quantity.

GOSE A nearly forgotten style of beer originating in Leipzig, which has risen to prominence in North America in recent years. Typically consisting of 50 percent wheat, gose's main attraction is that it is salted and dosed with coriander. It's an acquired taste on the road to triumph, despite its oddity.

GRISETTE A low-alcohol Belgian ale in the style of a saison, designed for refreshment. Typically includes a significant portion of wheat and very low bitterness. Popular with miners, historically speaking.

HECTOLITRE (HL) The more prevalent metric measurement of brewery volumes, a hectolitre is 100 litres. One hectolitre is approximately 0.85 barrels.

HEFEWEIZEN A German style of wheat beer typically redolent of banana, clove, or bubble gum yeast esters and featuring a creamy body. Often open-fermented. Asking for it with a slice of orange will get you hooted at in beer bars.

HELLES A style of lager developed in Munich in the late nineteenth century that is the culmination of a century of lightening malt character in the city's beer. Typically finds a balance between a simple grain character and an herbal, floral hop aroma.

HOPS The flowers of the rhizomatous plant *Humulus lupulus*, hops are to beer what spices are to cooking. Hops provide bitterness if used early in the boil and aroma and flavour if used later in the brewing process.

INDIA PALE ALE An English style of higher-alcohol, heavily hopped ale that acquired the name as a result of being shipped from England to India during the nineteenth century, surviving due to the preservative nature of the hops. An inspiration for North American craft beer due to its assertive bitterness and pronounced flavour.

IMPERIAL STOUT A type of export stout originally brewed in England for export to the court of Catherine II of Russia. It is typically high in alcohol with pronounced roasted- and dark–malt characters and a significant amount of sweetness due to residual sugars.

INTERNATIONAL BITTERING UNIT (IBU) The standard unit of measurement for bitterness in a beer, the IBU scale runs from 0 (no bitterness) to 100 (very bitter indeed). It is theoretically possible to exceed the scale, but the perception threshold in humans sits at around 100, raising the question, "Who are you brewing that for? Robots?"

KÖLSCH A style of beer from Cologne in Germany, kölsch is a hybrid style of beer fermented at ale temperatures and then lagered. It is noted for being lightly fruity and spicy, golden in colour and coming in 200 millilitre glasses in its native city.

KOYT A Dutch style of gruit recently in resurgence, featuring wheat and oats as significant percentages of the malt bill. Traditionally the style does not use hops, preferring instead sweet gale.

LAGER Beer produced with bottom-fermenting yeast strains and cold conditioned in storage. Typically central European in origin, lager styles are diverse and are frequently given a bad rap due to the prevalence of relatively bland pale lagers on the world stage.

MALT Any germinated cereal grain that has had its sprouting process arrested. In brewing, *malt* usually refers to barley that has been kilned to some extent, resulting in different treatments and flavour profiles.

MICROBREWERY In normal usage, the term *microbrewery* connotes a brewery that is independently owned and produces less than

15,000 BBL of beer annually. In general parlance, it's what craft breweries were called before the term caught on.

MILD	A low-alcohol English beer with regional variants (lighter in colour in the south U.K., darker in Wales and the north). Typically below 4% alcohol, mild is a sessionable option for refreshment.

MILK STOUT	Named for the use of lactose as a sweetening agent, milk stout tends to take on a sweeter body and creamier texture than regular stouts. A good choice if you like the sweetness of an imperial stout but not the alcohol.

MOUTHFEEL	The texture of a beverage in your mouth. It might be sparkling and fizzy, or slick and coating, or bone dry. Texture is an important sensory element to take into account.

NANOBREWERY	A very small brewhouse capable of producing an extremely limited amount of beer. If it could fit in your garage, it's a nanobrewery.

PALE ALE	A popular style of English beer brewed mostly with pale malt and usually moderately hopped, meaning that it can vary in flavour immensely. Pale ale has spawned a number of regional and international variants.

PHENOL	A group of aromatic organic compounds that make up aromas in beer. In low concentrations they are appropriate, spicy, and pleasant. In high concentrations they're a little like melting plastic or a dirty Band-Aid, and are therefore a brewing flaw.

PILSNER	A style of lager developed in the Czech town of Plzeň in 1842, which has spawned regional variants including a more lightly hopped German variety. Possibly the most influential beer style in history.

PORTER	A style of dark English ale brewed in London since the beginning of the eighteenth century, sometimes catastrophically as in the case of the London Beer Flood of 1814. Typically it includes a nutty malt presence in addition to dark malt flavours and roast. Historical recreations frequently include a souring note.

REAL ALE Cask conditioned rather than artificially carbonated, real ale still contains live yeast at time of service and is frequently a better treatment for subtle flavours and certain English styles like bitter and mild.

REINHEITSGEBOT A law enacted in Bavaria in 1516 that limited the ingredients to be used in beer to barley, hops, and water. The law was as much about crop management and ensuring food supply as it was about beer quality, but it did result in some nice lager, which we're all grateful for.

SAISON A Belgian style of farmhouse ale historically brewed for farmhands to drink during the summer planting and harvest seasons. It usually contains a significant amount of wheat and relatively few hops.

SCHWARZBIER A dark lager made in Germany that typically has a light roast quality with hints of coffee or chocolate, which fade away into the body and a clean finish. Currently growing in popularity in North America.

SESSION IPA A low-alcohol variant of the American IPA, which usually features large amounts of late and dry hopping in order to place the aromas of a regular IPA in a beer that you can drink all day. If you attempt to drink full-strength IPA all day, it's going to be a short day.

STOUT A dark style of ale that is usually defined by the presence of roasted barley, which gives the beer a lightly burnt character in addition to other features. Extremely popular on St. Patrick's Day.

STRONG ALE More than merely an ale with increased alcohol, strong ale tends to connote increased malt complexity and assertive flavour, regardless of national genre. In the case of England, it denotes a specific genre of bottled beer. In the case of American and Belgian styles, the descriptor is something of a catch-all.

TABLE BEER
A Belgian style of ale noted for its extremely low alcohol content, managed without sacrificing flavour. Until the 1980s it was served to schoolchildren at lunchtime. Belgian children are less belligerent now but no happier.

VIENNA-STYLE LAGER
An early style of lager developed in the 1830s whose hallmark is its reddish tint and malt-forward, caramel-accented body. Popular as a gateway craft beer style for those acclimatizing to flavourful beer.

VLB BERLIN
Versuch- u. Lehranstalt für Brauerei, a German institute that provides beer-making training and education.

WEST COAST IPA
Referring to the West Coast of the U.S.A., this IPA variant features American hops

WHEAT BEER
A catch-all term for a number of styles featuring wheat as a significant part of their makeup. If you can use a more specific term, you're wise to do so.

WEISSE
The German word for "white," not for "wheat." The name has to do with the light colour of wheat beers more than the content of their grist.

WITBIER
A Belgian ale made with a significant portion of wheat and featuring orange peel and coriander seeds as flavouring additions. The style nearly disappeared in the middle of the twentieth century but was revived by brewer Pierre Celis.

WORT
A technical brewing term for unfermented beer. Beer is wort right up until the yeast starts eating it, at which point you still want to wait a couple of weeks before drinking it.

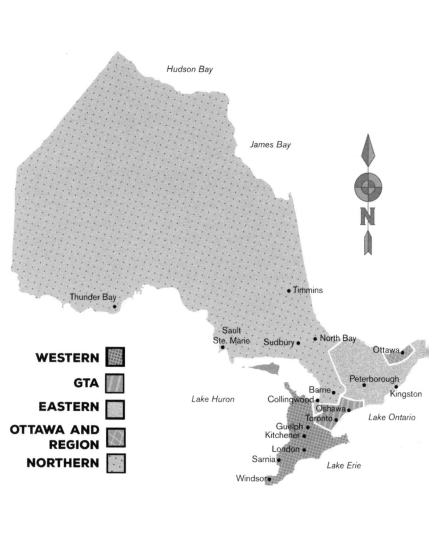

BREWERIES BY REGION

WESTERN

Abe Erb Brewery & Restaurant	Waterloo
Arch Brewing Co.	Guelph
Banded Goose Brewing Co.	Kingsville
Bayside Brewing Co.	Erieau
Beer Lab London	London
Bell City Brewing Co.	Brantford
Black Swan Brewing Co.	Stratford
Block Three Brewing Co.	St. Jacobs
The Blue Elephant Craft Brew House	Simcoe
Brew Windsor	Windsor
Brick Brewing Co.	Kitchener
Brimstone Brewing Co.	Ridgeway
Brothers Brewing Co.	Ridgeville
Brux House	Hamilton
Ceeps	London
Clifford Brewing Co.	Hamilton
Collective Arts Brewing	Hamilton

Craft Heads Brewing Co.	Windsor
Descendants Beer & Beverage Co. Ltd.	Wellesley
Elora Brewing Co.	Elora
Forked River Brewing Co.	London
Garden Brewers	Hamilton
Grand River Brewing	Cambridge
The Hamilton Brewery	Hamilton
High Road Brewing Co.	Niagara-on-the-Lake
Hockley Valley Brewing Co.	Orangeville
Innocente Brewing Co.	Waterloo
Lion Brewery Restaurant	Waterloo
London Brewing Co-operative	London
Mash Paddle Brewing Co.	Brantford
Merchant Ale House	St. Catharines
Motor Craft Ales	Windsor
Neustadt Springs Brewery	Neustadt
New Limburg Brewery	Simcoe
Niagara Brewing Co.	Niagara Falls
Niagara College Teaching Brewery	Niagara-on-the-Lake
Niagara Oast House Brewers	Niagara-on-the-Lake
Outlaw Brew Co.	Southampton
Railway City Brewing Co.	St. Thomas
Ramblin' Road Brewery Farm	La Salette
Refined Fool Brewing	Sarnia
Royal City Brewing Co.	Guelph
Silversmith Brewing	Niagara-on-the-Lake
StoneHammer Brewing	Guelph
Stratford Brewing Co.	Stratford
Strathroy Brewing Co.	Strathroy
Syndicate Restaurant and Brewery	Niagara Falls
Taps Brewhouse & Grill	Niagara Falls
Toboggan Brewing Co.	London
Together We're Bitter Co-operative Brewing	Kitchener

Walkerville Brewery	Windsor
Wellington Brewery	Guelph

GTA

All or Nothing Brewhouse	Oshawa
Amber Brewery	Markham
Amsterdam Brewing Co.	Toronto
Bellwoods Brewery	Toronto
Black Creek Historic Brewery	Toronto
Black Oak Brewing Co.	Toronto
Blood Brothers	Toronto
Brock Street Brewing Co.	Whitby
Burdock Brewery	Toronto
Bush Pilot Brewing Co.	Burlington
Cameron's Brewing Co.	Oakville
C'est What?	Toronto
Cheetah International Brewers Inc.	Toronto
Cheshire Valley Brewing	Toronto
Cool Beer Brewing Co. Inc.	Toronto
County Durham Brewing Co.	Pickering
Double Trouble Brewing Co.	Toronto
Duggan's Brewery	Toronto
5 Paddles Brewing Co.	Whitby
Folly Brewpub	Toronto
Granite Brewery	Toronto
Great Lakes Brewery	Toronto
High Park Brewery	Toronto
Hogtown Brewers	Toronto
Hop City Brewing Co.	Brampton
House Ales	Toronto
Indie Alehouse Brewing Co.	Toronto
Junction Craft Brewing	Toronto

Kensington Brewing Co.	Toronto
Lake Wilcox Brewing Co.	Richmond Hill
Left Field Brewery	Toronto
Liberty Village Brewing Co.	Toronto
Longslice Brewing Co.	Toronto
Louis Cifer Brew Works	Toronto
Magnotta Brewery	Vaughan
Manantler Craft Brewing Co.	Bowmanville
Mascot Brewery	Toronto
Mill Street Brewpub Toronto	Toronto
Mill Street Brewery (production)	Toronto
Muddy York Brewing Co.	Toronto
Nickel Brook Brewing Co.	Burlington
Old Credit Brewing Co.	Mississauga
Old Tomorrow	Toronto
Ontario Beer Co.	Toronto
Orange Snail Brewers	Milton
Pepperwood Bistro & Brew House	Burlington
Pitschfork Brewing Co.	Toronto
Radical Road Brewing	Toronto
Rainhard Brewing Co.	Toronto
Saint Andre Brewing	Toronto
Shillow Beer Co.	Toronto
Spearhead Brewing Co.	Toronto
Steam Whistle Brewing	Toronto
Stouffville Brewing Co.	Pickering
Sweetgrass Brewing Co.	Toronto
The 3 Brewers Adelaide St.	Toronto
The 3 Brewers Mississauga	Mississauga
The 3 Brewers Oakville	Oakville
The 3 Brewers Richmond Hill	Richmond Hill
The 3 Brewers Yonge St.	Toronto
Tracks Brew Pub	Brampton

The Trafalgar Club	Oakville
Triple Bogey Brewing & Golf Co.	Toronto
Woodhouse Brewing Co.	Toronto

EASTERN

Bancroft Brewing Co.	Bancroft
Barley Days Brewery	Picton
Cartwright Springs Brewery	Pakenham
Cassel Brewery Company Ltd.	Casselman
Church-Key Brewing Co.	Cambellford
Gananoque Brewing Co.	Gananoque
Kingston Brewing Co.	Kingston
Lake on the Mountain Brewing Co.	Prince Edward County
MacKinnon Brothers Brewing Co.	Bath
Northumberland Hills Brewery	Cobourg
Old Flame Brewing Co.	Port Perry
The Olde Stone Brewing Co.	Peterborough
Perth Brewery	Perth
The Publican House Brewery	Peterborough
Smithavens Brewing Co.	Peterborough
Stone City Ales	Kingston
Whitewater Brewing Co.	Foresters Falls
Wild Card Brewing Co.	Trenton
William Street Beer Co.	Cobourg

OTTAWA AND REGION

Ashton Brewing Co.	Ashton
Beau's All Natural Brewing Co.	Vankleek Hil
Bentley Brewers	Nepean
Beyond the Pale Brewing Co.	Ottawa
Bicycle Craft Brewery	Ottawa

Big Rig Brewery & Taproom	Kanata
Big Rig Kitchen & Brewery	Ottawa
Broadhead Brewing Co.	Nepean
Broken Stick Brewing Co.	Ottawa
Calabogie Brewing Co.	Calabogie
Clocktower Brewpubs	Ottawa
Covered Bridge Brewing Co.	Ottawa
Dominion City Brewing Co.	Ottawa
Gongshow Beauty Beer	Ottawa
HogsBack Brewing Co.	Ottawa
Kichesippi Beer Co.	Ottawa
Lowertown Brewery	Ottawa
Mill Street Brewpub (Ottawa)	Ottawa
Nita Beer Co.	Ottawa
The 3 Brewers Kanata	Kanata
The 3 Brewers Ottawa	Ottawa
Tooth and Nail Brewing Co.	Ottawa
Tuque de Broue	Ottawa
Waller St. Brewing	Ottawa
Whiprsnapr Brewing Co.	Ottawa

NORTHERN

Barnstormer Brewing Co.	Barrie
Bobcaygeon Brewing Co.	Bobcaygeon
Boshkung Brewing Co.	Minden Hills
Cecil's Brewhouse & Kitchen	North Bay
Creemore Springs Brewery	Creemore
Flying Monkeys Craft Brewery	Barrie
Haliburton Highlands Brewing Co.	Haliburton
Kilannan Brewing Co.	Owen Sound
Lake of Bays Brewing Co.	Baysville
Lake of the Woods Brewing Co.	Kenora

MacLean's Ales Inc.	Hanover
Manitoulin Brewing Co.	Little Current
Muskoka Brewery	Bracebridge
New Ontario Brewing Co.	North Bay
Northwinds Brewhouse & Eatery	Collingwood
OutSpoken Brewing	Sault Ste Marie
Redline Brewhouse	Barrie
Sawdust City Brewing Co.	Gravenhurst
Side Launch Brewing Co.	Collingwood
Sleeping Giant Brewing Co.	Thunder Bay
Split Rail Brewing Co.	Gore Bay
Square Timber Brewing Co.	Pembroke
Stack Brewing	Sudbury
Thornbury Beverage Co.	Thornbury
Tobermory Brewing Co. & Grill	Tobermory
Union Jack Brewing Co.	Sault Ste Marie

INDEX OF BEERS

INDEX OF BEERS

427

ACKNOWLEDGEMENTS

This book was a combined effort and we couldn't have done it without a little help, both direct and indirect, from the following. Thanks to Stephen Beaumont for his moral support and wise advice, and fellow beer scribes Jamie MacKinnon, Josh Rubin, Chris Burek, Ben Johnson, Crystal Luxmore, Alan McLeod, Dan Grant, Greg Clow, and Chris Schryer. Additional thanks to Mirella Amato, the OCB; our tenacious and brilliant agent, Clare F. Pelino; Brad Campeau of Brew Donkey; Aaron Brown and Milos Kral; and Kirk Howard, Karen McMullin, Kathryn Lane, Cheryl Hawley, Dominic Farrell, and Courtney Horner of Dundurn Press.

Finally, thanks to the Ontario breweries for being yourselves. Keep brewing, keep refining, keep evolving, and keep drinking.

FROM ROBIN LEBLANC:

Special thanks to my parents, Anya and Larry LeBlanc, for their unwavering support. Thanks also to Cheryl Weatherill, Liam Leadbetter, the Whitechapel Crew, and all the wonderful people in my life for their constant encouragement and help since I first started writing about beer in 2011. I'm happy to consider you folks my friends.

Additional thanks to Death in Vegas, whose song "Dirge" got me through the final leg of writing.

FROM JORDAN ST. JOHN:

Thanks to Matthew McCormick, who acted as chauffeur for the Niagara leg of the trip and to whom I still owe gas money. It is likely he will be paid in beer instead. Thanks also to my mother, Laurel Dempsey, for handling the driving on the Cobourg to Bath corridor.

Someday I really must get a car. Beer is heavy and the roads are poor.

JORDAN ST.JOHN

Jordan St.John has been writing about beer since 2010, and in that time has published four books, over 200 syndicated newspaper columns as Canada's only nationally syndicated beer columnist, 300 blog posts at saintjohnswort.ca, and several dozen magazine articles. He has appeared on *Storage Wars Canada*, CBC Radio One, *Global News*, and a number of other media outlets as a beer expert. He holds the ranks of Certified Cicerone and Prospective BJCP. He lives with his cat, Sweet William, who is named after a nineteenth-century Toronto brewer. Jordan spends much of his time attempting not to be a cautionary example.

———

JORDAN is best described as an acquired taste: robust, with a slightly over-full body, typically featuring an aroma of heavily roasted coffee and mild English accents (4).

ROBIN LEBLANC

Robin LeBlanc began writing about beer in 2011, shortly after becoming captivated with the deep complexities of the beverage. Her website, thethirstywench.com, has won multiple awards and was the first Canadian-based site to win the Saveur Magazine Best Food Blog Award in the Best Wine or Beer Blog category. She also writes two regular beer columns: the bi-weekly Inherent Weisse for Torontoist and the syndicated On Tap for Metroland North Media. She has appeared regularly as a beer expert on various media outlets such as *Rogers Daytime Toronto* and 680 News Radio. When not writing, she works as a photographer and publicist. She lives in Toronto and takes her coffee black with two sugars, thanks.

———

ROBIN is a fine example of an English/North American hybrid, with a distinct jab of bitterness balanced out by a gentle sweetness and a somewhat looming, dry finish (4).